Edgar Holt has written on a wide variety of historical subjects, including the Boer War, the Second World War, the Irish Troubles and, more recently the Carlist Wars in Spain and the Chinese Opium Wars. He has also published a biography of Mazzini.

RISORGIMENTO

By the same author

The World At War, 1935–1945
The Boer War
Protest In Arms: The Irish Troubles, 1906–1923
The Strangest War: The Story of the Maori Wars
The Opium Wars In China
The Carlist Wars In Spain
Giuseppe Mazzini: The Great Conspirator

RISORGIMENTO

The Making of Italy

1815-1870

EDGAR HOLT

MACMILLAN

First published 1970 by
MACMILLAN AND CO LTD
London and Basingstoke
Associated companies in New York Toronto
Dublin Melbourne Johannesburg & Madras

Printed in Great Britain by
WESTERN PRINTING SERVICES LTD
Bristol

To
CELIA HADDON

CONTENTS

LIST OF MAPS

Anthony Longo

ITEM ON HOLD

LIST OF ILLUSTRATIONS

ACKNOWLEDGEMENTS

All the photographs have been reproduced by permission of the
Istituto per la Storia del Risorgimento Italiano, Rome, with the
exception of numbers 3b, 4b and 7b, which are reproduced by
permission of the Radio Times Hulton Picture Library.

FOREWORD

THE events which attended the great Risorgimento – the making of Italy in the nineteenth century – seem to be less well known outside Italy than some of the other important happenings of the same period, such as the American civil war and the Franco-Prussian war. Most people have heard of Garibaldi, but very often that is as far as their knowledge of the Risorgimento goes. Yet Garibaldi, after all, was only one of the leading figures who played their part in uniting Italy.

The object of this book is simply to provide a reasonably concise answer to the questions, 'What was the Risorgimento and what happened in it?' I am acutely conscious that the subject is far too vast to be easily confined within the covers of a single book, and I must ask indulgence for sins of omission which I may have unintentionally committed.

For the writing of such a history, which attempts to give a conspectus of the whole Italian scene and the principal actors, it seemed both impracticable and unnecessary to make any new search in archives and record offices. Instead, I have tried to take every possible advantage from the works of modern and recent writers, especially Italian writers, who have studied the many problems of the Risorgimento and have opened up new lines of thought. In this way I hope that I have presented a modern view of what happened in Italy between 1815 and 1870, based on the findings of recent historical scholarship.

The bibliography, the references and the book itself will give some idea of the historians to whose works I am most indebted. In particular, I must gladly acknowledge how much I owe to important books by Denis Mack Smith in England, and Walter Maturi, Renato Mori, Adolfo Omodeo, Piero Pieri, Rosario Romeo, Luigi Salvatorelli, Gaetano Salvemini and Cesare Spellanzon in Italy. These are perhaps my 'front line' of obligations, but there are many other recent writers, such as Noel Blakiston, E. E. Y. Hales, Arturo Carlo Jemolo and Ruggero Moscati, whose books have been most helpful, while of older works G. M. Trevelyan's great Garibaldi saga and the histories of Bolton King, G. F.-H. and J. Berkeley and Carlo Tivaroni are still a most valuable framework for Risorgimental studies. On a small point of style I may say that I side with those English historians who prefer to use the anglicized names of Italian kings – Victor Emmanuel instead of Vittorio Emanuele, Charles Albert instead of Carlo Alberto, Ferdinand instead of Ferdinando, and so on. The English forms probably seem more natural to English readers, and I hope that no one will be worried by the slight inconsistency of calling Carlo Alberto Charles Albert while leaving others called Carlo (such as Cattaneo and Poerio) with the Italian style of their names.

I cannot end this foreword without giving particular thanks to Dr Emilia Morelli and the staff of the Istituto per la Storia del Risorgimento Italiano, Rome for allowing me to go through their fine collection of illustrations and helping me to make a selection. I am also especially grateful to the library staff of the Italian Institute in London for valuable advice and assistance, and to the staff of the London Library and the British Museum reading room. Finally I must thank the friends in London and in Rome who have encouraged me so much by their interest in the preparation of this book.

EDGAR HOLT

SOME LEADING FIGURES IN THE EVENTS OF THE RISORGIMENTO

ANTONELLI, Cardinal Giacomo, Pope Pius IX's secretary of state.

AZEGLIO, Massimo D', Piedmontese writer and politician.

BALBO, Cesare, Piedmontese writer and politician.

BANDIERA, Attilio, Venetian revolutionary.

BANDIERA, Emilio, Venetian revolutionary.

BUONARROTI, Filippo, Tuscan revolutionary and Carbonaro leader.

CATTANEO, Carlo, Lombard writer and revolutionary.

CAVOUR, Count Camillo Benso di, Piedmontese statesman and first prime minister of the kingdom of Italy.

CHARLES ALBERT, king of Piedmont, 1831–48.

CHARLES FELIX, king of Piedmont, 1821–31.

CONFALONIERI, Count Federico, Lombard revolutionary.

CRISPI, Francesco, Sicilian revolutionary and colleague of Garibaldi.

EUGENIE, Empress, wife of Napoleon III.

FARINI, Luigi Carlo, Romagnol historian and political colleague of Cavour.

FERDINAND I, king of the Two Sicilies, 1760–1825.

FERDINAND II ('King Bomba'), king of the Two Sicilies, 1830–59.

FRANCIS II, king of the Two Sicilies, 1859–60.

FRANCIS IV, duke of Modena, 1814–46.

FRANCIS JOSEPH, emperor of Austria, 1848–1916.

GARIBALDI, Giuseppe, Piedmontese general and revolutionary.

GIOBERTI, Abbé Vincenzo, Piedmontese writer and politician.

GREGORY XVI, Pope, 1831–46.

GUERRAZZI, Domenico, Tuscan revolutionary.

LAMBERTI, Giuseppe, Piedmontese revolutionary and joint organizer of Young Italy.

LEOPOLD II, grand duke of Tuscany, 1824–59.

MANIN, Daniele, Venetian revolutionary.

MARIO, Jessie White, English supporter of Mazzini and Garibaldi.

MAZZINI, Giuseppe, Piedmontese revolutionary and founder of Young Italy.

MENOTTI, Ciro, Modenese revolutionary.

METTERNICH, Prince Clement, Austrian chancellor.

MINGHETTI, Marco, prime minister of united Italy.

MONTANELLI, Giuseppe, Tuscan revolutionary.

NAPOLEON, Prince, cousin of Napoleon III and husband of Princess Clotilde of Savoy.

NAPOLEON III, emperor of the French, 1852–70 (formerly Prince Louis Napoleon).

ORSINI, Felice, Romagnol revolutionary.

PELLICO, Silvio, Lombard writer and revolutionary.

PEPE, General Guglielmo, Neapolitan revolutionary and defender of Venice.

PILO, Rosolino, Sicilian revolutionary.

PISACANE, Carlo, Neapolitan revolutionary.

PIUS IX, Pope, 1846–78.

POERIO, Carlo, Neapolitan revolutionary.

RADETSKY, Marshal, Austrian commander-in-chief in Italy.

RAMORINO, General Gerolamo, Piedmontese soldier of fortune.

RATTAZZI, Urbano, Piedmontese politician and prime minister of united Italy.

RICASOLI, Baron Bettino, Tuscan statesman and prime minister of united Italy.

SANTAROSA, Santorre di, Piedmontese officer and revolutionary.

SELLA, Quintino, finance minister of united Italy.

SETTEMBRINI, Luigi, Neapolitan author and revolutionary.

VICTOR EMMANUEL II, king of Piedmont, 1848–61, and first king of Italy, 1861–78.

VISCONTI VENOSTA, Emilio, foreign minister of united Italy.

Part I
1815-1846

Divided country: Italy in 1815

I
PROLOGUE

Risorgimento   Forerunners   The French in Italy   Murat

IN 1815, when the congress of Vienna had redrawn the map of Europe at the end of the Napoleonic wars, the present republic of Italy consisted of seven separate states, each under its own sovereign ruler. The seven were Piedmont (which also comprised Sardinia and was formally described as the kingdom of Sardinia), Lombardy-Venetia, Tuscany, Modena, Parma-Piacenza, the Papal States and the Two Sicilies (Naples and Sicily), together with two smaller duchies, Lucca and Massa-Carrara. The tiny states of San Marino and Monaco were also Italian.

Fifty-five years later all these states (except San Marino and Monaco) had been united in one kingdom, the kingdom of Italy. The final step in the process of unification was on 20 September 1870 when the troops of King Victor Emmanuel II, first king of Italy, entered Rome through a breach in the walls at Porta Pia and ended for ever the pope's temporal power over the city and its surrounding territory. The military act was confirmed a few days later by the overwhelming vote of the Roman people. 'A great nation was added to Europe; the most glorious of the world's cities became again one of its civil capitals.'[1]

The period in which the separate Italian states were welded into a single nation is known as the Risorgimento – the resurgence or resurrection of Italy and its people. The exact duration of this process is a matter of some dispute, and even the terminal date is not universally agreed. Some argue that the Risorgimento was complete when the kingdom of united Italy was established in 1861, though it is hard to see anything final in the creation of an Italian kingdom which at that time did not include the great cities of Rome and Venice. Others – those who were once called irredentists – believe that Italy was not truly Italy until Trieste and Trentino were brought within the national boundaries after the first world war. But the irredentist argument puts too much emphasis on the purely territorial aspect of the Risorgimento. Spiritually and morally Italy did not need Trieste and Trentino for its resurrection. It was fully reborn when the new kingdom regained the ancient capital of Rome.

Varying opinions are held also about the date when the national resurgence began. Though it was during the years 1815–70 that Italy won unity, constitutional freedom and independence from foreign domination, many Italian historians suggest that the Risorgimento began at an earlier date. 'Everyone agrees today', states Luigi Salvatorelli, 'that the beginnings of the Risorgimento should be put back from 1815 to the eighteenth century', and the treaties of Utrecht in 1713 and of Aix-la-Chapelle in 1748 have been suggested as starting-points. The treaty of Utrecht, by which the duke of Savoy gained the royal crown that he was soon to wear as king of Sardinia, seemed an appropriate beginning to historians in Italy's fascist period who wished to glorify the house of Savoy; the treaty of Aix-la-Chapelle, which reduced foreign domination of Italy and left most of the country under its own rulers, is favoured by those who think that the Italian resurgence really started with the reforms made by enlightened princes and ministers in the second half of the eighteenth century.[2]

The choice of either of these starting-points implies that the making of a united Italy began before the French revolution and the subsequent French occupation of the Italian peninsula. Yet many historians feel that this French influence was one of the determining factors of the Risorgimento. Adolfo Omodeo declares that the ferment left behind by Napoleon when he returned from Italy to France in 1797 really marked the birth of the new Italy.[3] Gaetano Salvemini says that 'without the arrival of the French armies in Italy the ancient regimes would have stayed on for who knows how many generations.'[4] Denis Mack Smith goes back to the 1790s for the first items in his collection of documents illustrating the progress of the Risorgimento.[5]

When the claims for an eighteenth-century origin of the

Italian resurgence are so much the vogue it may seem a little perverse to prefer the now unfashionable date of 1815. Yet a case remains for regarding the Risorgimento as essentially a nineteenth-century occurrence, since the period which began with the return of the Italian rulers displaced by Napoleon and ended with the inclusion of Rome in a united kingdom of Italy was the only active period of national resurgence. Eighteenth-century reformers, philosophers and patriots did much to awaken a new spirit in Italy, but no positive steps were taken towards the achievement of unity, freedom from foreign domination and the ending of absolute rule. Again, remarkable progress towards unification was made during the French occupation, but it was not *national* progress; independence was further away than ever, and the new administrative unity was soon destroyed under the settlement made by the congress of Vienna.

It can be argued, therefore, that the constructive resurgence of Italy did not begin until the Italian states had settled down under their old regimes in 1815. The years which followed were vital. Without the special impetuses, both revolutionary and governmental, which eventually destroyed the old system and created the new Italy, it is hard to see how the separate and firmly entrenched absolute sovereignties could have been merged so rapidly in just over a half-century. These impetuses, which operated between 1815 and 1870 – the conspiracies, insurrections, propaganda, diplomacy and wars of liberation – were the effective part of the Italian Risorgimento. Many of the preceding events were important and significant, but they must surely be regarded as only a prologue to the actual making of Italy.

2

What *was* the Risorgimento? Salvatorelli defines it as 'a resumption of autonomous national life through which Italy took its place again in the course of modern civilization and politico-social life, forming itself on the political plane into a unitary state, independent and free.'[6] But the word Risorgimento begs the question. If Italy was resurging, it must have been re-creating something which had previously existed. In fact, there was never an Italian state or nation before the nineteenth century.

It was during the congress of Vienna that Metternich first made his famous remark that Italy was 'merely a geographical expression'. His comment applies to the whole of the previous history of the Italian peninsula; even imperial Rome did not create an Italian nation, but succeeded only 'in converting Italy into a uniform Roman state'.[7] With the fall of the Roman empire this uniformity disappeared. When Italy reappeared after its dark ages it was a country of city-states, which formed temporary alliances for warlike purposes but were not joined in any kind of permanent confederation. The same separatism persisted when the city-states were replaced by larger territorial groupings.

Yet the use of the word Risorgimento suggests that some Italians felt, in spite of the contrary evidence, that Italy had once been a single nation and should become one again. This was the idea on which the Risorgimento was built.

It was not a new idea. Both Dante and Petrarch had visions of a united Italy. In the sixteenth century, when the peninsula was under Spanish domination, Macchiavelli ended *The Prince* with his memorable appeal for union, under the prince's leadership, against the 'barbarous tyranny' which 'stinks in everyone's nostrils'.[8] Two hundred years later, when Austria had replaced Spain as the chief foreign power in Italy, other writers took up the themes of unity and freedom.

The second half of the eighteenth century was a particularly fertile period for pre-Risorgimento writers. Though most of the states were subject to Austrian influence in one way or another, only Lombardy came directly under Austria's rule and the rest of Italy was enjoying the relative independence it had achieved through the treaty of Aix-la-Chapelle. The time was ripe for the development of a national consciousness.

Eighteenth-century patriotic literature began with Antonio Genovesi, who proclaimed in 1754, 'We are beginning to have a fatherland', and went on to urge the princes and dukes to develop some kind of concord and unity. But one aspect of Italian life which hindered any approach to unity was the way in which the people of one state or city treated men from other parts of the country as foreigners rather than as fellow-countrymen. It was to combat this attitude that Gian Rinaldo Carli wrote in 1764 his much-quoted article telling how a stranger entered a café in Milan and puzzled its occupants by saying that he was neither a foreigner nor a Milanese. 'Then what *are* you?' they asked. 'I am an Italian,' he explained, 'and an Italian in Italy is not a foreigner, just as a Frenchman is not a foreigner in France, an Englishman in England or a Dutchman in Holland.'⁹

One of the great men of these years was Vittorio Alfieri, who is said to have been the first Italian to assert the national will to become a nation-state.¹⁰ As tragedian and essayist he was an impressive exponent of conscious nationalism, and in later years significant lines in his tragedies were greatly applauded because of their anti-Austrian suggestions. He attacked tyranny in his notable *Della Tirannide*, published in 1777, and he condemned clerical interference in political affairs. But he had faith in the future of Italy, which, said the dedication of one of his books, 'some day will undoubtedly rise again, virtuous, magnanimous, free and one.'¹¹

It was in these years also that Italian writers began to put forward plans for federal union, either under the pope's presidency, as proposed by Gaetano Napione in 1780, or under the joint leadership of Piedmont and Naples, as suggested by Gaetano Filangieri in the same year. One man who has a special claim to be remembered is the Jesuit, Saverio Bettinelli: in a book published in 1773 he was the first writer to give the word risorgimento a political meaning, though he used it to describe the intellectual reawakening of Italy in the early Middle Ages.¹²

The projects of all these writers remained on paper only. No one tried to put them into action. Impressive though they were, these contributions to Italian liberal thought must be regarded, in Salvemini's phrase, as part of 'the proto-history of Italian national sentiment',¹³ and not as an integral part of the Risorgimento.

The half-century of peace after the treaty of Aix-la-Chapelle was a period of enlightenment and reform in the government and administration of the Italian states. The principle of absolute rule remained unchallenged. No progress was made towards the constitutional freedom and popular government which were to be sought by the nineteenth-century revolutionaries. Yet most of the

Italian rulers, influenced by the new ideas of economists and philosopher-ministers, made extensive reforms in their administrative systems.

Though varying from state to state, the general pattern of reform was to reduce the burden of the feudal system, to limit privilege, to restrict the powers of the Church, to simplify law, to humanize the penal code and to increase opportunities for education. But the importance of these changes should not be exaggerated. It seems too much to suggest that even before the French revolution Italy 'was advancing towards its own ends according to the forms and methods of an internal evolution.'[14] In fact, the reforms were geared to the system of absolute rule and were not designed to open the way to representative government, independence or unity. It was a long way from such well-meant proofs of enlightenment to a truly national Risorgimento.

3

The reform movement in Italy was abruptly checked by the outbreak of the French revolution in 1789. Enlightened sovereigns saw the danger of liberal policies and felt that it was more important to maintain their own authority than to make any further concessions to their subjects. But this authority, which had no strong military force to support it, could not be upheld against the arms of revolutionary France.

Pope Pius VI was the first Italian sovereign to lose territory to the French republic: the papal enclaves in France – Avignon and the Venaissin – were seized by the republican government in 1791 and were never restored to the papacy. In the following year Savoy and Nice, which were part of the combined kingdom of Piedmont and Sardinia, were also incorporated in the new France. Victor Amadeus III, king of Piedmont, formed alliances with Austria and England and sent troops along the Mediterranean coast in the hope of recovering Nice, but there was little profit for either side in a desultory campaign between the Piedmontese and a poorly equipped French army.

The conflict became wider in 1796, when the French republic, at war with a coalition of European powers headed by Austria on land and Britain at sea, gave its Mediterranean army a new task and a new commander. The task was to advance on Vienna through Piedmont and Lombardy while two other French armies struck at Austria through Germany. The commander was the twenty-six-year-old General Napoleon Bonaparte, the Italian-speaking Corsican who had recently broken up a dangerous rising in Paris. Though his forces were greatly outnumbered by the Piedmontese and Austrian armies which opposed him, his skill in attacking each of his enemies separately enabled him first to drive Piedmont out of the war and then to turn the Austrians' line and push them back behind the Mincio. In May he entered Milan as conqueror and liberator.

These were the two aspects of the French invasion of Italy – conquest of the Austrians, liberation of the Italians. The contrast between them was illustrated by the very different words which Bonaparte used to his troops and to the Italian people.

In addressing the French army of Italy at Nice before crossing the Ligurian Apennines into Piedmont, he said:

> It is my intention to lead you into the most fertile plains in the world. Rich provinces and great cities will be in your power; there you will find honour, glory and wealth.[15]

But to the Italians he proclaimed:

> Peoples of Italy, the French army comes to break your chains; the French people is the friend of all peoples; meet us with confidence. Your property, your religion and your usages will be respected. We make war as generous enemies, and we have no quarrel save with the tyrants.[16]

Power and wealth for the soldiers; liberty and respect of property for the Italians. The two promises were hardly consistent, and the Italians soon learned that neither the French commander nor his army had any intention of keeping his pledge to respect Italian property. Italy was a country to be sacked and pillaged. Works of art and other treasures were seized as loot by the self-styled liberators.

The reshaping of Italy after Napoleon's first campaign is of some significance in the prehistory of the Risorgimento, because it gave Italians their first indications of the benefits of unity. A tragic casualty was the ancient republic of Venice, which was given to Austria, in compensation for losses elsewhere, by the Franco-Austrian treaty of Campo Formio in October 1797. In this brutal way the long history of Venetian independence was abruptly ended. Except for its brief period of freedom in 1848-9 Venice was to be under foreign rule for nearly seventy years.

In the years 1797-9 republican governments under French protection were set up in the greater part of Italy. The first of these, which existed for only a few months, was the Cispadane republic, consisting of the four cities of Modena, Reggio, Bologna and Ferrara. Its special place in history is that it chose as its flag the white, red and green tricolour which had been first used in the summer of 1796 by Milanese troops enlisted to fight the Austrians.[17] It is paradoxical that one of the earliest results of the French conquest was the emergence of Italy's national flag.

In June 1797 the four cities of the Cispadane republic were merged in a new Cisalpine republic, together with the ancient duchies of Mantua and Milan and the cities of Bergamo, Brescia, Crema, Massa and Carrara. At the end of the same year the old republic of Genoa was given a new democratic existence as the Ligurian republic, and in 1798 Italian patriots in Rome set up a Roman republic, reclaimed the sovereign rights of the people and declared that the pope's temporal power was abolished. Pius VI was taken prisoner by the French and died at Valence in the following year.

Another substantial republic was set up in January 1799 – the Parthenopaean republic, covering the former kingdom of Naples, whose ruler, King Ferdinand IV, had fled to Sicily when French troops entered Neapolitan territory. In the same month the small republic of Lucca was 'democratized'; three months later republican government was imposed on the grand duchy of Tuscany and the kingdom of Piedmont was annexed to France. King Charles Emmanuel IV, who had succeeded Victor Amadeus III, at once abdicated and went with the royal family to Sardinia, which remained in Piedmont's hands throughout the two French occupations of the mainland.

Thus by the spring of 1799 almost the whole of Italy, except for Sicily, Sardinia and Venetia, had been either annexed to France or given republican government under French guidance.

Even greater changes were to come under the second French occupation, but already Italians could perceive the advantages of partial unity in such matters as the sweeping away of onerous customs barriers between the component parts of the Cisalpine republic.

Neither the French overlords nor the republican governments were popular in Italy, where men of all classes resented the introduction of conscription for service in the French armies. Many would have welcomed the return of their generally benevolent princes and dukes. In 1799, when a counter-attack by Austrian and Russian armies drove the French out of most of Italy, there were simultaneous risings by a sect of religious crusaders known as Sanfedists (because they claimed to protect the holy faith) and by other Italian reactionaries.

So the first French occupation was ended after three years. Ferdinand IV returned from Sicily to Naples. A new pope, Pius VII, resumed both temporal and spiritual power in Rome. But Italy was still in a ferment when Bonaparte led a new French army over the Great St Bernard pass in May 1800. Within six weeks a lucky victory at Marengo, where a desperate situation was retrieved by the timely arrival of French reinforcements, forced Austria to surrender Lombardy and leave the rest of Italy in Bonaparte's hands.

In the nine years which followed Marengo, the states of Italy were again regrouped under French control, but this time a different pattern was imposed on Italian life. The republics of 1796–9 were largely forgotten, though the big Cisalpine republic was revived under the name of the republic of Italy. When Napoleon became emperor of the French in 1804 the Italian republic was renamed the kingdom of Italy, and a year later Napoleon crowned himself king of Italy. He believed that his Italian conquest was final, for as he placed the crown on his head in Milan cathedral, he said: 'God has given it to me. Woe to whoever touches it.'

No move was made against either Pius VII or Ferdinand IV of Naples until peace was temporarily restored in central Europe after the French victory at Austerlitz in March 1805. Both rulers were then deposed – Ferdinand in 1806, the pope in 1809 – and their territories occupied, except for the island of Sicily, where Ferdinand resumed his reign under British protection. Napoleon's brother Joseph was made king of Naples and Sicily. The pope's temporal power was again abolished, and Pius VII was held prisoner by the French, first at Savona, on the Italian Riviera, and later at Fontainebleau.

For the remainder of the second French occupation Italy was divided into three parts. In the north was the so-called kingdom of Italy, enlarged by the addition of Venetia after the battle of Austerlitz; here Napoleon himself was nominally king, though the kingdom was actually ruled by his stepson, General Eugène de Beauharnais, who was made viceroy. In the south was the kingdom of Naples and Sicily, though the island was never held either by Joseph Bonaparte or by Marshal Joachim Murat, who succeeded Joseph when he became king of Spain in 1808. The rest of Italy, including Piedmont, Genoa, Tuscany, Rome and those provinces of the former Papal States which were not part of the kingdom of Italy, was directly annexed to France as provinces of the French empire.

Thus the whole of Italy was now a French dependency. Yet once again the French-imposed pattern did something to promote the unitary idea. Salvemini justly observes that 'a peninsula divided into three political sections is considerably nearer unification than a country divided into nine parts, even if it lacks national independence.'[18]

Italy, indeed, had never known such unity since the days of the Roman empire. The old differences between the various kingdoms, duchies and republics had largely disappeared. Internal customs barriers, which had previously been a great hindrance to all forms of trading, were abolished. Trade was further encouraged by road-building, and the confiscation and sale of ecclesiastical property led to a wider ownership of land by small proprietors. All parts of the country had similar legal codes, modelled on the French code. The remaining burdens of the feudal system and the special privileges of clergy and nobility were swept away, and a stronger middle class was created. The opening of new schools and universities marked a continuous advance in education, which was taken away from the Church and entrusted to local authorities. Conscription was revived and was more unpopular than ever, as tens of thousands of Italians were called up to serve in the French armies, but it had the merit of teaching young men the profession of arms.

This elaborate structure had no sure foundation. Like the French empire itself, it rested on the personal success or failure of the Corsican soldier who dominated Europe. Yet the stirring of new life in Italy under the French occupation is not an inglorious moment in its history. It showed that a new regime *could* be built in Italy. The many Italians who helped the French with their radical reforms were founding a tradition of Italian regeneration which others would follow.

4

Events in Sicily and Naples were of particular significance in the closing years of Napoleonic Italy. Though Ferdinand IV reigned in Sicily after his second flight from Naples, the effective governor was General Lord William Bentinck, commander of the British forces which were occupying the island to keep it out of French hands. The army's spending power brought great prosperity to Sicily, and the close association with Britain encouraged local liberals to hope that the island might move from the existing Bourbon absolutism to constitutional government on the British model.[19]

Bentinck shared their hopes. He was a lively and self-willed man in his late thirties, who had been governor of Madras and had served in the Peninsular war. As a faithful whig, he was convinced that British liberal institutions were the best form of government for all countries, and since Britain was providing most of the cost of the Sicilian administration he felt fully entitled to intervene in political affairs. It was due to his influence that a parliament was summoned for the purpose of preparing a new liberal constitution.[20]

This constitution was adopted in 1812. Though it had only a short life, it was an interesting attempt to bring Sicily into the nineteenth century under something not unlike the British system of government. It provided for annual parliaments with fiscal and legislative powers, subject to royal assent, for the abolition of feudalism, of private jurisdictions and of torture, and for the rebirth of Sicily as an independent monarchy under the rule of either Ferdinand himself or his eldest son, if Ferdinand went back to Naples. When parliament met, the moderate liberal government was opposed by both reactionaries and radicals and could make little use of its powers. But in theory, at all events, Sicily became Italy's first constitutional monarchy for the final years of the Napoleonic period.

The importance of Naples at this time was mainly due to the character and ambitions of its remarkable king, Marshal Joachim Murat, who had succeeded Joseph Bonaparte and reigned under the title of King Joachim Napoleon. He was a brilliant cavalry general who had married Napoleon's sister Caroline, an attractive young woman whose marital status had not deterred her from becoming the mistress of Metternich, the Austrian diplomat and statesman.* Napoleon had been anxious to give her a throne, and the treaty which sent Murat to Naples showed that the emperor was more interested in making Caroline a queen than Murat a king. It expressly referred to 'this princess who, by virtue of the present cession, made chiefly in her favour, establishes her descendants upon the throne.'[21]

Murat liked being a king. In 1812 he went to Russia as cavalry commander of Napoleon's Grand Army, but when the campaign collapsed in the disastrous retreat from Moscow he realized that the emperor's star was setting and his only desire was to get back to Naples and resume his kingship as quickly as possible. When Napoleon returned to Paris he tried to make Murat stay with the army by appointing him acting commander-in-chief, but the anxious king gave up his command in January 1813 with the excuse that he was beginning to suffer from jaundice. Napoleon was deeply angry. In a letter to Caroline he observed: 'Your husband is a very brave man on the battlefield, but he is weaker than a woman or a monk when he does not see the enemy. He has no moral courage.' More publicly he rebuked Murat in a curt

* It was said to have been Napoleon himself who threw his sister into the arms of the handsome Austrian. When Metternich came to Paris as a young ambassador in 1806 Napoleon pointed him out to Caroline at a reception with the remark, '*Amusez ce niais-là. Nous en avons besoin à present.*' (Bibl, *Metternich, 1773–1859*, p. 47.)

announcement in the *Moniteur de l'Empire*, stating that the king of Naples had given up the command of the army because of indisposition, and that General Eugène de Beauharnais, viceroy of the kingdom of Italy, had succeeded him. 'The latter', said the announcement, 'is more accustomed to great administrative duties.'[22]

Murat cared nothing for imperial rebukes. He was resolved to keep his throne, and he now thought that he was more likely to do so with Austria's help than with Napoleon's. With sublime treachery to his brother-in-law he offered Austria full military support against France in return for a guarantee that he could keep the kingdom of Naples.

The remarkable saga of Murat's betrayal of Napoleon had begun. After months of negotiations, in which Lord William Bentinck took part, it was still undecided whether he should keep Naples or be given some other kingdom in compensation. At this point – in August 1813 – he was called back to lead the French cavalry as Napoleon's army was driven back through Germany by the combined forces of Austria, Prussia and Russia. Even Murat's brilliance could not save Napoleon from defeat in the battle of Leipzig, but he fought so gallantly that Tsar Alexander I of Russia, who was watching the battle and knew of the secret negotiations, observed drily, 'Truly our ally is hiding his game too well.'[23]

From Leipzig Murat returned to Naples, where in January 1814 he at last signed a treaty of friendship and alliance with Austria. He then led the Neapolitan army north in the hope of securing all Italian territory south of the Po, but his campaign was ended by the Franco-Austrian armistice which followed Napoleon's abdication and withdrawal to Elba in April. Back in Naples again, Murat could do nothing but wait for the decisions of the peace-making congress of Vienna. Elsewhere in Italy the French remained in possession in spite of Napoleon's fall.

At first Metternich, the presiding genius of the Vienna discussions, was inclined to leave Murat on his throne. Later he decided to reinstate the Bourbon dynasty in deference to the wishes of Louis XVIII, the restored Bourbon king of France, but before Murat could be expelled from Naples the whole situation was changed by Napoleon's escape from Elba on 1 March 1815.

Murat now adopted a new role as the champion of Italian independence. An Italian rising, he thought, could be synchronized with Napoleon's return to France. He declared war on Austria and marched north with his Neapolitan army, calling on all Italians to free themselves from foreign domination. In a proclamation issued from Rimini he told the Italian people that their hour of destiny had come, providence was calling them to liberty and one cry was making itself heard – the independence of Italy: 'I summon all brave men to fight at my side. I call on all those who have reflected on the interests of their country to prepare the constitution and the laws which are henceforth to govern happy and independent Italy.'[24]

Many Neapolitans genuinely believed that the Italian people would join in a war for freedom, and even northerners were attracted by the idea of an Italy liberated by Murat.[25] But the venture was doomed from the start. There was no rush to join King Joachim. His army was weakened by desertions, and Austrian divisions closed in on the hopeful saviours of Italy. On 3 May Murat was decisively beaten in the battle of Tolentino. After leading the remnants of his army back to Neapolitan territory he left Naples for the south of France, while his wife found refuge in Austria.

Even then, and even after the battle of Waterloo, Murat could not believe that he had lost his Italian crown for ever. After three months in France he went to Corsica, where the presence of many of his old soldiers made him dream of a landing in Calabria, like Napoleon's return from Elba, and a triumphant march on the capital to evict King Ferdinand IV, whom the congress of Vienna had replaced on his throne.

It was a tragic error. In October he sailed for Italy with a small expeditionary force in six boats, but only one of these reached the Calabrian coast and Murat had exactly thirty men with him when he went ashore at Pizzo. His followers' cries of 'Long Live Joachim' drew no response from the local populace. In a few hours the enterprise had collapsed and Murat was a prisoner. On instructions from Ferdinand his case was considered by a military commission, which condemned him to death. He was shot on 13 October 1815.

Murat was dead, but Murattism lived on. The idea of a Murattist restoration in the Two Sicilies was to be mooted more than once in the formative years of the Risorgimento. King Joachim himself has a small place in its history as the first man who called upon all Italians to fight for their independence.

METTERNICH'S ITALY

Congress of Vienna   The Age of reaction   Privilege and
poverty   Secret societies

THE Italian rulers who left the peninsula during the French
occupation began to return within two months of Napoleon's
abdication in 1814. But Italy did not entirely return to its old
territorial divisions. There were important differences between
the old Italy and the new.

These were the fruits of the congress of Vienna, at which the
representatives of Austria, Prussia, Russia and Britain made
plans for the future of Italy and other territories which had been
conquered by France. The convener of the congress was Prince
Clement Metternich, a German nobleman who had gone to
Vienna as a young man and had been persuaded by the Austrian
emperor to take up a diplomatic career. After holding various
posts in foreign capitals, including the important position of
Austrian minister in Paris, he returned to Austria in 1809,
shortly before the battle of Wagram, and was appointed minister
of state and subsequently chancellor. For nearly forty years he
was the arbiter of Austria's destiny, and often of Europe's
also.

During the congress of Vienna he was much criticized for his
apparent neglect of work and excessive devotion to the balls and
parties arranged for the delegates,[1] but in spite of his delight in
social pleasures he kept his hold on the congress's work, and his
principles of the balance of power and the inalienable nature
of legitimate sovereignty were the basis of its decisions. The
republican and Napoleonic upheavals gave way to reaction.
Europe was to be planned in such a way that there would be no
more revolutions, and to uphold the principles of legitimacy and
absolutism the rulers of Austria, Prussia and Russia signed a

Holy Alliance, which declared that they would rule according to the precepts of justice, Christian charity and peace, and that governments and peoples must henceforth behave as 'members of one and the same Christian nation'. The British statesman Castlereagh called this agreement 'a piece of sublime mysticism and nonsense',[2] but Metternich was able to convert it into 'a definitely reactionary alliance of governments against the governed'.[3]

For Italy the congress ruled that most but not all of the old divisions should be restored, and that certain territories should have new forms of government. Republics, as Tsar Alexander I told a Genoese delegation, were no longer in fashion; in the remade Italy there was no place for the ancient republics of Genoa, Venice and Lucca. Genoa and its Ligurian hinterland were given to Piedmont. Venice was merged in the new Austrian province of Lombardy-Venetia. Lucca became a temporary duchy.

During the French occupation both Britain and Austria had promised the Italians independence and liberty in return for their support against France. These promises were now forgotten.[4] Italy was reconstituted into seven states and two smaller territories, all under absolute rulers and largely under Austrian influence.

Of these states only the kingdom of Piedmont (with Sardinia) and the Papal States had native Italian rulers. Members of the Austrian royal house ruled over Lombardy-Venetia (an Austrian province), Tuscany, Parma and Piacenza, Modena and the smaller duchies of Massa-Carrara and Lucca, and a Spanish Bourbon was ruler of the Two Sicilies. Massa-Carrara and Lucca were earmarked for later absorption by Modena and Tuscany respectively.

2

The diversity of the seven major states and their rulers is itself a sign of the immensity of the task of bringing them together in a single kingdom. Piedmont, the small sub-Alpine kingdom in the north-west, with Turin as its capital and a population of 3,500,000 out of Italy's 18,000,000, was the key to the future. It was the second largest and the most warlike of the Italian states; the Church and the army dominated its national life, and Turin was 'half barrack, half cloister'.[5] Its place as one of the secondary powers of Europe had been won by a succession of ambitious rulers who had profited from wars between greater powers.

At one time Piedmont had straddled the Alps as far as Geneva, and its upper classes still spoke and wrote in French more readily than in Italian; but at the time of the French revolution its territory consisted of Piedmont itself (excluding Genoa), the island of Sardinia, Savoy and the county of Nice. Its rulers were formerly the dukes of Savoy, but they had been raised to kingship after the treaty of Utrecht, and in the eighteenth and nineteenth centuries the ruler of Piedmont was officially known as the king of Sardinia. (For the purposes of this book it will be simpler to use the word Piedmont in preference to Sardinia, since events in Sardinia have little bearing on the history of the Risorgimento.)

Over the years the kings of Piedmont had not lost their ambitions. In the eighteenth century one of them had announced that Piedmont would eat Italy like an artichoke – that is to say, a leaf at a time. In the early nineteenth century Piedmont had its eye on the territory of its eastern and south-eastern neighbours, but it was disappointed in its hope of being given Lombardy by the congress of Vienna. In compensation it was allowed to annex Genoa and the whole of the Ligurian coastal area.

Legally and morally, the congress had no right to dispose of the old republic of Genoa in such a way. Lord William Bentinck, who had occupied the city on behalf of the anti-French coalition early in 1814, when he was hoping to persuade all Italy to rise against France, had promised the Genoese that their republican constitution would be restored after the war. The breaking of Bentinck's pledge was bitterly criticized in Britain, where Lord Buckingham called the annexation of Genoa 'foul and disgraceful' and Samuel Whitbread declared: 'In this one transaction is brought together all the perfidy, baseness and rapacious violence that could disgrace a country.' But Lord Liverpool, the prime minister, explained that it was necessary to incorporate Genoa in Piedmont, because Piedmont was the natural guardian of the Alpine passes.[6] Moreover, although the congress was not thinking of future Italian unity, it was undoubtedly right to avoid any unnecessary fragmentation of Italy.

Piedmont was the first Italian state in which the old order was re-established. In May 1814 two elderly brothers returned from Sardinia to Turin – Victor Emmanuel I, who had succeeded to the throne on Charles Emmanuel IV's abdication, and Charles Felix. Neither of these had a son, and since succession to the throne was governed by Salic law, under which no female could become sovereign, a young cousin was heir-presumptive after the brothers' deaths. This was Charles Albert, prince of Carignano, who belonged to a branch of the royal house which had been separated from the central line of succession for two hundred years.

Charles Albert had lived in France and Switzerland during the French occupation of Italy. He returned to Turin as a boy of fifteen soon after his cousin's restoration. Victor Emmanuel liked him, and described him as *'jeune homme de bon cœur, de très bonne volonté, dont l'education a besoin d'être commencée.'*[7] In spite of this favourable judgment it was rumoured that the king would rather have kept the crown of Piedmont in his own family. One of his daughters, Princess Maria Beatrice, had married the Austrian Archduke Francis, who became duke of Modena, and Victor Emmanuel seems to have thought of abrogating the Salic law, so as to bring his daughter and her husband into the line of succession. Such a change would have been contrary to the principle of strict legitimacy, and nothing came of the king's proposal.[8] Charles Albert's right to the throne was upheld by the congress of Vienna.

Victor Emmanuel's clothes when he returned to Turin were an indication of what lay ahead for Piedmont. Fashions had changed in the previous twenty years, but the Turinese, who turned out in their thousands to give their king a rousing welcome, were surprised to see that he and his brother were still dressed in the mode of 1789, with three-cornered hats, powdered hair and pigtails.[9] It was from this time that the word *codino* (pigtail) passed into Italian speech as a nickname for supporters of the *ancien régime*.

It was certainly a return to the *ancien régime* that Victor Emmanuel had in mind. 'I shall always remember this day of my entry into our faithful Turin,' he wrote to his wife, 'and I shall at once repay its joy by obliterating every trace of the enemy occupation.'[10] On the very next day he issued a decree ordering that all the laws and institutions in force in Piedmont in 1798 (its last year of independence) were to be restored, and all laws passed under the French occupation were to be cancelled, except those relating to taxes.

So Piedmont put back the clock. The legal and social reforms introduced by the French were swept away. The aristocracy and the Church regained their old rights and privileges; the ecclesiastical courts were revived, the Jesuits resumed control of education and all professors suspected of liberal tendencies were dismissed from the university of Turin. In the army and the public services rank and position were reinstated as they had been in 1798, and promotion to higher posts was made on the basis of age and seniority. Men who had held high positions under the French were demoted to make room for inexperienced courtiers who had been with the king in Sardinia. One of these sycophants even wanted to destroy the great bridge over the Po, simply because it had been built by the French. Fortunately the queen saved it. She had a villa on the far side of the river, and the bridge was preserved so that there could be easy transport between the villa and the royal palace.[11]

Liberals and radicals who had welcomed Napoleon's wind of change were distressed at the return of privilege and the suppression of progressive thought. Genoa was particularly resentful when it found that its republic had been destroyed to make way for royal absolutism. But there was always a bond of affection between the royal house of Savoy and the people of Piedmont. The country as a whole accepted the return to the old ways with resignation and indifference. Opponents of the king's government were relatively few.[12]

The Austrian archdukes who ruled in Modena and Tuscany were also given a warm welcome on their return. In Modena the people were so pleased to see Duke Francis IV that they took the horses out of his coach and pulled it to his palace. Like Victor Emmanuel, the duke of Modena ordered a general return to the laws and institutions of the 1790s, but he was wise enough to keep some of the French regulations, including one which abolished torture and others concerned with mortgages and wills.[13]

Of Tuscany, to which Ferdinand III came back in September 1814 to take up the grand dukedom he had surrendered in 1798, it has been said that 'no Italian state returned to its old regime with greater satisfaction'.[14] Ferdinand also thought it advisable to keep some of the best French laws, and he combined them with a benevolent absolutism which made Tuscany the freest country in Italy.[15] The press was free; arts and letters were honoured; political trials were rare. The grand duke's government was both personal and patriarchal; he was himself responsible for all public affairs with the aid of one minister and a number of royal secretaries.

Restoration was more complicated in the smaller duchy of Parma (or Parma, Piacenza and Guastalla, to give it its full title). Parma had previously been ruled by a Spanish Bourbon, but Metternich was anxious to find a throne for Napoleon's second wife, Marie-Louise, the Austrian princess who had been persuaded to marry the French emperor for political reasons. Parma seemed eminently suitable and was duly assigned to her. To pacify the previous ruling family Metternich arranged that they should return to Parma on Marie-Louise's death (which did not occur until 1847), and in the meantime the duke-presumptive was to be duke of the former republic of Lucca. When he succeeded to Parma, Lucca would be absorbed by Tuscany. (In the same way the small province of Massa-Carrara was made a duchy for the benefit of the Austrian Archduchess Maria Beatrice of Este, and was to be incorporated in Modena when the archduchess died.)

Marie-Louise did not take up her dukedom until 1816. When she did so Metternich felt that she was too weak and frivolous to be left on her own, and he sent the experienced Count von Neipperg, a man of thirty-nine, to act as her minister. His advice was so much to her liking that she also became his mistress. Until Neipperg's death in 1829 Parma was one of the most humanely governed states in Italy. Its citizens enjoyed genuine freedom of speech and the printed word, and it was the only state which kept (and improved) all the French laws.[16]

The remainder of Italy north of the Papal States was formed into the new kingdom of Lombardy-Venetia, governed by an Austrian viceroy, living in Milan, on behalf of the Austrian emperor. It was a component part of the Austrian empire, with separate administrations in Milan and Venice, and Italians had no effective share in its government. Italian regiments were disbanded and replaced by Croat militia. The chief official posts were held by Austrians, and although Italians sat on central and provincial councils known as 'congregations', these had no executive authority. Police control was rigid, and all Italian initiative was sternly suppressed.[17]

Lombardy-Venetia suffered both economically and financially under Austrian rule. Free trade was abolished; the province was brought into the Austrian economic system, and Lombard traders were obliged to buy from Austrian producers the goods which England and France could sell them more cheaply. Though the kingdom had only one-eighth of the population of the Austrian empire, it was forced to contribute one-third of the empire's tax revenue.[18]

The establishment of an Austrian province in the north of Italy put the whole country in Austria's power. From his northern base the Austrian emperor could send troops into any part of the peninsula; so long as the Austrians remained in Lombardy-Venetia there could be no Italian independence. The system was meant to be permanent. When the peace treaty with France was being discussed in Paris in 1814, Count Federico Confalonieri, a Lombard nobleman, took a Milanese delegation to France to plead the cause of Lombard independence. He got no satisfaction from the Austrian Emperor Francis II. 'It is essential,' the emperor told him, 'that the Lombards should forget that they are Italians. Obedience to my wishes will be the link which will bind the Italian provinces to the rest of the empire.'[19]

To emphasize Lombardy-Venetia's dependence on Austria, all holders of official posts had to take an oath of allegiance to the emperor. One who refused to do so was Ugo Foscolo, poet, author and patriot, whose romantic novel, *Jacopo Ortiz*, written in 1798, made such an impression on Giuseppe Mazzini that he learnt it by heart.[20] Rather than take the oath, Foscolo left his books and papers with his friend Silvio Pellico and became, in March 1815, the new Italy's first political exile.

Lombards found their own way of showing their dislike of Austrian rule. A few months after Foscolo's departure Pellico's play, *Francesca da Rimini*, was presented at the Theatre Royal, Milan, where its patriotic sentiments were warmly applauded. The Milanese were especially aroused by Paolo's speech towards the end of the first act, in which he threatens 'the foreigner' with massacre and pledges himself to fight for Italy.[21]

Lying across the centre of Italy were the Papal States, consisting of Lazio (the province in which Rome was situated), Umbria, the Marches and the Romagna (which included the legations of Ravenna, Bologna, Ferrara and Forli, each of which was administered by a cardinal-legate), together with the duchy of Benevento and the principality of Pontecorvo. Pius VII resumed his rule at Rome on 24 May 1814, with Monsignor Agostino Rivarola, an ignorant and fanatical Genoan priest, as his chief administrator.[22]

Rivarola's first action was to abolish almost the whole of the French legislative system, although, like the duke of Modena, he was prudent enough to retain some of the commercial and financial regulations introduced during the French occupation. Theocratic government resumed its sway; cardinals and other ecclesiastics administered the revived eighteenth-century laws and penal system; the lay population had to endure the hardships imposed by a callous and reactionary government, and those who had collaborated with the French were heavily penalized.* Pius VII was a humane man, but he had little influence on the ecclesiastics who exercised his temporal power.

An ominous sign for the future was that the congress of Vienna gave Austria a foothold in the north-east of the Papal

---

* The story was told that a Signor Morelli, who had been deprived of his public office because he had continued to hold it under French rule, tried to excuse himself to Rivarola by explaining that he had not served France of his own free will, but only to earn enough money to save the honour of his beautiful daughters. Rivarola shrugged his shoulders. 'You are trying to arouse my pity with an excuse that makes you more guilty,' he retorted. 'Rather than serve the French, you should have put your daughters on the streets.' (Spellanzon, *Storia del Risorgimento*, I, p. 732.)

States. The part of the Ferrara legation which lay on the left bank of the Po was transferred to Lombardy-Venetia. Austria was also allowed to maintain garrisons within the Papal States at Ferrara and Comacchio. More would be heard in time of the Austrian garrison at Ferrara.

The restoration of the Spanish Bourbon, King Ferdinand, to the throne of the Two Sicilies was at first complicated by the presence of Murat as a 'sitting tenant' in Naples. While other princes were resuming their rule Ferdinand had to stay in Sicily during the winter of 1814–15. It was a galling time for him because of the ineffectiveness of the liberal government which had taken office under the new constitution. At last, when the British troops had left Sicily and Murat had fled from Naples, Ferdinand took action. He dissolved parliament and went back to the mainland, where he entered Naples on horseback and without display on 9 June 1815. His simple manners, which led people to call him 'the countryman king', were in sharp contrast with Murat's theatricality and fondness for ceremonial.[23]

Ferdinand was wiser than some of his fellow-sovereigns in his attitude to the French laws and institutions introduced by Murat. He accepted the existing administrative pattern and promised to maintain civil liberties. Though he promulgated a new code of laws, it preserved the main features of the French code. The Church, however, regained many of its lost privileges, including the control of education and the censorship of the press.[24]

Ferdinand at once found himself in a dilemma as ruler of a joint kingdom. In Naples he had resumed absolute rule. In Sicily the constitution which he had granted in 1812, and had sworn to observe, was still in force. One of its provisions was that Sicily should be independent of all other states, including Naples. But Ferdinand had no intention of dividing his kingdom and making Sicily an independent state ruled over by another member of the royal family, and he found it inconvenient that the funds required for administering Sicily should have to be voted by parliament. He took the easy way out. At the end of 1816 he abolished the Sicilian constitution. At the same time he emphasized the permanent nature of the union between Naples and Sicily by changing his own title. Until then he had been formally known as King Ferdinand IV of Naples and King Ferdinand III of Sicily. He now became King Ferdinand I of the Two Sicilies.

3

By 1816 all the Italian states had returned to a system of government based on the sovereigns' absolute power. This was Metternich's Italy – a country of small states dependent on Austria's good-will and so organized as to be a bulwark against any revival of revolutionary tendencies. In the new spirit of the nineteenth century the inequities of this system were bound to encourage the revolutionary urge it was designed to suppress.

Privilege and poverty were the two extremes. Feudalism had been abolished except in Sicily, and even there it was ended by royal decree in 1818; but both the nobility and the clergy still enjoyed great privilege.[25] The influence of the clergy, who numbered about 150,000 out of Italy's population of 18,000,000, was paramount in education, which they entirely controlled.

More hopeful for Italy's future was the steadily growing middle class, consisting of civil servants, doctors, lawyers, business-men, authors, journalists and the new class of medium and small landowners which had come into existence when the French confiscated and sold ecclesiastical property.[26] The middle class provided most of the members of the secret societies which were being launched or enlarged in all parts of the country.

Lower in the social scale were the artisans in the large towns, whose numbers grew steadily as Italy slowly accepted the Industrial Revolution. But the great bulk of the population consisted of the peasantry, who knew nothing of politics and were solely concerned with the problem of keeping themselves and their families alive. Their conditions varied greatly from state to state. In Lombardy they had good cottages and a tolerable standard of living, but in Sicily some were dressed in goatskins as late as the second half of the nineteenth century. In the Papal States their conditions were deplorable, and they were reduced to starvation in years of bad harvests. The peasants' only property was the house or hovel they lived in, and their pay as land workers was miserably low. Very few could read or write.

Two other sections of the Italian population were the brigands, who were a constant danger to travellers in Naples, Sicily and the Papal States, and the beggars, who were especially numerous in Rome and in Naples, where they were known as *lazzaroni*. The *lazzaroni* were generally active at times of public disturbance, but there was no means of organizing them as a revolutionary force.

No Italian had any vote or direct share in the government of his state, which was carried on by the sovereign and the ministers of his choice. Personal liberty was everywhere subject to the surveillance of a strong police force.

The sharp divisions of Italian society, in which even the middle classes had little or no contact with the artisans and the peasants, made it an unpromising field for national revival. How could such diverse groups, living in such widely different territories and often speaking in dialects that were unintelligible in other parts of the country, ever be brought to feel that they all belonged to one nation? Omodeo sums up the problem when he states: 'The laborious construction of the Italian conscience is the real history of our Risorgimento.'[27]

Yet even in these early days of reaction there were men who had visions of revolutionary change. The restorations were hardly completed before the first plans for revolt were being discussed. The plotters were members of the secret societies.

4

It has often been said that Italians have a flair for conspiracy. It was not surprising, therefore, that secret societies should have proliferated all over Italy to counteract the post-Napoleonic reaction. Some had fanciful names like Knights of the Sun, Sons of Mars, White Pilgrims and even American Sharpshooters, though many of these were only local offshoots of a larger group. More substantial societies were the Federati, who flourished in northern Italy, the Guelfi and the Adelfi. The most important of all was the great society of the Carbonari – the charcoal-burners.

In addition to the societies founded in Italy some were established from outside the country by patriots who had left the country for fear of imprisonment. One of the persistent founders of secret societies was Filipo Buonarroti, a Tuscan revolutionary who lived at different times in Corsica and Geneva and established in turn the Friends of Italian Liberty, the Sincere Friends and the Filadelfi. These were set up at the end of the eighteenth century and in the first decade of the nineteenth; in later years Buonarroti went to live in Paris and became the recognized head of the Carbonari, whom he reformed and reorganized.

The Carbonaro movement was not, as is sometimes thought, derived from freemasonry, which was introduced into Italy in the eighteenth century. Except on rare occasions there was no connexion between the two movements, and the freemasons made little effective contribution to the Risorgimento. Freemasons and Carbonari had different objectives: freemasons were international and anti-clerical; Carbonari were national and patriotic. In the Papal States they were inevitably anti-papal, since they were always against the government, but in general they were not anti-religious. Indeed, they regarded Christ as their prototype and St Theobald (who made charcoal in the woods of Germany) as their patron saint.[28]

Though there is some doubt about the actual origins of the Carbonari it is certain that they existed in Naples and Sicily by 1806, and that their original function was to oppose French rule in Italy. Their name may have come from similar organizations in France and Germany, or it may have been meant to recall that the first Italian Carbonari hid in the mountains and pretended to be charcoal-burners in the intervals between their anti-governmental conspiracies. Their early opposition to the regimes of Joseph Bonaparte and Murat was encouraged by King Ferdinand and the British authorities in Sicily, but this kind of collaboration ceased after the restoration, when the Carbonari became anti-Bourbon and worked against the king. From Naples the movement spread to other parts of Italy, and in a few years the total number of Carbonari may have reached 300,000.[29]

Broadly their objectives were constitutional government and independence from foreign rule. Many Carbonari were also republicans.

Carbonarism was never a 'popular' movement. At times of great risings – in Naples in 1820 and in the Papal States in 1831 –

peasants would swell the insurgent ranks, but the movement was mainly supported by the middle classes, together with a number of army officers and aristocrats.

The middle classes joined the Carbonari because they felt that their new social and economic progress was threatened by the return of absolute government; the Carbonaro movement was their instrument for securing constitutional rule which would safeguard their interests. The army officers who became Carbonari were men who had served under Napoleon and were disappointed to find that their past service now counted for nothing. Both the officers and the aristocrats were patriots who longed to see the Austrians driven from Italy and wanted their states to have institutions which were more in keeping with the nineteenth century. The Carbonari also included a number of priests and friars.

Though fundamentally different from each other, the Carbonari were organized in the same way as the freemasons; they were formed in local groups and they had an elaborate ritual for admission to membership. They called fellow-members *buoni cugini* (good cousins), and to preserve the charcoal-burning fiction their meeting-places were known as *vendite* (sales centres, or, more simply, lodges). They had their own colours of black, blue and red – black for charcoal and faith, red for fire and charity, blue for smoke and hope.

Though their practical aims were political and national they regarded themselves as a moral and religious organization. One of their rules stated: 'To every Carbonaro belongs the natural and inalienable right to worship the Almighty according to his own intuition and understanding.'[30]

It was dangerous to be a Carbonaro, as the movement was officially prohibited, and the police seized every opportunity of putting their own informers into the local *vendite*. In the Papal States Carbonari had the added peril of opposition from the Sanfedisti, the counter-revolutionary secret society which claimed that its objects were to defend the holy faith, the pope's temporal power and the papal prerogatives, 'as well from the plots of innovators as from the aggressions of the Austrian empire'.[31] The Sanfedisti were especially active in the legations, where they were often in conflict with the Carbonari and other secret societies.

The Carbonari made no lasting contribution to the Risorgimento, but they were useful servants of the national cause in the years which followed the French occupation. At a time when the Italian people seemed to have no means of influencing the course of events the Carbonari kept alive the central issues of constitutional government and freedom from foreign rule. The gallant but unsuccessful leaders of secret society insurrections were worthy forerunners of the men who liberated and united Italy.

THE FIRST RISINGS

Macerata   Naples and Palermo   Piedmont   Pellico and Confalonieri   Charles Albert

SECRET societies had strong roots in the Papal States, which were the worst governed area in Italy. Exiles who went to live in other Italian states gave a grim picture of life under pontifical rule: 'There was no care for the cultivation of the people, no anxiety for public prosperity; Rome was a cesspool of corruption, of exemptions and of privileges; a clergy, made up of fools and knaves, in power, the laity slaves; the treasury plundered by gangs of tax farmers and spies; all the business of government consisted in prying into and punishing the notions, the expectations and the imprudences of the liberals.'[1] Civil government could hardly be said to exist in this atmosphere of theocratic oppression.

The chief secret societies in the Papal States at this time were the Carbonari, whose headquarters were at Macerata, and the Guelfi, whose central council met at Bologna. In the autumn of 1816 these two societies agreed to join forces for an insurrection which was timed to begin on the death of Pope Pius VII, who was said to be in failing health. It was hoped that the rising would spread all over central Italy, but there was no co-ordinated planning with societies in other states.

Like other ill-prepared plots in the ensuing years, the Macerata rising was sadly bungled. Paolo Monti, grand master of one of the Guelf lodges at Bologna, was put in charge of the operation and was given responsibility for choosing the right moment – probably in the spring or summer of 1817. During the winter the pope recovered, and Monti decided to postpone the insurrection. The Macerata conspirators did not agree. Feeling confident of success, they rose in revolt on the night of 2 3–4 June.

Unfortunately all their confidence disappeared at the sound of the first shots, which were actually fired by one of their own men. The conspirators dispersed, and the police and papal soldiers rounded them up without difficulty.[2]

The papal government brought the full rigour of the law to bear on this pitiful affair. After long delay three trials were held at Rome in the autumn of 1818. Five men were condemned to death, three sentenced to the galleys for life and many others given smaller sentences, but all the major sentences were later commuted to permanent or temporary exile. The significance of the trials was that the widespread ramifications of the Carbonaro movement were clearly revealed in the evidence. The rising was also important because it heightened the tension between the Sanfedisti and the Carbonari. Clashes between the two groups became more frequent, and the Romagna won a grim reputation as a scene of murder and bloodshed.

2

The first rising which can be regarded as part of the Risorgimento was in Naples in 1820. It was the result of nearly three years' plotting by the Carbonari, who had also found much support in the Neapolitan army. Its object was to force King Ferdinand to grant a constitution.

The inspiration for action came from Spain, where an army revolt at Cadiz in January 1820 compelled the king to restore the Spanish constitution of 1812. Where Spain led, Naples could surely follow. In May General Guglielmo Pepe, one of Murat's veterans and the commander of the Naples garrison, began to work out the details of a military rising with Carbonaro support, but his orders to begin the revolt were anticipated by two cavalry sub-lieutenants at Nola, who raised the black, blue and red colours of the Carbonari on 2 July. From Nola, accompanied by a Carbonaro priest, they rode to Avellino, where they were joined by the colonel commanding the garrison. Thereafter the rising spread rapidly through the army, while thousands of Carbonari hurried to join the troops. General Pepe, fearing discovery and arrest if he stayed in the capital, led part of the Naples garrison into one of the insurgent camps.

The revolution was not directed against Ferdinand himself, whose government, according to an unprejudiced Neapolitan exile, was one of the best in Europe.[3] It was solely designed to secure constitutional government, and the mutineers rallied to the slogan of 'For God, the king and the constitution'. Their march on the capital was irresistible. The troops sent against them deserted and went over to the insurgents' side. Ferdinand was obliged to yield. A decree promising Naples a constitution was signed on the night of 6–7 July.

Two days later the insurgents entered Naples, with bands, army, militia and Carbonari all marching in one great column. To avoid meeting them, Ferdinand appointed his eldest son, Francis, duke of Calabria, to act as regent. As the procession passed the royal palace, where Francis was watching from the balcony with the king's ministers and members of the royal family, he pinned the Carbonaro colours to his breast and told the others to follow his example. The revolution was over. The army and the Carbonari had won.

Ferdinand then resumed his authority, and at the request of the Carbonari he gave Naples the Spanish constitution of 1812, which, in spite of its length and complexity, had an almost legendary importance among European revolutionaries. In the royal chapel on 13 July Ferdinand swore on the Bible that he would observe the constitution, and after repeating the agreed formula he added on his own initiative: 'Omnipotent God, if I am lying or if one day I am to be untrue to this oath, in this moment strike me with Thy thunderbolt.' The king's request was not granted. There was no thunderbolt. For the moment no one doubted his sincerity.[4]

This was the greatest triumph of the Carbonari. With the army's help they had won constitutional government for Naples, and they could fairly hope that the rest of Italy would follow suit. But there was trouble, almost from the beginning, because of rivalry between the Carbonari and the army.

Under the new constitution the king retained his power to choose his ministers. He chose them from nobles and army officers who had served under Murat and had had no jobs since the restoration. Thus the ministry was Murattist, while the

Carbonari were left to exert their liberal influence in parliament, in the press and generally in the national life. This rivalry would have had grave consequences if the constitution had lasted longer.

Further trouble came from Sicily. News of the Naples rising was welcomed at Palermo, and the nobles at once demanded the restoration of Sicily's own constitution of 1812. They regarded this constitution, which provided for two-chamber government and left the Church and the nobility with many of their privileges, as more suited to Sicilian conditions than the Spanish one, under which there was single-chamber government and the powers of the nobles and clergy were severely curtailed; and they were deeply offended when a royal decree ordered that Sicily as well as Naples should accept the Spanish constitution. Under the barons' leadership Palermo rose in revolt. Disturbances followed in many parts of the island, though Messina and a number of other towns held back through jealousy of Palermo.[5]

The barons' demand for the island's old constitution was only one reason for the Sicilian rising. It was also an expression of anti-Neapolitan feeling and of Sicily's desire for independence. Sicily disliked the legal changes and administrative centralization introduced by Ferdinand since his restoration. So the rising of 1820 was actually 'the explosion of popular discontent with the reforms of the previous five years, and the people of Palermo were the true protagonists and authors of the revolt.'[6]

A Sicilian independence movement was unwelcome to the new constitutional government in Naples. Florestano Pepe, brother of Guglielmo, was sent to the island with 7000 troops and an offer to summon an assembly to vote on the issue of union or independence. This did not satisfy the Sicilians. In the face of their intransigence the Neapolitans attacked Palermo by land and sea and forcibly suppressed what was virtually 'an insurrection within an insurrection'. In October Sicily accepted the Spanish constitution and agreed to remain in the kingdom of the Two Sicilies. But the Neapolitan government was not convinced that it would keep the agreement, and General Pietro Colletta was sent to the island to carry out further repressive measures.[7]

For a few months the Neapolitan revolution seemed to be

holding its own, Alone among the Italian states, the Two Sicilies now had constitutional government. But Metternich was not prepared to accept this drastic change in the Italy he had planned at the congress of Vienna. He regarded the Italians as 'an ignorant and semi-barbarous people, whose last word is the dagger',[8] and he knew that Austria's position in Italy would be endangered if the people got the upper hand over their rulers. He decided to intervene and restore the *status quo*, but before doing so he invited Russia, Prussia, France and Britain to send representatives to a conference at Troppau, to discuss the Neapolitan situation. The conference was inconclusive. The five powers condemned all political changes brought about by military risings or popular insurrections, and claimed the right to armed intervention. But action was postponed until the king of Naples had been able to meet the powers and explain the situation at a further conference to be held at Laibach.

Under the new constitution Ferdinand had to ask for parliament's permission if he wished to leave the country. In doing so he promised to uphold the constitution, and he sailed from Naples on 14 December with a Carbonaro ribbon in his buttonhole.

That was the end of constitutional government in Naples. On arriving at Laibach Ferdinand broke his promise to parliament; he told the conference that he had agreed to the constitution under duress, and that he was willing to accept the powers' decisions about his country's future. Metternich undertook to send an Austrian army to restore the king to his old position.

This was a good illustration of Austria's mastery of Italy. From the Austrian province of Lombardy-Venetia an army of 60,000 men marched through the Papal States to the kingdom of Naples. The Neapolitan government resisted its advance. Two columns were sent north, but one, commanded by General Guglielmo Pepe, was soundly beaten by the Austrians at Rieti, and the other was so much weakened by desertions that it could not go to Pepe's assistance. The Austrian white-coats entered Naples on 23 March 1821. The constitution was annulled, and Ferdinand returned a few weeks later to resume his absolute rule. He had killed the revolution, but he had lost his people's trust. By going back on his oath to preserve the constitution he had destroyed the moral basis of the Bourbon dynasty.[9]

It has been argued that the Neapolitan rising of 1820 was guided by elderly men and had none of the spirit of the new generation.[10] Certainly it was an isolated rising, and its leaders had no idea of promoting Italian unity or of driving the Austrians out of the peninsula. But even the temporary establishment of constitutional government in an Italian state was no small matter, since constitutional rule was an integral part of the Risorgimento. Pepe and his colleagues were old-fashioned, but they were working – unconsciously, perhaps – towards the fulfilment of Italy's destiny.

3

The Neapolitan example of a rising to force the grant of a constitution was followed in Piedmont in the spring of 1821. The leaders were army officers, who were joined by the Federati, a secret society with civil servants, professors, ecclesiastics, doctors, lawyers, engineers and other professional men among its members, but not a single representative of the urban working class or the peasantry.[11] The conspiracy had no republican element. Its leaders were loyal to King Victor Emmanuel I. They wished to induce him to give Piedmont a constitution and declare war on Austria.

This was essentially a patriotic movement. The conspirators wanted to see the Austrians driven out of Lombardy-Venetia, and they hoped that the Lombards would rise in sympathy when the time came for the attack. Secret negotiations between Lombard and Piedmontese conspirators were conducted for some months in the winter of 1820-1, when a leading negotiator on the Piedmontese side was Prince Charles Albert, the ultimate heir to the throne.

The prince was neither a liberal nor a member of a secret society, but he was certainly an Italian patriot. 'One can never tire of repeating, "Oh, Italy, why are you so beautiful and not stronger?" ', he wrote to a friend after seeing the ruins of Rome in January 1820.[12] Though he had married an Austrian princess – Maria Teresa, daughter of the grand duke of Tuscany – he had no love for his wife's country, and the heads of the

Piedmontese conspiracy were greatly encouraged by his obvious sympathy with their plans.

They were not very subtle conspirators. Their first and most blatant error was in not striking when the Neapolitan revolution seemed to have won the day. A simultaneous rising in the north would have stirred all Italy, but the Piedmontese misjudged the situation and thought that there was no need to hurry because the Neapolitans could be trusted to resist the forces of reaction. This is shown in a letter from Santorre di Santarosa, one of the leading conspirators, to Cesare Balbo in October 1820. 'If the Austrians attack Naples it will be at the beginning of December', wrote Santarosa. 'I do not believe that the army of Naples will melt away as in previous wars. A country which has a parliament cannot be easily subdued ... And perhaps there will then be born the great occasion for the Italian war.'[13]

So the Piedmontese conspirators waited, and did not even take advantage of the tense situation created by a students' 'rag' at a Turin theatre in January 1821. On this occasion four students were arrested for wearing red berets with black pompoms as they sat in the theatre. Their comrades at the university staged a 'sit-in' as a protest; they refused to leave the university buildings and barricaded them against intruders. Troops had to be used to drive them out. Thirty-four students were wounded, and though no one was killed the incident became popularly known as 'the students' massacre'.

Prince Charles Albert now openly ranged himself against the 'establishment' of which he was nominally a part. He sent gifts of money and sweets to the wounded and imprisoned students.[14] This generous and rather rash act caused the army officers who were planning the rising to look still more confidently to the young price as the natural leader of their insurrection.[15] But they still hesitated to act, though it was becoming clear that the Neapolitan experiment would soon collapse under Austrian pressure.

At the beginning of March they realized that they could wait no longer. Letters from secret society members overseas were intercepted by the Turin police; they mentioned plans for a revolution and indicated that Charles Albert was involved in it. Some arrests were made. More were expected. The leaders of the rising decided to put detailed plans before Charles Albert and ask for his approval and co-operation.

Much controversy has raged over Charles Albert's actions at this critical moment. It is beyond dispute that Major Santorre di Santarosa and three of his brother officers went to Charles Albert's home, the Palazzo Carignano, on the evening of 6 March and were joined there by Marquis Robert d'Azeglio (whose brother Massimo later became prime minister of Piedmont). Plans for military risings at Turin and Alessandria were explained to the prince. It was emphasized that this would not be a revolt against the king's authority, but an attempt to make him use his authority by granting a constitution and making war on Austria.

There are different versions of Charles Albert's reaction to this information. According to Santarosa, who published an account of the meeting soon after the rising had collapsed, 'Charles Albert agreed to everything, and reserved to himself the role he wished for – one which suited his rank', the role, in fact, of 'mediator between the insurgents and the king'.[16] But Charles Albert himself, in writing an account of his conduct for the governments of the great powers, said that he tried to dissuade the conspirators and show them the folly of their enterprise, and that he threatened to oppose them with artillery if they went on with their plans.[17]

So far the two accounts are in open disagreement, but it is undisputed that on the following morning Charles Albert had a further meeting with two of the conspirators and said clearly that he could not take part in the rising. The problem is whether he was breaking a pledge he had given the night before or was merely confirming an earlier statement.

Santarosa was a truthful man, and his account has never been contradicted, except by Charles Albert. It can be assumed, therefore, that the conspirators honestly thought that the prince had given his full consent to their plans. On Charles Albert's side it is claimed that the midnight talk was less definite and more conditional than the conspirators thought, and that he had never suggested that he would actually oppose the king. Probably there was a genuine misunderstanding between the prince and the officers, though even one of Charles Albert's defenders admits that 'there are elements of culpable illusion and weakness in the prince's conduct'.[18]

The upshot of Charles Albert's final refusal was that Santarosa and his friends tried to countermand the revolution. Their orders were effective at Turin, but did not reach Alessandria in time to prevent a rising. Four days later the insurrection spread to Turin. A group of officers and men captured the citadel and raised the revolutionary tricolour.

Though deeply disturbed by the rising, the king refused to grant the rebels' demand for a constitution, and in view of the growing unrest he decided to abdicate in favour of his brother Charles Felix, who was then visiting Modena. For the time being he appointed Charles Albert as regent.

Turin was shocked when Victor Emmanuel and his family left for Nice at dawn on 13 March. Even the rebels were dismayed, since their aim had been to bring the king himself into their movement. Crowds paraded the streets all day, calling for the constitution. In the evening lights went up all over the city when Charles Albert gave way to the insurgents and issued a proclamation adopting the Spanish constitution for the state of Piedmont.[19]

But the revolution had been only partly successful. The army was divided between troops which were loyal to the king and troops which supported the revolution, and the national junta which had replaced the king's ministers had no real power. From Modena Charles Felix disowned the constitution, and sent a proclamation to Turin denouncing all supporters of the insurrection as rebels. Charles Albert was ordered to leave the country and go to Tuscany.

The revolution was dying, though Santarosa, who had become minister of war in the national junta, still dreamed of saving the situation. He decided that the constitutionalists' best hope was to defeat or win over the loyal counter-revolutionary troops which were concentrated at Novara. But the cause was lost already. Charles Felix had asked for Austrian help, and Metternich had agreed to send troops. The constitutional army, which could muster between 4000 and 5000 men, had to face some 7000

royalist troops, under General Vittorio de la Tour, and 2000
newly arrived Austrians.

On 7 April the constitutionalists made their camp close to
Novara. On the following day they slowly advanced towards the
town, hoping that the royalist troops would come out and greet
them as brothers. The hope was vain. The Novara batteries
opened fire, and when the rebels began to retreat they were
dispersed and routed by an Austrian cavalry charge. De la Tour
and Count Bubna, the Austrian commander, then entered Turin
and Alessandria without opposition, the rebel leaders fled and
Piedmont returned to absolute rule under a lieutenant-governor
appointed by Charles Felix. An unhappy legacy of the rising
was that more Austrian troops had crossed the Ticino and were
ranging all over the country.

Charles Felix himself did not return from Modena till October.
In the interval judical tribunals tried those who had taken part
in the insurrection. Seventy death sentences were passed, but
most of those sentenced had already left the country, and only
three soldiers were actually executed. More than 300 officers
were dismissed or put on retired pay.

4

The Naples rising had tragic results in Lombardy, whose
Austrian rulers were alarmed at the evident strength of the
Carbonaro movement. Lombard patriots were soon to pay for the
Neapolitans' success.

In August 1820 membership of the Carbonari was scheduled
in Lombardy-Venetia as an act of high treason, for which the penalty was death. Arrests of Carbonari and Federati soon followed.

One of the leading Carbonari in Lombardy was Piero Maron-
celli, a native of Forli, in the Papal States, who had come to
Milan in 1815 and founded a *vendita* there. Shortly before the
Austrians issued their anti-Carbonari edict he had enrolled
Silvio Pellico, the distinguished playwright and joint editor of a
progressive magazine, *Il Conciliatore*, as a new member.

It was a fateful enrolment. A few weeks later one of Maroncelli's letters fell into the hands of the police. It mentioned that
he had initiated Pellico and several others into the rites of the

Carbonari. Most of those named in the letter were arrested, and were tried in the following spring. Maroncelli, Pellico and one other were sentenced to death, but the Austrian emperor commuted their sentences to fifteen years' imprisonment in the grim fortress of Spielberg, in Moravia. Their sentences were later curtailed, and Pellico was released in 1830. In 1843 he published his famous account of his imprisonment, *Le mie prigioni*, a book, says Tivaroni, 'whose gentle moderation did more harm to the Austrian domination of Italy than a lost battle'.[20]*

Another important political prisoner joined Pellico in the Spielberg in 1824. This was Count Federico Confalonieri, one of the leading figures in Milanese life, who had been concerned with public affairs since 1814, when he went to Paris to plead the Lombard cause after Napoleon's abdication. It was on that visit that he came to know the exiled patriot, Buonarroti, and was introduced by him into the world of secret societies. In Milan he showed his liberal sentiments by contributing to the foundation of *Il Conciliatore*, and as leader of the Lombard group of Federati he looked forward to the end of Austrian domination and the birth of a kingdom of Italy. He was the chief Lombard negotiator with Charles Albert and the Turin conspirators over the possibility of a Lombard rising if the Piedmontese invaded Lombardy-Venetia.

Though the Austrian police suspected Confalonieri, they had no proof against him, and even a search of his house in July 1821 yielded no result. But in November of that year two of his friends were arrested. During the police interrogation about their activities they carelessly mentioned Confalonieri's name. This was the corroboration for which the police had been waiting, and they began to close their net around him.

He still had a chance of escape, for the Austrian general, Count Bubna, tried to save him from arrest. As a friend of the beautiful Countess Confalonieri, Bubna went to her box at the opera and tactfully suggested that she should persuade her

---

* Pellico's book was translated into all the languages of Europe. Denis Mack Smith considers that 'possibly no other person except Mazzini had such an effect in arousing national indignation'. (*The Making of Italy, 1796–1866*, p. 66.)

husband to take an immediate trip abroad for the sake of his health. But Confalonieri preferred to stay in Milan. He was unwilling to condemn his wife to a life of exile, and he was sure that everything in his house was so well hidden that the police would find no incriminating material.

He was too confident. Another search of his house produced evidence that led to the arrest of the count and many of his friends. Other Federati were arrested at Brescia. After a long trial Confalonieri was sentenced to death for high treason, but once again the Austrian emperor commuted the sentence to imprisonment in the Spielberg. He was nominally imprisoned for life, but was released in 1836.

5

Prince Charles Albert was unmistakably the 'odd man out' after the collapse of the Piedmontese insurrection. The revolutionaries accused him of treachery because they believed that he had given his word to support them and had then deserted them at the eleventh hour. The royalists called him disloyal because of his known contacts with the revolutionaries and because he had not revealed the whole plot to the king as soon as he had heard of it. King Charles Felix was so much shocked by the young prince's behaviour that he decided to bar him from succession to the throne. He ordered his lieutenant-governor in Turin, Count Thaon di Revel, to find out how far Charles Albert was compromised by the depositions taken at the trials.[21]

This was not a matter on which Charles Felix could act alone. Charles Albert's right of succession was written into the treaty signed after the congress of Vienna. He could not be deprived of it without the great powers' agreement. First and foremost, this meant that Metternich would have to agree.

Metternich saw finer shades in 'the Carignano question' which were hidden from the less perceptive Charles Felix. The principle of legitimacy was one of the cornerstones of the treaty of Vienna; to disinherit Charles Albert would go flatly against it. Again, if Charles Albert were barred from the throne, Piedmont would have to abrogate the Salic law and allow the succession to pass to Victor Emmanuel's daughter and her husband, the duke of

Modena. From the Austrian point of view Piedmont would be safer under the rule of a discredited and unpopular prince than if it were handed over to an ambitious duke who would unite the territories of Piedmont, Modena and eventually Massa-Carrara. Finally, Charles Albert's complicity in the insurrection was not clearly established. In a circular to Austrian ambassadors in Europe in December 1821 Metternich wrote: 'There is no material proof against the Prince of Carignano positive enough to make it possible to judge and condemn him legally.'[22]

The issue remained undecided until the great powers met at Verona in October 1822 to discuss the political situation of Europe. By this time Metternich was certain that any interference with legitimate succession would shake the foundations of all governments. To Charles Felix's disappointment, the great powers agreed that the young prince should keep his inheritance on condition that he would give a guarantee for his future conduct, to ensure that he would never again become 'the plaything of the factious'.

But Charles Albert had still to expiate the events of 1821. During two years in Tuscany, where he was virtually an exile from Piedmont, he became sombre and reserved, and even toyed with thoughts of suicide or leaving Italy for ever.[23] It was at this time that he showed the first signs of the intense absorption in religious matters which he retained all his life.

His redemption was won on the battlefield. The powers agreed at Verona that Louis XVIII of France should send an army to Spain in 1823 to rescue King Ferdinand VII from the clutches of the liberal government established after the revolution of 1820. They had the happy thought that Charles Albert should march with the French, since any links he still had with Piedmontese liberals would surely be broken for good if he went to shoot liberals in Spain.

It was not a severe campaign. The French, who were fighting under the Bourbon lily for the first time since the revolution, were rarely in action and were generally welcomed as the liberators of the Spanish people from an unpopular, if constitutional, government. Charles Albert fought with complete disregard of danger; at the storming of the Trocadero he was so much at ease that the French soldiers said of him, 'Carignan goes into battle as though he were going to a wedding.'[24] Louis XVIII regarded this military promenade as a great victory, which would make 'a fine page in his history',[25] and he was delighted with Charles Albert's prowess. At a Tuileries reception to the returning warriors he said to the young prince: 'You have shown Europe that Piedmont will one day have for its king a valiant soldier whom I love and esteem.'[26]

Louis XVIII's patronage was a useful factor in Charles Albert's rehabilitation, but Charles Felix was unwilling to have him back in Piedmont until he had given the guarantee which the powers had asked for at Verona. This was to be an oath that, when he came to the throne, he would make no alteration in the fundamental principles of the Piedmontese monarchy.

The question of whether this oath was ever taken has been a matter of much debate, but satisfactory proof seems to have been found in a memorandum bearing a marginal note by Pralormo, Charles Felix's ambassador at Vienna. The note reads: 'On the prince of Carignano's return from his Spanish campaign the count of Pralormo was ordered by King Charles Felix to tell Emperor Francis that the prince of Carignano had taken a solemn oath to make no innovation in the laws and fundamental bases of the monarchy.' Correspondence between the Piedmontese foreign minister and his ambassador to France indicates that the oath was taken at the end of December 1823 in the Piedmontese embassy in Paris.[27]

This was the end of Charles Albert's exile. He returned to Piedmont, where Charles Felix, after grumbling that 'One is born royal highness, one doesn't become it', agreed that he should have all the honours due to an hereditary prince. He also named Charles Albert his universal heir, but the young prince was given little part in public affairs. He lived in the country with his family, writing books, making plans for the reform of civil administration and faithfully keeping up his religious devotions. His revolutionary days were over. Piedmont had an impeccable, if apparently uninspiring, heir presumptive. Italy was quiet again after the first flames of the Risorgimento had blazed up and gone out.

THE ESTE CONSPIRACY

After the risings Roman fantasy Menotti and Francis IV
Revolt in Romagna The powers and the pope New kings

THE risings of 1820–1 were the first examples of direct action towards an Italian Risorgimento. Their immediate results were disastrous. Many of Italy's most fervent patriots were jailed or exiled, Austrian troops were in Naples and Piedmont. Yet the sight of Italians rising to claim their political freedom was at least a step towards the reawakening of the national consciousness.

In the decade which followed the insurrections it seemed that Metternich's Italy was safely re-established. All the Italian rulers were sitting securely on their thrones. Charles Felix was soon master in his own house, for the Austrians left Piedmont after the congress of Verona. In Tuscany a happy era began in 1824 with the accession of Grand Duke Leopold II, a prince who enjoyed the nickname of 'Daddy' and of whom it has been said that 'he was content with the good-humoured affection which his subjects gave him, and his chief ambition was to promote their happiness.'[1] In Lombardy the bitter emotions aroused by the trials of Pellico and Confalonieri gave way to a mood of resignation; the nobility accepted Austrian domination without demur, and the Austrian emperor was given a splendid reception when he visited Milan in 1826. On that occasion 57,000 lire were spent on a single night's illuminations and 36,960 lire on an arch of triumph, while a young Frenchwoman was paid 11,000 lire for her aeronautical displays.[2]

Under a new pope, Leo XII, who was elected in September 1823, the Papal States remained in the grip of reactionary misgovernment; the clergy were given still further privileges and the Jews were deprived of the right to own real estate. In the kingdom of the Two Sicilies, from which also the Austrian troops had been withdrawn after the congress of Verona, constitutional government gave way to reaction, and there was no change for the better when Ferdinand was succeeded by the weak King Francis I in 1825. Government was based on military force, and most of the national revenue was spent on the army.[3]

This was Italy in the 1820s. Everywhere absolute rulers were in control, the people were subservient and often oppressed. But the spirit of conspiracy was not dead. Carbonari and others were still plotting. Central Italy was the scene of the next explosion.

2

The first signs of imminent insurrection were given in December 1830, when an abortive plot was hatched by a group of conspirators, mostly noblemen, in the city of Rome. Pius VIII, who had succeeded Leo XII, had died a year after his election, and the cardinals were gathering to elect a new pope. The conspirators' plot was conceived in the grand manner. It involved the seizure of Castel Sant'Angelo, the armoury and the arsenal, the opening of the prisons and, as a final master-stroke, the arrest of all the cardinals as they were going in procession to the papal conclave. No part of this fantasy was even attempted. The plot was discovered by the police and the conspirators were arrested. A young Frenchman who had been in touch with them was let off with an order to leave the Papal States at once.[4]

The young man was Prince Louis Napoleon, the future Napoleon III, who was a nephew of Napoleon I and was then twenty-two. His elder brother, Prince Napoleon Louis, was married and living in Florence, and in the autumn of 1830 Prince Louis Napoleon and his mother, ex-Queen Hortense of Holland, came from their Swiss home to visit him in Italy. From Florence they paid one of their regular visits to Rome, where a year earlier the English Lord Malmesbury had found Louis Napoleon 'a wild, harum-scarum youth ... apparently without serious thoughts of any kind'.[5] It was presumably the harum-scarum side of the prince's nature which made him join his aristocratic friends in their half-baked conspiracy. His one public contribution to the unsuccessful coup was an indiscreet ride through the streets of Rome on a horse decorated with Carbonaro colours.

Having escaped arrest by the young aristocrats, the cardinals continued their conclave. On 2 February 1831 they chose Cardinal Mauro Capellari as the new pope. He took the name of Gregory XVI, and he had barely ascended the throne before he was faced with an insurrection in Romagna.

3

The year 1831 seemed a hopeful time for rebellion. Italian liberals and members of secret societies had won new hope from the brief French revolution of 1830 which had put Louis-Philippe on the throne in the place of Charles X. Though the new king was soon to show that he was almost as conservative as his Bourbon predecessors, he was seen at first as a people's king, and his accession was as welcome to revolutionaries all over Europe as it was unwelcome at the courts of absolute rulers.*

Liberals were particularly heartened by the new French government's denunciation of the great powers' right to intervene in other countries' affairs and its insistence that the principle of non-intervention was 'sacred' and must be observed. Italians who were preparing insurrections felt that the last obstacle to a successful revolution was now removed. This time, they thought, there would be no repetition of 1821, when the Austrians had interfered in both Naples and Piedmont; if a new revolution took place in Italy, either Austria would not intervene for fear of provoking France, or France would come to Italy's defence in the sacred name of non-intervention. It was a reasonable belief, but those who held it were soon to be disillusioned.

The new risings were in three Italian states – Modena, Parma and the Papal States. They had been planned for many months, chiefly under the guidance of a Modenese patriot, Ciro Menotti. Modena was the pivot of the risings. Another Modenese, Enrico Misley, had made several secret journeys abroad, and was in

---

* In Piedmont Prince Charles Albert resented Louis-Philippe's accession as a blow at the principle of legitimacy, and he was disgusted when the new French government was recognized by the powers of the Holy Alliance. '*Le triomphe de crime est accompli*,' he observed bitterly in a letter to Marquis Michele di Cavour. (Rodolico, *Carlo Alberto*, I, p. 450.)

touch with the Italian exiles in France, headed by Buonarroti, who had formed a committee to support revolution in Italy. Both Misley and Menotti had consulted Francis IV, duke of Modena, who was rather surprisingly expected to lead the insurrection.

Francis IV was the son of an Austrian archduke and the heiress of the Este dynasty which had previously ruled in Modena. He kept his mother's family name, and the strange plotting which preceded the 1831 risings is always known as the *congiura estense* - the Este conspriacy. There is no complete record of how it was conducted. Even the painstaking Spellanzon has to admit that 'everything in this conspiracy is obscure, mysterious, equivocal'.[6] But it is certain that the duke had discussions with Misley and Menotti before the insurrections in central Italy. What they talked about is by no means so clear. Liberal historians claim that the duke promised to take part in the risings and treacherously withdrew at the last moment through fear of Austria; conservative writers say that the talks were not political at all but were solely concerned with commercial affairs.[7]

Politically, Francis was as reactionary as any of his fellow-rulers. He was notorious for his harsh treatment of the Modenese Carbonari. Why, then, should liberal patriots like Misley and Menotti have thought that he would take the lead in a movement designed to set up constitutional governments in central Italy?

The most likely explanation is that they offered the duke the prospect of territorial aggrandizement if he joined them. Misley's plan was to establish Modena as a constitutional principality, and then to enlarge it by the annexation of Parma and the papal legations, and possibly even Tuscany and Lucca.[8] Since Francis had been disappointed in his hopes of becoming king of Piedmont he may well have been tempted by the idea of expansion in central Italy, and it seems probable that he genuinely intended to join the conspiracy.

In promoting the *congiura estense* Menotti travelled widely in the central Italian states, urging patriots to join in a rising designed to secure civil liberty. He met liberal and Carbonaro leaders in Parma, Bologna and Florence, and it was in Florence that he visited Prince Louis Napoleon and his brother and unwisely persuaded them to join the conspiracy. It was later realized that he had made a mistake in linking the revolution with the dangerous name of Bonaparte.

The risings were not to be strictly Carbonarist, though the Carbonari did much of the spadework. They were to be organized by local municipal leaders, and the Carbonari would be strongly behind them. It was their last attempt at mass insurrection.

Menotti's plan was that Modena, Parma and Bologna (in the papal legations) should rise simultaneously in the first week of February, while Rome was still preoccupied with the election of the new pope. This timetable was upset by Francis IV's decision to arrest the Modenese conspirators. The mysterious *congiura estense* had reached its unhappy end.

By this time Menotti had come to realize that he would not have Francis on his side, and he was ready to act without the duke's support. But the duke knew too much about the conspiracy. On the evening of 3 February, when final arrangements for the rising in Modena were being made by the leading conspirators at Menotti's house, he sent a detachment of soldiers to arrest them. Menotti and his friends barricaded the house and put up a desperate resistance for some hours, but at last were forced to surrender. Proof of the duke's callous repudiation of his own share in the *congiura estense* is given in the message he is understood to have sent (though it does not survive in any archives) to the governor of Reggio that evening. It said: 'A terrible conspiracy against me has broken out tonight. The conspirators are in my hands. Send me the hangman.'[9]

But the duke had not crushed the Modenese insurrection by arresting its leaders. Outlying towns and villages rose in accordance with the general plan, and the duke sent an urgent request to Verona for Austrian troops. When the garrison commander refused to intervene without higher authority the duke left Modena on 5 February and put himself under Austrian protection at Mantua. Menotti, chained and guarded by armed men, was taken with him.

The duke's departure left Modena in the hands of the revolutionaries. The whole duchy was free. One provisional government was set up in the city of Modena, and another at Reggio, where the national tricolour of green, white and red was hoisted and Giuditta Sidoli, a pretty young widow who had taken a big part in preparing the rising, proudly walked through the streets in a dress made in the same patriotic colours.[10]

Modena's example was quickly followed in Parma. It was an unusual revolution, for the people of Parma had great affection for their duchess, the former Empress Marie-Louise of France, and a bitter hatred of Baron Werklein, the Austrian colonel who had been Parma's effective ruler since the death of Count Neipperg. The count's rule had been mild and tolerant; Werklein's was cold and hard. When revolution broke out in the second week of February, crowds surged round the ducal palace crying alternately, 'Long live Marie-Louise' and 'Death to Werklein'. Werklein fled the country, and though the duchess was urgently pressed to stay she slipped away by night and went to Piacenza, where the Austrians were allowed by treaty to maintain a garrison. A provisional government was set up in Parma after its bloodless revolution.

4

In Bologna too the revolutionaries seized power without bloodshed. The papal authorities made no resistance when a resolute body of men took down the papal arms and raised the national tricolour in their place. A provisional government was established, and inevitably its first act was to declare that the pope's temporal sovereignty was ended for ever.

In the following days the revolution spread over the greater part of the Papal States. A makeshift army was enrolled at Bologna and marched southward to free the rest of Romagna. Wherever it went there was no opposition from the papal authorities, the papal troops fraternized with the revolutionaries and the whole operation had 'the ease and gaiety of a flower-show'.[11] At Pesaro the army was put under the command of Major Sercognani, a Napoleonic officer who was soon promoted to be general, and the triumphal advance continued through the Marches and Umbria. Ancona surrendered, and by 23 February Sercognani had reached Ascoli, where he turned south-west to march on Rome.

For a brief spell it seemed that the great prize was within his grasp. By this time the pope's authority was maintained only in

Rome itself, and at Orvieto, Rieti, Civita Castellana and a few smaller places. But Sercognani's volunteers had neither cavalry nor artillery; after their long march nearly all of them were without boots and penniless.[12] Enthusiasm was not enough, and the few remaining papal strongholds proved an effective barrier to their further advance. From his temporary headquarters at Terni, Sercognani decided to attack Rieti, which threatened his left flank. On 7 March he moved against it with a thousand men, but the two hundred defenders, mostly volunteers and provincial militia, held out gallantly, and the revolutionaries' bullets made little impression on Rieti's strong walls. After three hours' vain assault they were discouraged by a heavy thunderstorm. Sercognani ordered the retreat. It was the end of a remarkable march, which so nearly achieved the liberation of Rome.[13]

While Sercognani was on the road to Rome the papal provinces which had risen in revolt came under one government at Bologna as the United Provinces of Italy. This new government promptly withdrew the commissions granted to the two Bonaparte princes, who had been serving in Sercognani's army. The reason for this rather ungenerous action was that the revolutionaries still hoped for help from King Louis-Philippe if Austria moved against them, and they feared that the presence of two Bonapartes in their army might be a bar to French assistance. The princes were ordered to leave the army and return to Bologna. They then went to Forli as civilians, and it was while they were waiting to escape from Italy that Prince Napoleon Louis, the elder brother, died of fever at Faenza, thus leaving Louis Napoleon to become the future head of the Bonaparte family. Louis Napoleon was also taken ill, but he escaped from Italy with his mother's help and resumed the adventurous career which was to take him to the Tuileries, Villafranca, Sedan and Chislehurst.

Central Italy's freedom was short-lived. The new pope, Gregory XVI, called for Austrian help, and Metternich had no hesitation in giving it. Once again it was shown that possession of Lombardy-Venetia gave Austria complete mastery of the peninsula. The Lombard town of Mantua was a convenient starting-point for a new Austrian invasion of central Italy, which began on 4 March.

This was the moment when Louis-Philippe of France should have stood up for his 'sacred' principle of non-intervention. He did not do so. The Italians were left to face the Austrians without the French support they had hoped for. The French king's innate conservatism was one reason why he declined to back a revolution; another was that Metternich had cleverly played on his fears of a Bonapartist restoration, and Louis-Philippe was not prepared to put his own crown at hazard by opposing Austria in Italy. Early in March he said to the papal nuncio in Paris: 'I must confess that our proclamation of the principle of non-intervention was a mistake.'[14]

The Austrians had no difficulty in replacing the duke of Modena and the duchess of Parma on their thrones. General Zucchi, a Napoleonic veteran who commanded the small Modenese army, was too heavily outnumbered to be able to offer any resistance. He thought it wiser to make his way to Bologna, where he was invited to organize and command a second revolutionary army. On his advice the government of the United Provinces left Bologna for Ancona. The Austrians entered Bologna on 21 March.

Zucchi had one moment of glory before the revolution collapsed. On his way to Ancona with 4000 men and four cannons he bivouacked outside Rimini, where he was attacked by the Austrians. They had double the number of Zucchi's men, but the rebels fought a gallant rearguard action before continuing their retreat to Ancona. It was a plucky fight, for Zucchi's army consisted largely of civilians, armed with sporting guns, pikes and scythes. Patriots were excited to hear that an Italian force had resisted the Austrians for even a few hours.

That was the end. Since no French help could be expected the rebels were at Austria's mercy, and it was useless to fight on. The rebel government capitulated. The pope's temporal power was restored all over the Papal States. An amnesty was included in the terms of surrender, but Gregory XVI withdrew it from thirty-eight of the revolutionary leaders, many of whom were imprisoned for nine months by the Austrians in Venice and then exiled by the papal government. In Modena the duke's restoration was followed by the trial and execution of Ciro Menotti.

The 1831 risings in central Italy were a turning-point in the history of the Risorgimento. They had shown that it was easy enough to topple an Italian sovereign from his throne, but impossible to prevent the Austrians from putting him back. They had also shown that a different approach was needed for the creation of a new Italy.

Some reasons for the failures of the risings of 1821 and 1831 were subsequently analysed in an essay by Giuseppe Mazzini. The risings, he felt, had been made by the wrong people, by old-fashioned liberals who descended in direct line from the French revolution. They were atheists, materialists, utilitarians, Macchiavellians, and their true faith and patriotism had grown lukewarm through endless compromises with different kinds of regime. They had made the 1831 rising on two hypotheses – that there would be no foreign intervention in Italy (or that if Austria intervened, France would support the revolution) and that the rulers themselves could be induced to join the liberal movement. Both assumptions were incorrect, and a movement based on such false hypotheses could neither arouse the fervour of youth nor win the support of the people. 'These men wished to use the art of diplomacy, and diplomacy smothered them.'[15]

The analysis is searching and justified. Menotti and his friends had proved that Carbonarism and vague liberal patriotism would never be strong enough to set Italy free. Mazzini himself was soon to suggest a better way.

5

The revolt in the Romagna and the pope's action in calling for Austrian help had brought papal misgovernment to the forefront of European politics. The Austrians could not be allowed to stay in the pope's territory. But when they left, what guarantee would there be against further grave disturbances in the heart of Italy? It was felt by the great powers that only extensive reforms in the Papal States could ensure genuine tranquillity. The ambassadors of Britain, France, Austria, Prussia and Russia were asked to meet together in Rome and consider what measures of reform they could recommend to the pope's ministers.

The ambassadors' memorandum, which was presented to the

papal government on 10 May, need not be examined in detail, for it had little effect on the life of the Papal States. It was a sensible document, and its suggestions, if put into operation, would have made the temporal power more bearable for many of the pope's subjects. Its chief proposals were that laity should be allowed to undertake all administrative and judicial functions, that municipal councils should be elected by popular vote, and that these councils should choose some of the members of a new supreme board of finance, which would be responsible for auditing the public accounts and supervising the public debt. This board 'might or might not form part of a council of state, to be chosen by the sovereign from among the persons most distinguished in birth, property or talent.'[16]

These proposals were too much for the papal court, which had no intention of changing the state from ecclesiastical to lay and was equally opposed to popularly elected municipal councils and to public financial accountability. 'Accordingly,' says Farini, 'it did not take in good part these over-comprehensive counsels, but temporized, shifted about, and met the wishes of the diplomatists, not only piecemeal, but even that more in promises and appearances than in reality, while it disgusted the people.'[17] Some show of reform was made. Laymen were allowed to administer one or two of the northern provinces, and municipal councils were established, though their first members were nominated by the government and their powers were extremely limited. (Rome itself had no municipal council.) It was all very lukewarm, and provided no genuine guarantees of better rule, but the ambassadors may have felt that it was an achievement to make the pope's government accept any reforms at all. Austria withdrew its troops from the legations in July. The ambassadors continued to meet for several months, though the papal government paid little further attention to their recommendations.

One result of the government's neglect was another rising in Romagna in the following year. Austrian troops were again called in, and Louis-Philippe sent French troops to occupy Ancona, partly to counterbalance Austria's occupation of Bologna and partly to establish France's right to intervene in Italy if it thought fit. The once sacred principle of non-intervention had now been completely discarded by Louis-Philippe and his ministers.

6

The rest of Italy had not been affected by the risings of 1831. Neighbouring Tuscany had remained calm, and the grand duke had politely refused an Austrian offer to send in troops to prevent a revolution. He preferred to enrol a civic guard of his own – a liberal gesture which the Austrians hardly expected from an archduke of their own royal house.[18]

In the kingdom of the Two Sicilies a new king was beginning his reign in an atmosphere of general good-will. The young and soldierly Ferdinand II, who came to the throne in 1830, seemed a great improvement on the weak and incompetent Francis I, and in view of the grim reputation he was later to win as 'King Bomba' it is noteworthy that at first he showed a real desire to reconcile his Sicilian subjects. He went to Sicily four times in the first ten years of his reign, and under the governorship of his brother Leopold the island felt that it was almost enjoying self-government.[19]

Within two years of his accession Ferdinand gave his country a saintly queen in the person of Princess Maria Cristina of Savoy, youngest daughter of Victor Emmanuel I, the former king of Piedmont.* Though many stories are told of Ferdinand's boorish behaviour towards Cristina, including such an oafish practical joke as pulling away her chair when she was about to sit down, all her surviving letters speak of her great happiness with her husband. Good reports of their married life were also given by the Piedmontese envoy at Naples in his dispatches to Turin, but it is not true that the king's more liberal tendencies in the early years of his reign were due to his wife's influence. She took no part in politics; Ferdinand was responsible for his own political conduct.[20] It was as he grew older that the reactionary side of his nature took command of his actions.

---

* A happy portrait of this 'charming and perfect princess', as Cavour once called her, is painted by Benedetto Croce in *Maria Cristina di Savoia* (Naples, 1924). She enjoyed gaiety, such as masked balls, but she was deeply religious, and her concern about public morals once led her to make suggestions about appropriate underwear for the ballerinas at the Teatro San Carlo (*op. cit.*, p. 70). She died young.

A month after the surrender in Romagna, Piedmont also had a new king. Charles Felix died in April 1831 and was succeeded by Charles Albert.

The new king had long abandoned his early liberalism. He could no longer have contemplated any such innovation as the constitution he had granted during his brief regency in 1821. He had pledged his word that he would make no change in the monarchical system, and the pledge was entirely in keeping with his sentiments. He believed, and would always believe, in the principle of absolute rule, by which kings and princes wisely exercised the authority bestowed on them by God. He was deeply religious, and he saw the Church as a powerful guardian of public morality. The clergy would have no need to fear encroachments on their privileges so long as Charles Albert remained on the throne.

But he was in no sense a despotic ruler. His intention to govern humanely was soon shown by his abolition of some of the more barbarous features of the judicial system, such as various forms of torture; and he also established a council of state, consisting of three sections dealing respectively with justice, home affairs and finance. Two of the leading councillors were Count Prospero Balbo and the marquis of Villamarina; the latter was also made minister of war when Charles Albert began to build up the army, which had been allowed to run down since the restoration. This was a matter of national prestige; it was not a warlike gesture. The new king was on good terms with Austria, and his insistence on military reform did not imply that he was already dreaming of driving the white-coats out of Italy.

On the face of it Charles Albert was just another of the humane but reactionary sovereigns who were not uncommon in eighteenth- and nineteenth-century Italy. Yet already it was possible to look on him as a man of destiny, a tall young soldier-prince who would draw his sword and set the whole country free. This picture was drawn with great skill and feeling in an open letter addressed to him by Giuseppe Mazzini in the autumn of 1831.

MAZZINI

The young Carbonaro   *The letter to Charles Albert*
Young Italy   *Guiding principles*   *Preparing for action*
      The Genoa plot   *Savoy fiasco*

GIUSEPPE MAZZINI, the author of the open letter to Charles Albert, was a Genoese who was born on 22 June 1805 during the French occupation of Italy, and became a native of Piedmont when the former republic of Genoa was annexed to it under the treaty of Vienna. He was the son of a doctor who had married a talented Genoese girl, and he soon gave proof of precocious intellectual powers. At the age of four he was reading easily. When he was seven a cousin of his mother's, a Colonel Patrone of the Pavia artillery school, wrote prophetically in a letter to Signora Mazzini: 'Believe me, signora, this dear boy is a star of the first magnitude, shining with a true light and destined to be admired one day by all the culture of Europe.'[1]

At the age of fourteen Mazzini began a preliminary course at Genoa university, where he was admitted to the medical school in 1821. It was in this year, when he was nearly sixteen, that he had an experience which he never forgot. After the collapse of the Piedmont rising many of the revolutionaries were leaving Italy by boat from Genoa. Walking one day near the harbour with his mother and one of her friends, Mazzini saw 'a tall, black-bearded man, with a severe and energetic countenance and a fiery glance', who was collecting money 'for the refugees of Italy'.

Years afterwards Mazzini described what he felt as his mother put money in the handkerchief held out by the bearded man. 'That day was the first in which a confused idea presented itself to my mind – I will not say of country or of liberty – but an idea that we Italians *could* and therefore *ought* to struggle for the liberty of our country.'² At that moment the Italian Risorgimento found its priest and its prophet.

Though of no great height Mazzini was already a striking figure in his university days, with his 'high and prominent forehead, black, flashing eyes, fine olive features, set in a mass of thick black hair, a grave serious face that could look hard at times, but readily melted into the kindest of smiles.'³ He had soon transferred from the medical to the law school, and he had a wide circle of friends, who admired his brilliant intellect. One of the formative influences of his adolescence was his warm friendship with the Ruffini family – particularly Signora Ruffini, a cultured woman who entertained at her house the advanced young liberals of Genoa, and three of her sons, Jacopo, who had been born on the same day as Mazzini, Agostino and Giovanni.

On leaving the university in 1827 Mazzini began to practise at the bar in a rather desultory way, but his ambitions leaned more towards a literary career. As a first step he began to contribute to the small periodicals which published progressive articles and were usually suppressed by the police after a few issues. This was the fate of the first paper Mazzini wrote for, the *Indicatore Genovese*, and also of the second, the *Indicatore Livornese*, founded at Leghorn, in Tuscany, by the notable Domenico Guerrazzi, a lawyer who had left the bar to write patriotic historical novels. The most important of the papers for which Mazzini wrote was *Antologia*, which the Swiss-Italian journalist Vieusseux managed to publish at Florence from 1821 to 1833, although its insistence on 'love of country' aroused suspicions in both the Tuscan and the Austrian governments.

But Mazzini was not destined to be solely a man of letters. He had been interested in the Carbonari since the days of the Piedmont insurrection. In his last year at the university he discovered a fellow student who belonged to the movement and he was himself initiated as a 'good cousin'. From that moment his life was given a new direction.

Mazzini's experiences of the Carbonari were disappointing. At the initiation ceremony he was surprised to find that the oath he was asked to take was nothing but a formula of obedience. He had already begun to think about Italian regeneration, but the

Carbonaro oath said nothing about federation or unity, nothing about republicanism or monarchy, nothing even about the objects of the movement except that it was 'a war against the government'.[4] In spite of his doubts he found himself well received by the Carbonari, and he became secretary of a *vendita* known as Speranza. After a year or two he was delighted to hear that Raimondo Doria, who was described as the grand master of the Spanish lodge, was coming to Genoa to reorganize the movement.

Doria's influence on Mazzini's life was profound and unexpected. He was impressed by the young lawyer and found his knowledge of French and English useful in dealing with correspondence. But Mazzini did not know that the new leader was a traitor to the Carbonari.

Doria's motives were obscure. E. E. Y. Hales, who has studied Mazzini's relations with the Carbonari, thinks it inconceivable that Doria decided to betray the movement in the hope of getting some reward from the Piedmontese government; it is more probable, he believes, that Doria had really come to hate the movement and wished to destroy it.[5] Mazzini was one of his first victims.

In September 1830 Mazzini was sent by Doria to Tuscany to found a Carbonaro lodge there. It was the first time that he had left Piedmont. With the help of Carlo Bini, who had worked with Guerrazzi on the now defunct *Indicatore Livornese*, he set up a lodge at Leghorn, and he also visited Guerrazzi at Montepulciano, where the fiery nationalist was interned for six months because of the strong Italian sentiments he had expressed in a public lecture after the suppression of his paper.[6] Mazzini hoped to go on to Bologna to meet the Carbonari of Romagna, but the Tuscan police were suspicious of his activities and would not allow him to go. It was when he went back to Genoa that he walked into Doria's trap.

Soon after his return Mazzini was ordered to go to an inn to initiate a new member of the Carbonari. The new member was really a police spy, whom Venannson, the governor of Genoa, had sent to the inn by arrangement with Doria. A disguised policeman looked into the room while the initiation was taking place. A few days later Mazzini was arrested, but in some way (which he does not explain in his memoirs) he managed to get rid of all the incriminating material, including documents, bullets and a sword-stick, which he had with him when the police seized him. At his trial he stoutly denied everything, and since the spy was unwilling to appear in court the evidence of a single policeman was not enough to convict him. But Venannson declined to let him go free. For ten weeks he was interned in reasonable comfort in the fortress of Savona, and then, when Venannson had reported the affair to King Charles Felix, he was offered the choice between living away from Genoa in some small town in Piedmont or going into exile. He chose exile, since he knew that if he stayed in Piedmont all his movements would be watched by the police.

2

Mazzini's internment in Savona in the winter of 1830–1 marked a decisive stage in his life. It gave him a breathing-space for reconsidering his position and deciding on his future course of action. Like another prisoner in the German fortress of Lands-berg nearly a century later, Mazzini began to make his plans to overthrow the existing order of government, though without developing them into the elaborate pattern of Hitler's *Mein Kampf*.

He was disillusioned with the Carbonari, not only because of his betrayal but because he saw little future for a secret society whose members did not even know what they were working for. Carbonarism, he felt, was a senile institution without a constructive programme, and one which would never awaken the people to a sense of mission.[7] But what was to take its place? Years afterwards he wrote: 'It was during these months of imprisonment that I conceived the plan of the association of Young Italy. I meditated deeply upon the principles upon which to base the organization of the party, the aim and purpose of its labours – which, I intended, should be publicly declared, the method of its formation, the individuals to be selected to aid me in its creation, and the possibility of linking its operations with those of the existing revolutionary elements of Europe.'[8] This was the idea he took with him when he crossed the Alps for the first time in February 1831, to become Italy's most distinguished exile.

Mazzini's first problem was to find the most suitable centre for working with other Italian exiles. He was not impressed by the Italians he met in Switzerland, and he went on to Lyons, where he found that his fellow-exiles were forming an expedition to join the revolt in Romagna. He at once enrolled and went with them to Corsica, but there was so much delay over chartering ships that the revolution had ended before the exiles could sail for Italy. Mazzini went back to France and settled at Marseilles.

It was a fortunate choice. In Paris Buonarroti presided over his Italian committee; Mazzini would have found it hard to impress his own ideas on the old revolutionary. Marseilles gave him more scope for leadership, and was also the most popular French centre for Italian exiles. Soon after his arrival there were probably between 150 and 200 exiles living in the city.[9]

Mazzini was twenty-five when he went to Marseilles, where his black hair and beard, black hat and black velvet suit were soon to be well known to his compatriots. He at once began that remarkable output of propagandist writing which was to have such a powerful influence on Italian thinking for years to come.

His first article, which appeared in the French newspaper, *Le National*, on 19 April, was based on conversations with exiles who had left Italy after the collapse of the recent risings.[10] It was entitled '*Une nuit de Rimini en 1831*' and it described Zucchi's rearguard action on his way to Ancona. For all its purple passages it was an impressive piece of writing, which paid due honour to the Italian rebels and savagely denounced the French government for having refused to come to their aid.

The Rimini article showed that a vigorous propagandist had arrived among the Italians at Marseilles. The same point was made still more forcibly by the 'open letter to Charles Albert' which was printed in Marseilles and privately circulated in Italy in June. Mazzini's name did not appear on it. The authorship was simply ascribed to 'An Italian'.

Mazzini's real purpose in writing this letter is a matter of controversy. But its message is not in dispute. It was a call to the new king of Piedmont to give his country free institutions, expel the Austrians and become the first king of Italy.

The letter was written in terms which were entirely complimentary to Charles Albert. 'If I believed you to be a common king, with a narrow tyrannical outlook,' it stated, 'I would not address you in the language of a free man . . . But you, Sire, are not such a king. Nature, in creating you for the throne, has given you strength of mind and high principles.' The new king, the letter continued, should guarantee free institutions, recognize the rights of humanity and yield to the popular demand for 'laws and liberty, independence and union'; he should expel the Austrians and become the first king of Italy. 'There is a crown more brilliant and sublime than that of Piedmont, a crown that awaits the man who dares to think of it, who dedicates his life to winning it . . . Place yourself at the head of the nation, write on your flag Union, Liberty, Independence. Free Italy from the barbarian, build up the future, be the Napoleon of Italian freedom . . . Your safety lies on the sword's point. Draw it, and throw away the scabbard.' Charles Albert, the letter concluded, could become 'either the first of men or the last of Italian tyrants'. But if he did not take up the cause of freedom, others would do it without him and against him.[11]

Like other 'open letters' which Mazzini was to write in later years, the letter to Charles Albert called for action which the king could hardly have been expected to take. At the very time when Mazzini was urging him to make war he was concluding a treaty of mutual defence with Austria, and it was actually signed in the month after the letter had been circulated. But if the appeal had no influence on Charles Albert, it had important results for Mazzini himself, for it soon became known in Italy that 'An Italian' was the Genoese lawyer, Giuseppe Mazzini, who was thus revealed as the leader of the exiles at Marseilles. He was now a national figure, and it was announced in Piedmont that he would be imprisoned if he attempted to return there. He was to remain an exile for the rest of his life, though in times of crisis, conspiracy and commotion he often went back to his homeland in defiance of authority.

The letter to Charles Albert also raises a question about Mazzini's political attitude. Throughout his life he claimed to be a republican. He was soon to make republican government one of the essential aims of his new political association. Yet in this

letter he offers support to the monarchical system, if only Charles
Albert will grant political freedom and will liberate and unite
Italy. He seems, in fact, to be offering to sacrifice his republi-
canism in exchange for Italian unity.

It is this point which made the letter controversial almost
as soon as it was written. Mazzini himself resented the suggestion
that it indicated any weakening in his republican faith. 'Those
who in later days have quoted that letter to the king either as a
justification of their own desertion of the republican banner, or
in order to accuse me of inconsistency or of too great readiness to
abandon my convictions, attack me on a false ground,' he wrote
in 1861. His real purpose, he said, was to show that Charles
Albert was unfit to be a national leader. 'By publicly declaring
to him all that his own heart should have taught him of his duty
towards Italy, my object was to prove to my countrymen his
absolute lack of those qualities which alone could have rendered
the performance of that duty possible.'[12]

It may still be wondered whether Mazzini's later explanation
really explains his attitude when he wrote the letter to Charles
Albert. Giovanni Gentile has asserted that 'Mazzini oscillates
between republican intransigence and faith in the house of Savoy,
according to the turn of events,'[13] and Salvemini, who is certainly
not unsympathetic to Mazzini, takes a sceptical view of his explanation of why the letter was written. Would Mazzini, he asks,
'have put so much fervour into exhorting Charles Albert to choose
the path of glory if he had really, in his heart, believed him to be
both cowardly and treacherous? The evidence points to the
conclusion that Mazzini, whose early hopes had given way only
too soon to disillusionment, had wanted, in later years, to present
what had been a sincere and youthful impulse as a calculated
dissimulation.'[14]

It is a matter of opinion. Though the warmth of the letter
makes one feel that it meant what it said, it is known that some of
the exiles in Marseilles were cherishing a quite irrational belief
that everything would be changed in Italy now that Charles
Albert had come to the throne. It is not impossible, as Omodeo
suggests, that Mazzini's explanation is correct, and that he wrote
the letter 'without hope, to overcome the remaining Carbonarist

illusions of the exiles, and to be able to give free rein to republicanism'.[15]

3

In the next few months of 1831 Mazzini was occupied with one
of the greatest achievements of his life, and one which had a profound effect on the progress of the Risorgimento. This was the
establishment of *Giovine Italia* – Young Italy. In its original
form it flourished for about two years, and it was revived in the
1840s. Though its plans for action ended in failure, its significance
was that it helped to build up a national consciousness in Italy
and to give the idea of national unity pride of place over any
federal solution. In this way Mazzini and his friends at Marseilles
provided the psychological and spiritual foundation on which
Cavour, Garibaldi and Victor Emmanuel II were to build the
new Italy.

Young Italy was both an organization and an ideology. It was
at first envisaged as a simple brotherhood: 'You may tell young
men', Mazzini wrote to a friend on 21 July, 'that this is not a
society like the others; there are no mysteries, no hierarchies of
rank, no symbols; it is a brotherhood of young men, who unite
to work together with frankness, sincerity and confidence.'[16] In
the ensuing weeks the idea of a simple brotherhood was seen to
be insufficient. On 8 October Mazzini wrote that his aim was 'to
organize a truly Italian movement, to link all parts of Italy in a
single bond, to form a *great Italian national association*', and in
the same month he drew up a plan of 'the great national association with the object of liberating Italy'.[17]

As an organization Young Italy had its central council (*congrega*),
which was always to meet outside Italy, provincial offices in Italy
which reported monthly to the *congrega*, local organizers, recruit-
ment officers and ordinary members, all grouped in *vendite*, or
lodges, in Carbonaro fashion. Each member paid a monthly
subscription of fifty centimes (or more if he could afford it) and
had to equip himself with a dagger, a rifle and fifty cartridges.
Except in special cases, no one over forty was admitted as a
member, for Mazzini believed in the power of youth and intended
the new organization to be Young Italy in fact as well as in name.

Its colours were the white, red and green of the national revolution; its banner had the words, Liberty, Equality, Humanity on one side and Unity, Independence on the other. It had its own publication, *La Giovine Italia*.

Though Mazzini had said that the movement had no mysteries it had still to be wrapped in a certain amount of secrecy. In Italy it was a secret society, and its members had to be on guard against discovery. Every member was given a pseudonym, a name taken from medieval Italian history, and every province had its own signs and passwords, which were changed every three months. These methods of preserving secrecy were very successful. Except for the tragic episode in Genoa in 1833 most of the lodges of Young Italy seem to have done their business without betrayal to the police.[18]

The aims of Young Italy were described as the improvement of Italy's political condition and the making of preparations for a revolutionary outbreak on as general a scale as possible. These aims were amplified in the society's statutes.

'Young Italy,' it was stated, 'is a brotherhood of Italians who believe in a law of *Progress and Duty*, and are convinced that Italy is destined to become one nation . . . They join this association in the firm intent of consecrating both thought and action to the great aim of reconstituting Italy as one independent sovereign nation of free men and equals.

'The aim of the association is revolution; but its labours will be essentially educational, both before and after the day of revolution . . . By raising its flag in the sight of Italy, and calling upon all those who believe it to be the flag of national regeneration to organize themselves under its folds, the association does not seek to substitute that flag for the banner of the future nation. When once the nation herself shall be free, and able to exercise that right of sovereignty which is hers alone, she will raise her own banner, and make known her revered and unchallenged will as to the principle and the fundamental law of her existence.

'Young Italy is *Republican* and *Unitarian*.' It is republican 'because all true sovereignty resides essentially in the nation, the sole progressive and continuous interpreter of the supreme moral law', and 'because our Italian tradition is essentially republican'.

It is unitarian 'because without unity there is no true nation; because without unity there is no real strength, and Italy, surrounded as she is by powerful, united and jealous nations, has need of strength before all things,' and 'because federalism, by reducing her to the political impotence of Switzerland, would necessarily place her under the influence of one of the neighbouring nations.

'The means by which Young Italy proposes to reach its aims are – education and insurrection, to be adopted simultaneously and made to harmonize with each other . . . Education, though of necessity secret in Italy, will be public out of Italy . . . Insurrection – by means of guerrilla bands – is the true method of warfare for all nations desirous of emancipating themselves from a foreign yoke.'

The great objective of the movement is restated in the central words of the oath to be taken by all members: 'I give my name to Young Italy, an association of men holding the same faith, and swear to dedicate myself wholly and for ever to the endeavour with them to constitute Italy *one free, independent, republican nation*.'[19]

Such was the pattern of the Risorgimento, as Mazzini saw it in 1831. Young Italy, as Omodeo observes, 'was completely divorced from sectarian forms; it kept only what it could preserve of their policies. It wished to be above all a society for the propagation of an Italian thought and faith, it wished as far as possible to reach the popular masses.'[20]

A curious point about the statutes of Young Italy is the insistence that insurrection by means of guerrilla bands was the method by which Italy should be liberated from its foreign yoke. In fact, guerrilla warfare, as practised by the Carlists in Spain and the Boers in South Africa, played no part in the Risorgimento; Garibaldi himself was rather a general in command of an irregular force than a guerrilla leader.

The explanation of Mazzini's mistaken faith in guerrilla fighting is that this kind of war had been strongly advocated by his friend Carlo Bianco, a Piedmontese exile who had fought for the constitutionalists in Spain and had heard much of the Spanish people's heroic resistance to the French between 1808 and 1814.

Bianco had published a book on the possibilities of guerrilla fighting in Italy, and Mazzini had been greatly impressed by it.[21] (In the fifth issue of *La Giovine Italia* he acclaimed Bianco as the first to have indicated a new way of safety for Italians.) But this was one of the Mazzinian dreams which never came true. The Risorgimento did not attract the kind of widespread popular support which would have made guerrilla warfare a practical possibility.

4

In these statutes of Young Italy, which Mazzini produced as a young man of twenty-six, we can see the broad outlines of the principles which guided him throughout his long career of conspiracy for the liberation of Italy. It can be said of him that he had 'no originality of thought, no new ideas about government',[22] but his system was coherent and for the most part practicable. In any case he was not primarily a thinker. Salvemini rightly declares that 'Mazzini was above all a man of action. Thought was only of value to him in so far as it could be translated into action.'[23] So the programme of Young Italy was a programme of action, based on certain fundamental beliefs which he was never to abandon.

Some of his beliefs were religious. Mazzini was neither a philosopher nor a theologian, he belonged to no Church, but he believed in the existence of God, the unity of the human race and the constant, unlimited progress of mankind towards the goal which God has created for it. He had, indeed, 'an essentially religious spirit', and he was convinced that there must always be a religious faith at the basis of political action. How he envisaged God is slightly obscure. De Sanctis suggests that he hesitated between two concepts – a personal God and an impersonal God. When he spoke to the people he depicted God as the supreme being from whom all human laws derive; in his more contemplative moments his God seemed rather to be the mysterious force of universal thought, order and harmony.[24]

If Mazzini was not clear about his interpretation of God, there can be no doubts about his devotion to humanity. He had an unshakeable faith in the popular will and the need for social justice. He saw the ideal world as consisting of 'God and the people; God at the summit of our social structure, the people, the university of our brothers, at its base.' Life was a mission, its end the development in action of all human faculties. Duty and self-sacrifice were the essential virtues needed for the achievement of the better world which would one day be made.[25]

His goal for Italy could be deduced from these general principles. He wanted to see an independent unitary republic, with full rights for every citizen and complete freedom from both foreign domination and the temporal power of the pope. The capital of the Italian republic would be Rome. There had been Rome of the Caesars, Rome of the popes; now Mazzini dreamed of a third Rome, Rome of the people. To this national design he added the hope of a closer association of nations, so that, when all countries had free governments, there could be a great confederation of all mankind.

Politically Mazzini was always on the left; some of his views may have seemed to be Marxist, but he was never a Communist and in basic principles he entirely rejected Marx's teaching. In the kind of socialist state Mazzini had in mind only the public services would have been state-owned and industry would have been run by producer-consumer associations.

Most of these trends of Mazzinian thought could be found in the constitution of the Young Italy movement, which 'combined the old Buonarrotian tradition, contemporary socialism and French republicanism into a new political language and sensibility permeated with romantic religiosity and a mystical sense of the destiny of all nations.'[26] Buonarroti had never made much impact on the general public. Young Italy was the first movement which sought to associate 'the people' with the resurgence of Italy.

5

The two years which followed the formation of Young Italy were in some ways the best period of Mazzini's life. They were also of great significance for the future of Italy.

Young Italy was a revolutionary organization of a new kind. It was both public and secret. Its existence was well known to the governments of France and the Italian states, but its plans for insurrection were the secret of its leaders. It was both propagandist and practical; in Mazzini's view these two sides of the movement formed a single whole, since he believed that the national character must be remade by education, so that people would know how to sacrifice themselves on the day of insurrection.[27]

In Marseilles Mazzini worked tirelessly; the numerous letters he would write in a single day were a valuable factor in building up the movement and holding it together. And he had many able associates. Giuseppe Lamberti and Angelo Usiglio were among his closest colleagues in France; in Piedmont his old friends Jacopo and Giovanni Ruffini helped to form a powerful lodge at Genoa, Guerrazzi and Bini were active at Leghorn and strong support was given by committees in Lombardy, Umbria, Romagna and Rome. In Naples Carlo Poerio and others had their own revolutionary organization, but they were sympathetic towards Young Italy and kept up a correspondence with Mazzini.

The chief propaganda medium was the periodical called *La Giovine Italia*, of which six numbers were issued, each with more than 200 pages – three in 1832, two in 1833 and one in 1834. Mazzini wrote many of the articles himself, and Jacopo Ruffini and Buonarroti were among his contributors.

An ingenious scheme was devised for getting Young Italy's pamphlets into the hands of its Italian members. With the connivance of friendly merchant seamen packages of propaganda were carried to Italy by sea, each package bearing a label with a reputable address for a port *beyond* its intended destination. A parcel for Genoa would be labelled Leghorn, one for Leghorn would have a label for Civita Vecchia, and so on. Police and customs officers would take no notice of them at the earlier port of call, since they appeared to be only goods in transit, but while the ship was in harbour conspirators would go on board, secretly open the parcels and smuggle the material ashore for distribution to the faithful.[28] The circulation of *La Giovine Italia* was not large, but it was important enough to make Metternich ask one of the Austrian representatives in Italy to send him a couple of copies.

In 1832, while a stream of inflammatory propaganda was flowing from the exiles' printing press in Marseilles and the revolutionary network was being extended over Italy, two important events occurred in Mazzini's life. In February Giuditta Sidoli came to Marseilles. In July he was ordered by the French police to leave France.

Giuditta Sidoli was blonde, beautiful and twenty-seven. She was the widow who had played a leading part in the Reggio (Modena) rising in 1831; she had then been exiled for her revolutionary activities and had gone to Geneva, leaving her four children in Italy. Though she had not remarried she was pregnant when she joined the Italian exiles in Marseilles, where she and Mazzini fell deeply in love. She became his mistress, and when her child was born in August she chose Giuseppe as the first of his four Christian names.* By this time she was a prominent member of Young Italy, and her house in rue Saint-Ferréol was a regular meeting-place for its members. Though her liaison with Mazzini was fated to last for little more than a year, and sixteen years were to pass before he saw her again, she was always the great love of his life.

In August of the same year the French government decided that Mazzini was becoming an embarrassment, and he was formally exiled from France. He refused to obey the order, as he felt that he was still needed at Marseilles. Instead of leaving the country, he went into hiding at Marseilles, first in Giuditta's house and later in the house of Demosthène Ollivier, father of Emile Ollivier, who was Napoleon III's chief minister in 1870. In this way, he recalled later, he 'remained for a whole year in Marseilles, writing, correcting proofs, corresponding, and even at midnight holding interviews with any members of the National party who came from Italy and some of the leaders of the Republican party in France.'[29]

* Some writers – for example, E. E. Y. Hales – believe that the child was Mazzini's. (Hales, *Mazzini and the Secret Societies*, pp. 218–20.) The dates prove that this was impossible. Evidence collated by Salvo Mastellone shows that Giuditta was still in Geneva in January 1832 and did not arrive in Marseilles until the following month; and the baby was born on 11 August 1832. She must therefore have been three months pregnant when she met Mazzini. The casual nature of Mazzini's references to the child in his letters to Giuditta is a further indication that he was not the father. The child lived only a couple of years. (Mastellone, *Mazzini e la 'Giovine Italia'*, pp. 124–6.)

Throughout the year the membership of Young Italy continued to grow; by the beginning of 1833 it had 60,000 members. Mazzini was impatient for action. No doubt he realized that he was living on borrowed time in Marseilles, as sooner or later the French police would catch up with him.

It seemed, too, to be the right time for a rising. His agents in Italy had been actively engaged in propaganda, especially in the Piedmontese army, and Mazzini had high hopes of a popular insurrection with army backing. It was always his weakness to over-estimate the amount of support that would be given to a rising started by a few brave men, and time was to prove him disastrously wrong in his bold assertion that 'Every revolution put into operation among a people who have been asleep for centuries develops volcanically the latent forces it possesses.'[30] But in 1833, as Young Italy went from strength to strength, he had some excuse for thinking that after two years' preparation the moment for action had come at last.

6

The moving spirit of the planned insurrection was Mazzini's boyhood friend, Jacopo Ruffini, who had been spreading dis-affection among Piedmontese troops. Many officers and non-commissioned officers, as well as ordinary soldiers, had joined Young Italy, not only in Genoa, where Ruffini lived, but also in Turin and Alessandria, and at Chambéry in Savoy. Mazzini's plan was for a simultaneous rising by military and civilian members of Young Italy in Genoa and Alessandria; the insurgents would seize barracks, arsenals and government offices, arrest governors and public officials and be prepared, if necessary, to assassinate the king. From these beginnings Mazzini hoped that an irresistible revolution would spread from state to state.

Unhappily for Young Italy, it never even began. Jacopo Ruffini's efforts to win over the Piedmontese army were always liable to discovery by the police or the army authorities, and in the event it was mere chance which put the Genoese police on the trail of Mazzini's plot. One day in April, a quartermaster and a sergeant began to quarrel in the army barracks at Genoa. They both used the same prostitute, and one accused the other of having told the girl about the plans for a rising. After angry words they struck at each other with their sabres, and the quartermaster was slightly wounded. The wound brought the matter to the notice of the military authorities. The soldiers were asked why they had been quarrelling, and their answers gave away the secret of the plot, so that the Genoese police were able to round up many of the leading conspirators, including Jacopo Ruffini.

Charles Albert was deeply angry when he heard of the attempt to tamper with the army's loyalty. More arrests were made, and the king insisted that no prisoner should be allowed to escape the full penalty of the law. A series of trials followed. Twelve conspirators, mostly private soldiers, were shot, and about a hundred received other sentences. A number of suspected persons including a Turin priest, Vincenzo Gioberti, were ordered to leave the country, and sentences of death were passed *in absentia* on some men who had escaped, including Giovanni and Agostino Ruffini, and on Mazzini himself. Jacopo Ruffini committed suicide in prison.

The conduct of the 1833 trials has been a subject of controversy among historians. At one time the sentences were regarded as a shocking example of despotic brutality. Bolton King, for example, observed that the Piedmontese government 'threw itself on its prey with a savage vengeance that has had no parallel in Italy since the days of Fra Diavolo';[31] Tivaroni described the executions as 'the greatest hecatomb of the century';[32] and Vidal called them 'a sombre page in the history of Piedmont, for the house of Savoy was not accustomed to drowning sedition in blood'.[33] More recent writers who have re-examined the trials in the light of the existing law feel that they were the necessary act of a government faced with a dangerous conspiracy, and that there is no evidence to show that they were carried out with undue brutality. Alessandro Luzio thinks that 'there is no trace of censurable deviation from the law of the time, and still less of real injustice and unnecessary ferocity';[34] and Rodolico considers that there was nothing illegal in the way in which the military tribunals interpreted and applied the existing penal code.[35] In spite of this changed verdict of history, Charles Albert himself must still be blamed for becoming personally involved in the

trials and for being so eager to press on with every possible
execution. Many years were to pass before Italian liberals for-
gave him for his conduct in 1833.

7

The Genoa executions and the death of Jacopo Ruffini were heavy
blows to Mazzini, but he was still determined to arrange a large-
scale insurrection in Italy. He now left Marseilles for a safer
refuge in Geneva; Giuditta Sidoli stayed with him for a few
weeks during the summer and then went back to Italy, where, in
spite of the danger of arrest, she was resolved to see her children.
In his new headquarters Mazzini was busy with plans for
an invasion of Savoy, which was designed to begin a general
rising.

It was in this summer that Mazzini was involved in the bizarre
incident of Antonio Gallenga's plot to assassinate Charles Albert.
Gallenga, a young man of twenty-two, had been exiled from
Parma after the insurrection of 1831 and had joined Young Italy
at Marseilles with the pseudonym of Procida. In July 1833 he
told one of Mazzini's close friends that he was making plans for
the stabbing of Charles Albert and asked him to obtain Mazzini's
approval. The request was passed on to Geneva, and after a
short interval Mazzini replied: 'I accept Procida's offer.' In
August Gallenga went to see him and asked for a dagger with
which to kill the king. Mazzini gave him a stiletto he had on his
desk, and Gallenga duly departed for Turin. It was only when he
arrived there that he began to realize how difficult it would be to
carry out his plan. His self-confidence waned, and in the end he
left Piedmont without having tried to fulfil his own mission. [36]

Though nothing came of Gallenga's plot, Mazzini's approval
of it has a certain historical importance. Years later, in the
course of a newspaper correspondence in London, he indignantly
denied that he had ever accepted 'the theory of the dagger'. The
Gallenga episode shows that this denial was disingenuous, for he
certainly approved of a plan for regicide in 1833.

After the fine fervour of its beginning Young Italy had entered
a period of difficulty and disappointment. In the autumn and
winter Mazzini continued to work on the project for invading

Savoy. He hoped to have a force of about a thousand men, consisting of Italian, German and Polish exiles and French and Swiss sympathizers, and their invasion was intended to synchronize with another attempt at insurrection in Genoa.

General Gerolamo Ramorino, a native of Genoa and a former Napoleonic officer, was chosen to command the expedition. He had gone into exile after supporting the Piedmontese revolution of 1821, and had later fought in a Polish rising against the Russians. He was engaged for the Savoy command in October and was sent to Paris with 30,000 francs to get arms and men for the invasion force.

It was a futile quest. As leader of the Italian exiles in Paris, Buonarroti had become jealous of Young Italy and was launching a new and reformed organization of 'democratic universal Carbonari'. He thought that the plans for invading Savoy were imprudent and had no chance of success, and he advised the Italians in Paris to take no part in them.[37] It was said by the exiles at Geneva that Ramorino gambled away their money in Parisian gaming-houses. This may or may not be true, but in one way or another the money had gone when he went back to Geneva at the end of January 1834. He brought with him precisely three volunteers instead of the expected hundreds.

Even without reinforcements from Paris Mazzini claimed to have recruited an international force of 783 men. But when the time came for action some 160 Germans and Poles were arrested and disarmed by Swiss gendarmes when trying to sail across the lake from Nyon, other volunteers had drifted away, and Mazzini had only 223 followers when he mobilized his force at Carouge, near the frontier of Savoy, on Saturday 1 February. This was the 'army' with which Ramorino was expected to invade Savoy and attack the fortress of Saint-Julien, garrisoned by 500 Piedmontese troops.

The venture was doomed. After a day of waiting the impetuous leaders of Young Italy urged Ramorino to start the attack on Sunday evening, but when he tested the volunteers' spirit by sounding an alert at 2 a.m., the poor response confirmed his professional view that the enterprise was hopeless. An hour later he called a council of war and announced that the force must be disbanded. Mazzini fainted when he heard the general's decision.[38]

The plan for a simultaneous rising in Genoa had no better fortune. The Savoy fiasco put the Piedmontese authorities on their guard; a number of precautionary arrests were made and there was no insurrection at all.

One of the Genoese conspirators was Giuseppe Garibaldi, a young sailor from Nice, which had been part of the duchy of Savoy, and subsequently of the kingdom of Piedmont, since the fourteenth century, except for the period of the French occupation of Italy. He was a merchant seaman who made frequent voyages to the Levant; on returning from one of these voyages in the late summer of 1833 he was told about Young Italy by some fellow Italians in a Marseilles café, and he was so much impressed that he was soon enrolled as a member, though probably not by Mazzini himself.* Early in 1834 he was in the royal Piedmontese navy at Genoa, doing national service as a conscript second-class sailor. His orders from Young Italy were to subvert his comrades and to seize a warship when the rising began.[39] His activities as propagandist were disclosed when the police began to make inquiries, and his arrest was ordered; but he escaped in disguise to Nice and later went to France. In his absence from Italy he was sentenced to death for high treason. After a year of voyages in French ships under assumed names he decided to try his luck in South America.

The first phase of Mazzini's Young Italy was virtually over. After two years of spreading the gospel of unity, independence and republicanism its attempts at action had been pitiful failures. But its work had not been wasted. Mazzini had charted a course for Italy's future.

* There is an old tradition that Mazzini personally enrolled Garibaldi as a member of Young Italy, and artists have drawn pictures of their meeting. A check on the dates of Garibaldi's voyages shows that Mazzini was in Geneva by the time that Garibaldi came to Marseilles in 1833, and they could not have met at that time. Their first meeting must have been in Lombardy in 1848. (*See*, John Parris, *The Lion of Caprera*, pp. 38–40.)

THE WAITING YEARS

Piedmont and its neighbours   *Mazzini in London*
Savigno rising   *The gallant brothers*   *An exile's friends*
     Manifesto di Rimini   *The salt dispute*

THE years between the Savoy fiasco of 1834 and the election of
Pope Pius IX in 1846 were in some ways an intermission in the
history of the Risorgimento. They were not uneventful years.
Such incidents as the Savigno rising, the Bandiera brothers'
landing in Calabria and the Rimini manifesto were signs of the
growth of an Italian national consciousness; the famous books
by Gioberti, Balbo and Azeglio and Cavour's essay on railways
pointed the way to a peaceful revolution on different lines from
those advocated by Young Italy. All these were important developments, but they were less dramatic than the great risings
of 1821 and 1831 which had shaken thrones and given Italy its
first experience of constitutional government. Those days were
over. The principle of absolute sovereignty seemed to have been
successfully reinstated.

Nowhere was this more evident than in Piedmont, where King
Charles Albert was firmly convinced of the necessity for absolute
power. Though he had turned his back on his old liberal ways
he was not hostile to modest reforms: he welcomed the sub-
stitution of reasonable legislative and administrative procedures
for the chaos which had ruled in Piedmont since the restoration,
he encouraged agriculture, commerce and railway-building (which
began in Italy at the end of the 1830s), and he gave special
attention to the problems of Sardinia, which was afflicted by the
combined hardships of feudalism, poverty and banditry. Army
reforms continued, but were more effective on paper than in
practice, owing to the low standard of the officers, who were
chosen because of their birth and social standing without regard

to their professional merits; and a notable innovation was the
foundation of the famous corps of bersaglieri (sharpshooters) by
General Alessandro La Marmora in 1836. But Piedmontese life
was still dominated by a reactionary clericalism. Under a king
who claimed that he reigned 'to advance as much as in my power
the glory of God and our holy religion', the Jesuits had greater
influence than in any other part of Italy and were generally hated
for their effrontery.[1]

In the early years of Charles Albert's reign there was little
evidence of the hatred of Austria which some writers have chosen
to regard as his 'secret'. It is true that in 1838 he refused to go to
Milan for the coronation of the new Austrian emperor and
preferred to meet him privately at Pavia. This has been described
as the first public sign of changed relations between Turin and
Vienna.[2] It was more probably an astute diplomatic move which
the king made on the advice of his foreign minister, Solaro della
Margarita, a staunch conservative who was jealous of Piedmont's
dignity and was opposed to any action that might appear to
depict his country as an Austrian vassal.

Whatever may be the truth about Charles Albert's 'secret',
few could have guessed in the 1830s that he was to end his reign
as the champion of Italian freedom and was to lead Italy in its
first attempt to drive out the Austrians. At this time Piedmont
seemed firmly embedded in reaction and there was more progressive thought to be found in Tuscany and Lombardy than in
the sub-Alpine kingdom.

In Tuscany, Guerrazzi and Bini were still the great protagonists
of the patriotic movement, and occasional spells in prison did
not deter them from promoting liberal ideas and devising new
ways of annoying the police, who regarded Guerrazzi as Tuscany's
evil genius. But Tuscan government was always benevolent;
when the two revolutionaries were imprisoned at Portoferraio
in 1833 they were treated with great consideration. This was the
year in which Vieusseux's great periodical, *Antologia*, at last
gave the Austrians an opportunity for effective protest. Both the
Austrian and Russian envoys in Florence complained to the
grand duke about articles in *Antologia* which were supposed to
have insulted their respective countries. The paper was sup-

pressed, but the incident strengthened the Tuscan liberals' desire to free their country from Austrian influence.[3]

Liberal sentiments were being advanced in Lombardy also by Carlo Cattaneo, Giandomenico Romagnosi and other distinguished writers. Cattaneo has been called 'the most vigorous figure in the Lombard Risorgimento'[4] and 'the only realist among so many romantics and theorists'.[5] He had been a teacher, but he gave up his profession in 1835, when he married the English girl Anna Pyne Woodcock, a descendant of the family of Milton's second wife, and from that time he was first and foremost a writer, dealing with such varied subjects as railways, commerce, agriculture, customs, finance, irrigation, charity and the penal code. In 1839 he founded his own monthly paper, which was called the *Politecnico*, and counted mathematicians, jurists, economists and doctors among its contributors.

Cattaneo and his friends were not practising revolutionaries. Their aim was to show the course of progress, so that their fellow-citizens would become conscious of their rights and capabilities. This was also the aim of the many Lombard journalists who agreed with Romagnosi, editor of the *Annali*, that 'there is an inexorable connexion between the advance of "civilization" and political ends'.[6] Romagnosi's followers oversimplified Italy's task in expecting that economic and social progress would inevitably lead to freedom from foreign rule, but they undoubtedly helped to develop national feeling in Lombardy during the long years of Austrian domination. Their work in Italy was the more important because it was done at a time when national leadership from outside the country had been damped down by the failures of the Savoy invasion and the Genoa insurrection.

2

Young Italy had not recovered from the double blow it had suffered in 1834. Mazzini stayed in Switzerland, but for the time being his political interests were mainly international. He always maintained that nationalism was only a step towards internationalism, and he soon founded a Young Switzerland movement, to be followed in subsequent years by Young Europe,

Young Germany and Young Poland. It was because of these activities that the Swiss authorities ordered him to leave the country in May 1836.

These were hard years for Mazzini. He went through a period of great disillusionment, which was at its most poignant in the winter of 1835–6. He was emotionally upset, because Giuditta Sidoli had refused his plea that she should come back to Switzerland, and he was also afflicted by doubts about the value of the work he was doing. 'Perhaps I was wrong and the world was right,' he pondered. 'Perhaps the idea which I pursued was a dream . . . How many mothers had already wept because of me? How many more would weep if I persisted?'[7]

At times he feared that he was going mad, and that his spirit was dying in his body. Reason was no help to him; he needed the blinding flash of intuition. It came at last. 'One day', he wrote afterwards, 'I awoke with my soul at peace and my intellect serene and the feelings of one who has been saved from an extreme danger.'[8]

His Swiss interlude was nearly over. After being ordered to leave the country he managed to evade the police by hiding in various places, but it was an uncomfortable existence, and his close companions, Giovanni and Agostino Ruffini, urged him to give it up. England, the political asylum for refugees of all kinds and from all countries, was there to receive them. On 12 January 1837, Mazzini, the two Ruffinis and Angelo Usiglio came to London, where Mazzini noted at once that the atmosphere was filled with something 'which seems like a light smoke'. He was to stay in London for nearly eleven years on his first visit, and was then to return for an even longer period. He had found his second home.

Mazzini's first years in London were a time of much financial hardship, which was only partly alleviated by the small sums he earned for his contributions to literary reviews. Poor though he was, he threw himself whole-heartedly into the life of his compatriots, whether exiles or voluntary immigrants, and helped to establish an Italian working men's association and a free school for Italian children. He also founded a newspaper with the odd name of *Apostolato popolare* (popular apostleship).

r Emmanuel I, king of Piedmont,
1802–1821

Charles Felix, king of Piedmont,
1821–1831

Prince Charles Albert with the conspirators, 1821

The Shooting of the Bandiera Brothers, 1844

But it was not long before he returned to the main work of his life. In 1839 he wrote to his friend Giuseppe Lamberti, who was then in Paris: 'We are not doing our duty.'[9] Next year he and Lamberti began to revive both Young Italy and Young Europe. Many of the former members of Young Italy refused to rejoin. This did not worry Mazzini. His eye was always on the young generation. The schoolboys of 1831 were now young men, and it was to their imagination that he appealed. 'This is the banner of youth – your banner,' his new manifesto declared. 'That one generation of young men should achieve its triumph has never been said. But this has been said: that one generation shall receive it from another until the day of victory!'[10]

So Young Italy was reborn. Mazzini's capacity for writing dozens of letters a day was again used to the full. In 1840 and 1841 his letters flowed to Italian exiles all over the world. Agents were appointed and revolutionary committees established in Italy itself and in many countries of Europe and North and South America. Central councils were set up in Paris, New York and Montevideo; in the United States there were branches in Boston, New Haven, Philadelphia, Richmond and Charleston, and others were set up in Canada, Uruguay, Cuba and the West Indies. Mazzini was no longer calling for guerrilla war or encouraging local revolts, though he was later to return to his old dream of freeing Italy by means of armed insurrection. But this seemed barely possible in 1841. His immediate aim was to persuade all Italians, both inside and outside their homeland, that they must build up their national consciousness and be ready, when occasion offered, to support a concerted plan of action for the resurgence of Italy.

3

Though Mazzini was currently devoting his attention to propaganda and education rather than to plans for action, other exiles were still in a militant mood. One of these was the Modenese Nicola Fabrizi, who had been a close friend of Ciro Menotti.

Fabrizi had left Italy after the risings of 1831, and had fought, like other Italian exiles, in the first Carlist war in Spain. From 1834 onwards he began to receive disconsolate letters from Mazzini, who at that time had no hope of reviving Young Italy, and he decided to start a patriotic association of his own. This was the Italian Legion, which Fabrizi set up in 1839 with head-quarters in Malta. Its aims and ideas were largely those of Mazzini; its statute proclaimed its objectives of independence, unity and liberty; but its programme was for guerrilla warfare in the mountains of central and southern Italy.

Mazzini was disturbed when he heard of Fabrizi's new move-ment. He was just on the point of issuing his new manifesto to Young Italy, and he feared that the multiplication of patriotic organizations might weaken the national movement. Well-mean-ing friends tried to persuade the two men to merge their societies; Mazzini was willing, but Fabrizi preferred to go his own way. It was thus the Italian Legion, and not Young Italy, which made plans for a synchronized rising in Naples, the Papal States and Tuscany in 1843.[11]

It was the old story over again. Italy was not capable of staging a co-ordinated insurrection. August was the chosen month but when the time came the conspirators in each centre hesitated to strike and waited hopefully to hear that the rising had begun elsewhere. Nothing happened in Naples and Tuscany, and there might have been no rising in the Papal States if the papal gendarmes had not forced the conspirators' hands. They had been correctly informed that two men of Savigno, Dr Pasquale Muratori and his brother Severio, were planning a revolt. They surrounded the Muratoris' house, but except for one man, who was captured, all the conspirators escaped to the countryside. There they began a short-lived guerrilla campaign against the pope's government that has been dignified with the name of *moto di Savigno* (Savigno rising).

The Muratoris' band consisted of about eighty men, who were well armed and had plenty of ammunition. They knew the country well, and thanks to this knowledge they were able to make a successful raid on Savigno, where they overpowered the handful of papal troops before withdrawing to the mountains with six hostages. Larger papal forces were soon on their heels. In their panic-stricken retreat before superior numbers the rebels shot two of their hostages dead and gravely wounded another; the papal forces then caught up with them and soon overcame their resistance. The rising was over. Some of the insurgents fell into their enemy's hands; others escaped through Tuscany into France.[12]

Even now this new revolt in Romagna was not entirely ended. Ribotty, an exile who had served as an officer in the Carlist war, had come back to Italy and was waiting at Leghorn with seventeen other officers to join any revolutionary movement. When they heard of the collapse of the *moto di Savigno*, they went to Bologna, where they recruited a number of followers. They then set off for Imola, with the interesting idea of capturing three cardinals who were staying there. But the cardinals were warned in time. Their house was resolutely and successfully defended against Ribotty's attack, and Ribotty himself left the country when he realized that there was no hope of a general rising in the papal legations.

A year later a military commission was set up at Bologna to try the Savigno prisoners and others involved in the conspiracy – 116 people in all. Twenty were sentenced to death, but thirteen of these were reprieved by the pope and only seven were actually shot. One prisoner who was sentenced to the galleys for life was a young lawyer called Felice Orsini, whose name was to ring round the world fifteen years later. He had joined Young Italy on its rebirth in 1840, and had taken part in several minor Romagnol plots against the papal government. His arrest at this time was due to the discovery of an incriminating letter.[13]

Once again an ambitious plan for co-ordinated insurrection had collapsed ignominiously. Yet the miniature *moto di Savigno* was significant because it marked the beginning of a more active revolutionary phase after a relatively quiet period. Uprisings of one kind or another were now to figure intermittently in Italian history until the final achievement of freedom, independence and unity.

To many Italians, however, the Savigno affair seemed to be another demonstration of the failure of Mazzinian tactics, for although Mazzini had been against the rising, and had tried to dissuade Fabrizi from action, it was inevitably believed that he had some share in it. Liberals were strengthened in their growing belief that the way of advance lay through moderate reforms rather than violent revolution.

4

Another incident in the month of the Savigno rising was also a
portent for Italy's future. Piedmontese customs officers and
Austrian soldiers were involved in a brawl at the small village of
Castelletto-Ticino, on the Piedmontese-Lombard border. Six
Austrians were arrested by the Piedmontese. On the following
day an Austrian officer crossed the frontier with a body of troops
and demanded his men's release. The mayor of Castelletto-Ticino
timorously handed the prisoners back.

Charles Albert was indignant when he heard what had
happened. In a letter to Villamarina, his minister of war, he
declared that the mayor should have rung all the bells and levied
the people *en masse* to fall on the Austrians. If that had failed he
would himself have had all the bells rung from the Ticino to the
last village of Savoy, and if the Austrians had not apologized he
would have launched an attack to set Lombardy free.[14]

Since the incident was over the king confined himself to sending an official complaint to Metternich through the Piedmontese
minister in Vienna, but his anger indicates an impressive change
in his attitude since the time when he had willingly signed an
Austro-Piedmontese treaty. There is no doubt that by 1843
Charles Albert was beginning to picture himself as the patriot
king who would free Italy from foreign domination. It was a year
later that he had a medal designed for his personal presentation
to distinguished men of letters. It bore on one side the old device
of Amadeus VI of Savoy, *J'atans mon astre.*[15]

While Charles Albert awaited his star, rasher men were ready
to risk their lives in the hope of setting Italy ablaze. In the spring
of 1844 Mazzini in London and Lamberti in Paris worked out
another elaborate plan for a number of simultaneous risings in
different parts of Italy. Like Fabrizi's plot of the previous year
it reduced itself in the end to a single small rising – this time at
Cosenza, in Calabria, and there a mere handful of insurgents
were easily dispersed by gendarmes.[16] Suspected plotters were
then rounded up in Naples, where the republican leader, Carlo
Poerio, was among those arrested.

This trifling incident at Cosenza helped to inspire a more

famous though equally unsuccessful exploit – the Bandiera brothers' landing in Calabria. Attilio and Emilio Bandiera were two young Venetians serving as officers in the Austrian navy, in which their father was an admiral. The father was one of the many Italians who were satisfied with Austrian rule over Lombardy-Venetia and were content to find careers in Austria's service; the sons were more idealistic and believed that all Italy should belong to the Italians. Attilio had met some of the exiles on his voyages, and had been excited to hear of the revival of Young Italy. With his brother and another officer, Domenico Moro, he formed a secret society in the Austrian navy and affiliated it to Young Italy in 1842. From this time the brothers were resolved to fight for Italy's freedom. They made contact with Mazzini, but got little encouragement from him, as he felt that they had no chance of success.

The Bandieras soon became objects of suspicion to their superior officers. Early in 1844 they discovered that their letters were being opened, and they knew that they had been betrayed. The two brothers and Moro deserted from the navy and joined a small group of Italian exiles in Corfu. News of the Cosenza rising made them believe that all Calabria was on the brink of revolt and needed only the right kind of leadership. Though both Mazzini and Fabrizi tried to dissuade them, they set off from Corfu, accompanied by Moro and fifteen others, drawn from various Italian states, and landed on the coast of Calabria in June. (It was afterwards remembered with pride that this was the first revolt in which men from different Italian states had fought together.)

It was a disastrous venture. As they went ashore the gallant brothers knelt to kiss the Calabrian earth, exclaiming as they did so: 'This is our fatherland! Thou hast given us life. We spend it for thee!' They soon found, as Murat had found nearly thirty years earlier, that the hope of enlisting local support was illusory. The Cosenza rising had cowed Calabria rather than aroused it. No peasants joined the brothers as they and their comrades marched on, and the brave eighteen were soon surrounded by Neapolitan gendarmerie. In an unequal fight some were killed, and the others wounded and taken prisoner. None escaped.

King Ferdinand II himself decided the prisoners' fate. Nine, including the Bandieras and Moro, were ordered to be shot. The executions took place in the valley of Rovito, near Cosenza. As they waited for the firing squad the brothers sang proudly, 'Who dies for his country has lived long enough.' Their last words were 'Long live Italy!'

5

As usually happened, it was thought in Italy that Mazzini must have planned the Bandieras' adventure, and it was regarded as still further proof of the futility of Mazzinian plotting. In London the brothers' death had unexpected repercussions on Mazzini's career.

It was about this time that he began to suspect that the British government was opening his letters. Simple tests confirmed his opinion,* and he reported his discovery to two acquaintances who were members of parliament. They concluded, quite wrongly as it turned out, that the British government must have found out about the Bandieras' plot from Mazzini's letters and passed the information on to the governments of Austria and Naples. One of them raised the matter in the House of Commons, where Sir James Graham, the home secretary, at first denied that Mazzini's letters had been opened at all, but was later obliged to admit that they *had* been opened – under powers, it appeared, contained in a statute passed in the reign of Queen Anne.

The news of government interference with private correspondence caused a great sensation in England. *The Times* observed: 'It is a question vital to us all that sealed letters in an English post-office be, as we all fancied they were, respected as things sacred.' People began to mark their letters 'Not to be Grahamed', and although, as was later revealed, the Austrian government's information about the Bandieras' plot had come from another source, and not from the British government, Sir James Graham

* Mazzini used various methods of detection to make sure that the government was tampering with his letters. Sometimes he posted two letters simultaneously – one addressed to himself, one to a fictitious name at the same address. The letter bearing his own name arrived two hours after the other. On other occasions he had letters sent to him with poppy-seeds inside the envelope or with a hair laid across the seal. Both seeds and hair had vanished when the letters reached him. (E. F. Richards, *Mazzini's Letters to an English Family*, II, p. 101.)

was denounced as 'the assassin of the Italian patriots'. The episode ended, rather characteristically, with an 'open 'letter' from Mazzini to Sir James Graham. In this he was able to discuss publicly the whole Italian question.[17]

The controversy helped Mazzini by making English people more aware of him. Thomas Carlyle, indeed, told a friend that 'the best thing that had ever befallen Mazzini was the opening of his letters'. Editors asked him to write articles for them, and greater interest was taken in Italian affairs. It was also through the letter-opening incident that Mazzini became acquainted with the Ashurst family, who were his closest friends for the rest of his life.

This friendship, which is delightfully recorded in the three volumes of *Mazzini's letters to an English Family*, began when William Ashurst, a solicitor of progressive views, sent his son William and his unmarried daughter Eliza to call on Mazzini with a letter of sympathy after the first House of Commons debate on the letter-opening. Mr Ashurst lived at Muswell Hill, which was then considered to be 'in the country', and his home was the centre of a clever and unconventional family circle to which Mazzini was cordially admitted. The Ashursts had three other daughters – Matilda (Mrs Joseph Biggs), Caroline (Mrs James Stansfeld) and Emilie (Mrs Sydney Hawkes, later Signora Venturi). Their charming family background gave Mazzini a happier personal life than he had known since he came to England.*

* Mazzini's friendship with the Ashurst girls was greatly resented by Jane Welsh Carlyle, wife of Thomas Carlyle. She and her husband had often entertained Mazzini at their home in Chelsea, and she was clearly jealous of his new acquaintances. In a letter to her sister Babbie in 1847 she referred cattily to 'a Miss Eliza Ashurst – who does strange things – made his acquaintance first by going to his house to drink tea with him all alone, etc., etc.! and when she had got him to *her* house she introduced him into innumerable other houses of her kindred.' (*Jane Welsh Carlyle: Letters to her Family, 1839–1863*, p. 300). Agostino Ruffini said that Jane Carlyle had an affair with Mazzini. This would certainly have accounted for her jealousy of the Ashursts, but the affair may, in fact, have existed only in Ruffini's imagination. Dr Emilia Morelli, who has studied the relationship, thinks that Mazzini 'may have passed unscathed through the flames and succeeded in keeping himself within the limits of an affectionate cordiality'. (*Mazzini in Inghilterra*, p. 27.)

6

More than a year after the Bandieras' exploit Mazzini was invited to support a projected rising at Rimini, in the Papal States, which was being planned by a rather unusual partnership of moderate liberals and republicans, who had acquired a few arms from French sources and aspired to overthrow the papal government. He refused to become involved in it, since he felt that there was not enough real strength behind it. On reflection the intended leaders, of whom the most prominent was Luigi Carlo Farini, came round to the same way of thinking; they decided to postpone their rising and they withdrew to Tuscany.

Their decision was not accepted by Renzi, an Italian exile who had come from Paris to assist the revolt. He took the leaders' place, called out as many supporters as he could rally and attacked the papal barracks, which he successfully occupied after a fight in which three papal soldiers were killed and seventeen wounded. Renzi was master of Rimini for three days, but gave up the struggle when a large papal force was reported to be approaching. There was no more fighting, and Renzi and his followers escaped from the Papal States – some overland to Tuscany, others by boat to Trieste.

This militarily unimportant rising is remembered because Farini, after his flight to Tuscany, issued a document which became famous as the *Manifesto di Rimini*. Written by Farini himself, and revised and modified by Giuseppe Montanelli, a leading Tuscan patriot, it was a strong condemnation of the misgovernment of the Papal States and a dignified protest against ecclesiastical privilege, the Inquisition and clerical control of education. Many of the evils it attacked would have disappeared long since if Gregory XVI had genuinely accepted the ambassadors' memorandum of 1831, and the manifesto 'was virtually an appeal to the great powers to make the papal government carry out the terms of the memorandum or their equivalent'.[18] Its chief demands were for an amnesty for all political prisoners, reform of civil and criminal law in accordance with general European practice, the establishment of genuinely elective municipal councils, the admission of the laity to all kinds of civil, military and judicial offices, the modification of press censorship, the removal of all foreign troops from the Papal States and the formation of a civic guard.[19]

Though bad government in the Papal States was an old story, the manifesto was a useful re-statement of the abuses of the pope's temporal power. Its authors insisted that it was a message of peace, not a declaration of war. The pope and his court took no notice of it.

7

A new pope was soon to take a more sympathetic attitude towards his subjects' complaints, but before his appearance the vexed question of Austrian domination was sharply raised in Piedmont. The Austrian and Piedmontese governments had been at logger-heads for two or three years over the supply of salt to the Swiss canton of Ticino. By a treaty of 1751, which was confirmed by the congress of Vienna, this trade was an Austrian monopoly; but in the 1840s the Swiss became dissatisfied with the Austrian supply and arranged to buy salt in the south of France and have it transported through Piedmont.

Technically this was not a breach of the treaty, which only prevented Piedmont from supplying its own salt to Ticino, but the Austrians chose to regard Piedmont's action as being in contravention of the agreement. After much acrimonious argument Austria took its revenge in 1846 by increasing the duty on the import of Piedmontese wines into Lombardy, thus seriously damaging Piedmont's wine-growing industry.

Charles Albert had not yet made any public declaration of hostility towards Austria. This piece of Austrian effrontery gave him a chance of doing so. He sent an indignant note to Vienna, and broke with precedent by having it published in the official *Gazzetta Piemontese*. In Turin the liberals were delighted and arranged to hold a demonstration in the king's honour when he reviewed the garrison troops; but on the day of the review Charles Albert stayed in his palace, as he felt that the time had not yet come for public displays of anti-Austrian sentiments. None the less, his publication of his note to the Austrian government was an impressive sign of Italy's wish for independence. For the first time an Italian prince had openly condemned an Austrian act of injustice.[20]

While the public applauded, some of the royal councillors were alarmed at the king's boldness. What would happen, they asked, if Austria broke off relations with Piedmont over the salt dispute? Charles Albert had his answer ready for them – and for history. 'If Piedmont loses Austria,' he said, 'she will gain Italy, and then Italy will go it alone.' This was his great, though mistaken, vision of future events – *l'Italia farà da se*.[21]

THE PRINTED WORD

Gioberti's Primato *Balbo's* Speranze *Azeglio's* Gli ultimi
casi di Romagna *Cavour on railways*

THESE years of comparative inaction in the physical progress of
the Risorgimento were also the years in which Italian thought was
profoundly influenced by the publication of three important
books. The first of these was Vincenzo Gioberti's *Del primato
morale e civile degli Italiani*, which is usually known as the
Primato.

Gioberti was the Turin priest who was ordered to leave Piedmont after the discovery of the Genoa plot in 1833. He was not,
and never had been, a member of Young Italy, as Mazzini
wrongly asserted in his memoirs; but he was a liberal thinker,
and he was certainly in touch with one of the surviving coteries
of the dying Carbonaro movement. After leaving Piedmont he
taught philosophy in Brussels, and he was still in exile when he
wrote the *Primato*, which was published in 1843. Though he
was to write other books, one of which had a great influence on
Charles Albert's eldest son, and he was also to play a brief part in
Piedmontese government, the *Primato* is the chief reason for the
claim that he and Mazzini were the greatest figures in the
heroic and dramatic period of the Risorgimento.[1] Each had a
vision of Italian unity, but while Mazzini wished to build that
unity on the people's will Gioberti preferred to base it on the
historic foundation of the Roman Catholic Church.

The general line of Gioberti's thought was that Italy and the
Catholic Church should go forward together. There would be,
he hoped, a complete reconciliation between the Church and
modern civilization and between the Church and the Italian
nation. In Belgium, Ireland and Poland Catholic sentiment was
associated with the national movement. Would it not be possible

to create in Italy a similar movement of national Catholicism and so avoid the greatest rock on which, up till then, national progress had been shipwrecked – the antithesis between traditional religion and the Italian national movement?[2]

This union of patriotism and religion was the theme of the *Primato*. Its title is explained by Gioberti's belief that Italy once enjoyed the civil and moral primacy of the world, and though it had lost its place through long centuries of division and servitude it was still capable of regaining its former leadership.

How could this be done? To Gioberti the answer was clear. The last period of Italy's greatness had coincided with the greatness of the popes. The great Guelf tradition of the Middle Ages, when the Guelfs stood for the papacy against the emperor and the Ghibellines, was Italy's only truly consecutive national tradition. Italy was then, as it still should be, the capital of the world, because Rome was the religious capital of the world, and Rome should be the seat of the civil and federal court of the peninsula.

It was therefore in association with the Catholic idea that Italy would regain her world primacy, but this could not be won unless the country were politically united. Gioberti saw no advantage in a union created by fusing all the Italian states into one, and little likelihood of such fusion ever becoming practicable. His solution was to unite Italy as a confederation of states under the presidency of the pope. The true principle of Italian unity lay in the papacy. The confederation he envisaged would have its national armed forces and would rank as a great nation.

Gioberti went on to appeal to the people to support the national cause, and to Charles Albert, as the head of Italy's most militarily-minded state, to fulfil his royal house's destiny by 'binding the Alpine people to those of the Apennines and forming them all into one single family'. The need for war with Austria as a prerequisite of Italian unity was never formally stated, though it may have been implicit in his final words to Charles Albert: 'Therefore, brave prince, Italy is confident that from out of your house will come forth her redeemer.'

Gioberti also proposed a programme of reform for the Italian states. It was a modest programme, since his book was in no sense an attack on absolute power; but he felt that there must be better relations between rulers and ruled if the different states were to come together in unity. His idea was to make the monarchies 'consultative', by setting up in each state a consultative assembly, mainly elected, which would advise the sovereign on any matters he wished to discuss with it. Freedom of the press should also be guaranteed, though it would be kept within bounds by a council of censors.

Omodeo has described the *Primato* as 'the Trojan horse'. It found enthusiastic readers all over Italy, and it is doubtful if many of them realized that its doctrines implied a peaceful revolution which in time would have overturned the existing governmental system. Mazzini's own ideals of liberty, unity and independence were all to be found in Gioberti's book, though the liberty was only a shadow of true democratic freedom, unity was by federation rather than fusion and independence from foreign domination was only hinted at and never expressly demanded. Even so, it was a remarkable advance in political thought, which was no less significant because of its apparent harmlessness. 'It seemed perfectly orthodox. It revealed the possibility of reconciling national sentiments with the Catholic religion, with the love of established order, with what were regarded as the Italian traditions ... It was now possible to speak openly of Italy. The beginning of the movement of public opinion was Gioberti's greatest success.'[3]

It was not, of course, everyone's book. The reactionaries disliked it: Solaro della Margarita, Charles Albert's conservative foreign minister, called it sentimental medievalism.[4] The Jesuits vehemently attacked both the book and its author.[5] And there were even doubters among the liberals. What hope could be put in the papacy while the illiberal Gregory XVI was pope? And was not the talk of federation utopian while the Austrians remained in Lombardy-Venetia? These were valid criticisms. The Risorgimento did not, in fact, proceed on the lines suggested by Gioberti. But his book was a momentous contribution to the rediscovery of political consciousness and a valuable text-book for the new political group which had arisen in Piedmont and elsewhere. These were the so-called moderates, who believed that Italy's problems should be solved by peaceful reforms, on which princes and peoples could agree, and not by violent revolution.

It was also of some importance that two readers of the *Primato* who were much impressed by its arguments were Charles Albert of Piedmont and Cardinal Mastai-Ferretti, bishop of Imola, the future Pope Pius IX.

2

Those who disliked the *Primato* could dismiss it as the work of an exile who was out of touch with contemporary Italian affairs. The same charge could not be brought against another vital book on national problems which appeared in the following year. This was written by an Italian who was living in Italy, a Catholic monarchist and a member of the Piedmontese aristocracy.

Count Cesare Balbo, author of *Delle speranze d'Italia*, had held military and diplomatic posts in Piedmont after the restoration, and had been exiled in 1822 because of his association with the leaders of the 1821 rising. He had been allowed to return two years later, on condition that he lived quietly in his country villa and took no part in public life. There he wrote books, including his famous essay on the hopes of Italy.

Balbo's book, which was dedicated to Gioberti, was an improved and more practicable version of the *Primato*. Both writers agreed that a federation of Italian states was the desirable end, but Balbo put Piedmont in the very centre of the picture and set less store by the papacy's part in it. One of his hopes for Italy, was that Austrian ownership of Lombardy-Venetia should be ended, not necessarily by war but possibly by Austria's own willingness to withdraw from Italy in exchange for increased territory in the Balkans, where the Ottoman empire was expected to collapse in the near future. He argued that the pope was the wrong leader for an Italian federation, for if in the end a war of independence had to be fought the pope would be unable to lead the Italians against Catholic Austria.

In Balbo's opinion, the leadership of a federated Italy should go to Piedmont. Indeed, when the Austrians eventually surrendered Lombardy and Venetia, these territories should be joined to Piedmont, thus forming a strong northern Italian kingdom. Even that enlargement might not be the end of Piedmontese aggrandizement, for Balbo observed that Italy was divided naturally by the Apennines into a northern and southern part. Since the papal legations of Bologna, Ferrara, Ravenna and Forli were north of the Apennines, he was clearly hinting that these too should be incorporated in the new Piedmont. In this revised form of Gioberti's Italian federation the pope would be only one of the sovereigns taking part in it, though he would still remain, as he was bound to remain, the spiritual head of the Catholic world.

These were Balbo's most definite proposals. On liberty, in the sense of liberal institutions, he refused to be dogmatic. The first aim was to win independence, and liberty came second. Independence, he wrote, 'is to nations as modesty is to a woman; what do all the virtues matter if that one is missing?' When independence was won, the princes themselves should decide on the right time for extending civil and political liberties.

Gioberti's plan for making the pope president of a federal Italy is known as the neo-Guelf theory because of his insistence that Italy was at its greatest in the days of the Guelfs. In Balbo's *Speranze* the neo-Guelf theory was changed into a plan for Piedmontese hegemony. As a straightforward political study it had wider influence than Gioberti's more philosphical treatise, and it was well received by Charles Albert, who observed that 'What Count Balbo has done is very good.' In view of the book's anti-Austrian attitude the king would not allow it to circulate openly in Piedmont, but the fact that he said nothing against it in public was taken to indicate that he sympathized with its views.[6] The book was secretly read in Piedmont in spite of the official ban, and it circulated widely in other Italian states.

3

The third author who contributed to this remarkable phase in Italian political writing was Massimo d'Azeglio, another Piedmontese aristocrat but one who had not previously been concerned with public life. Azeglio had given up an army career to become an artist, and had won considerable popularity and success in a period when he had no particularly distinguished rivals. He had also written two historical novels.

While visiting Rome in 1845 Azeglio was persuaded by some politically-minded friends to undertake a mission for them. This was to tour Romagna, make contact with the leaders of secret societies and warn them that it would be foolhardy to begin insurrections on the death, which was expected in the near future, of Pope Gregory XVI.

Azeglio duly fulfilled this curious assignment, which took him to Rimini a few weeks before Renzo's rising; but he did not restrict himself to the warnings he had been asked to give. He was a close friend of Cesare Balbo, and he fully accepted the arguments of the *Speranze*. In Romagna he made it his business to expound Balbo's theories and to persuade liberals and secret society leaders that Charles Albert was the one man who could successfully lead a movement for Italian regeneration and the expulsion of the Austrians. Many of the Romagnol liberals were not convinced by his arguments; they were suspicious of Charles Albert because of his anti-liberal past and they feared that his leadership might result in Piedmontese domination of the rest of Italy.[7]

On his return to Piedmont Azeglio wrote a book about Romagna, but before doing so he asked for an audience with Charles Albert. The king, as was his custom, received him early in the morning. He listened carefully while Azeglio told him of the liberal and anti-Austrian sentiments he had found everywhere in Romagna, and finally said with great earnestness: 'Tell those fellows that they must keep quiet for the present, because nothing can yet be done; but they may rest assured that, when the occasion comes, my life and the life of my sons, my arms, my gold, my troops – nay, my all will be spent in the cause of Italy.' Azeglio was impressed by Charles Albert's forthright declaration of his intention to liberate Italy, but he was not wholly convinced by the king's words. He felt that there was something cold and even funereal about Charles Albert in spite of his apparent friendliness.[8]

It was in 1846 that Azeglio published his small book entitled *Degli ultimi casi in Romagna* (Recent Events in Romagna). It had only a hundred pages, but in its own way it was a worthy successor to the more imposing works of Gioberti and Balbo. Azeglio examined the recent insurrections and trials in Romagna, and denounced the papal court's misgovernment, under which wages were low and taxes exorbitant, while the people were harassed by a brutal secret police and savagely punished if they committed offences. At the same time he warned the secret societies against futile insurrections, and recommended political agitation as the best course for Italy.

'The first, the greatest protest, which we should never tire of making, which should be on every tongue, and flow from every pen, must be against foreign occupation, and in support of our right to full control over our own soil, of our nationality and of our independence,' he wrote. 'Let protests follow against the injustices, the abuses and evil orders of our own governments.'

Agitation, in Azeglio's view, could help the Italians to secure free institutions from their rulers; then there could be a great national movement to drive out the Austrians. 'This conspiracy in open daylight,' he declared, 'with its own name written on the brow of everyone, is the only kind useful, the only kind worthy of us and of the favour of opinion, and in this manner of conspiracy I also declare myself a conspirator in the view of all; in this manner I also incite every good Italian to conspire.'

Azeglio made no contribution to the question of how Italy could achieve unity, but his moral was plain to all. Neither Mazzinians nor members of local secret societies could save Italy; only the king of Piedmont could lead a great national crusade. Independence from Austrian domination and influence was shown to be Italy's most desirable goal.

The new idea of an anti-Austrian campaign led by Charles Albert pushed both Young Italy and neo-Guelfism into the background. Azeglio's book was widely read and was regarded as a call to action. Its effect on Azeglio himself was to turn him from painter into politician.

4

These were the three books which provided a political basis for the development of the new moderate party. The case for an

Italian federation was now clearly stated; the respective arguments for neo-Guelfism or Piedmontese hegemony could be
studied at leisure. The importance of expelling the Austrians
was also emphasized. A course was openly set for Italian patriotism.

One other example of political writing deserves to be mentioned
though it had not the wide circulation enjoyed by the books. This
was an article on Italian railways by a Piedmontese nobleman,
Count Camillo di Cavour. It was published in Paris in the
Revue nouvelle in 1846.

At this time in Italian history the meetings and annual con-
gresses of scientific or agricultural associations provided a useful
means of inculcating liberal ideas. One of these societies, which
came into being in 1842, was the Sub-Alpine Agrarian Association, sponsored by Count Cavour and other aristocrats. Although,
as its name implied, the association was mainly concerned with
agricultural improvement, its members had also the secret aim
'of devoting all their efforts, and all the authority of their association, to the development of national sentiment and the search
for liberal institutions'.[9] Something of this spirit was reflected in
Cavour's article on railways.

It was a timely article, for railway development in Italy was
making slow progress through lack of private capital. The first
lines to be built were those from Naples to Caserta in 1838 and
from Milan to Monza in 1839, and various projects were mooted
in Piedmont, Lombardy and Venetia in the early 1840s. These
were held up because of a clash between Austria and Piedmont
on the course of development: Austria wished to make Trieste,
in its own territory of Venezia Giulia, the railhead for central
Europe, but Charles Albert thought that Italian interests would
be better served by a line from Milan to Genoa, which would
continue into France. Piedmont's point of view was expressed,
with Charles Albert's approval, in a book by Count Illarione
Pettitti, which was published in Paris. It was this book which
inspired Cavour's article.

The subject was one on which he could write with some
authority, for he had been keenly interested in railways since 1837,
when he had made a journey in France on the newly opened

railroad from Paris to St Germain. Two years later he had joined the administrative council of the Savoyard railway company as a representative of the Piedmontese and Lombard shareholders.[10]

Cavour argued in his article that a railroad from Turin to Chambéry, which was then proposed, would remove the distances which separated London and Paris from Venice, Milan, Genoa and Turin and would bring 'incalculable benefits' to Italy. Moreover, railways would be one of the factors which would help Italy to gain its independence. 'The time of conspiracy has passed', he wrote. 'The emancipation of peoples cannot result from mere plots or a surprise attack; it has become a necessary consequence of the progress of Christian civilization and the spread of enlightenment.'

Cavour also discussed railways in relation to the general Italian position. Italy's troubles were primarily due to foreign political influence, and the obstacles of internal divisions, rivalries and antipathy between different parts of the peninsula made it difficult for that influence to be thrown off. 'If the action of the railways diminishes these obstacles and perhaps even abolishes them, it will have given the greatest encouragement to the spirit of Italian nationality.'

From these arguments Cavour advanced to the question of Italian independence. 'Here', he wrote, 'is a supreme good which Italy can obtain only by the combined effort of all her children. Without independence Italy cannot hope for any durable improvement or be confident of any real progress.' But the triumph of Italian nationality, he insisted, would not come from military or democratic revolutions, but from 'the combined action of all the live forces in the country, that is to say, of the national rulers openly supported by every party'. Only union between the different branches of the Italian family 'will enable the country to profit from such favourable political circumstances as the future must bring, and so free itself from foreign domination.'[11]

Cavour's message was clear. Italy must unite, its rulers must lead the people and the Austrians must go. His article was a worthy postscript which helped to prepare Italians for the great tasks ahead of them.

Part II

1846—1860

Part II

1846—1860

VIII

PIUS IX

The man and the myth   Amnesty and reforms   Austrian
reprisal   Mazzini's 'Open Letter'   Lord Minto's mission
Charles Albert's call for independence   The tobacco riots

WHILE Italian political thought was being adjusted to the new
ideas the national scene was dramatically changed by the
appearance of a reforming pope. The reactionary Gregory XVI
died on 1 June 1846 and the conclave to elect his successor met
on 14 June. Cardinal Lambruschini, who had been the late
pope's secretary of state, was thought to have the best chance of
election; but he had enemies as well as friends, and though he
led on the first count of votes he was far short of the necessary
majority. In further counts he was overtaken by Cardinal Mastai-
Ferretti, bishop of Imola, who had long been absent from Rome
and had no involvements in central ecclesiastical politics. Mastai
himself was scrutineer when the fourth count gave him thirty-six
votes – two more than were needed for election. He exclaimed,
'My, lords, what have you done?' and fainted. The last pope
who was to exercise temporal power in the papal dominions had
begun his long reign.

Cardinal Mastai-Ferretti, who took the title of Pius IX, was a
handsome, broad-shouldered man of fifty-four, whose ecclesiastical career had not been seriously hampered by his affliction of
epilepsy. Though he was little known to the general public,
except in the dioceses where he had served, he had been well
thought of in Rome since his visit to Chile in 1823 as secretary
to a papal envoy. (He was thus the first pope who had been to
America.) Pope Leo XII made him archbishop of Spoleto in
1827, Gregory XVI translated him to the more important
bishopric of Imola in 1832, and the cardinal's hat followed in

1840. Since he had the reputation of being an enlightened churchman his election to the papacy seems neither surprising nor undeserved.

Unlike his reactionary predecessors the new pope was sympathetic towards liberal thought. During his fourteen years at Imola one of his liberal friends was Count Giuseppe Pasolini, of Monterico, whose son later put up a marble tablet in the family home, recording that Cardinal Mastai had often visited there before his election as pope and that the count and countess had given him copies of Balbo's *Speranze* and Gioberti's *Primato*.[1] These were useful homework for a reforming pope.

Before considering the extent of his reforms something must be said about the 'myth of Pius IX', which assumes that there were two phases in his life as pope – the period of 1846–8, when he was praised as a political reformer and an Italian nationalist, and the long years after 1848–9, when his experiences of revolution seemed to have shattered his liberal faith and to have placed him among the reactionaries.

This view of his career was widely accepted by his contemporaries and was crystallized in Alessandro Manzoni's epigram, '*Pio IX prima ha benedetto l'Italia, poi l'ha mandato a farsi benedire.*' ('Pius IX first blessed Italy, then he told it to bless itself, i.e., to go to the devil.') For years afterwards the theory of the two phases of Pius IX's pontificate was part of the Risorgimental tradition, and he was duly condemned for having betrayed Italy. But this is a mythical picture of a pope who was only a rather woolly liberal, and never a radical or a fervent nationalist; and it has now come to be realized that the historical facts do not support the old tradition.

'Recent Italian critical historiography tends ... to modify this traditional judgment,' Dr Walter Maturi wrote in 1960, 'and to define precisely what Pius IX really meant to do and did in the first two years of his pontificate. And Cesare Spellanzon, in whom this revisionary process culminates, has come to the conclusion that the Italian patriotic tradition's complaint against Pius IX is not justified, because Pius IX meant his reforms to be only of an administrative character, but never proposed either a solution of the Italian question or the liberalization of the pontifical state. The pope's intentions and acts were transformed by patriotic propaganda, which created the myth of Pius IX.'[2]

The new emphasis on the essentially limited scope of Pius IX's reforms helps us to understand his real intentions, which were not clear to his contemporaries. Their blindness was natural: in an Italy where new political ideas were fermenting and revolution was always round the corner, even the hint of liberalism in the occupant of St Peter's chair was seen throughout the country as a tremendous portent. It was not Pius's fault if people read more into his modest and well-meaning gestures than they were meant to convey.

2

It was in June that Pius IX took up his residence at the Quirinal. The first sign of change was seen in Rome two hours before sunset on 17 July, when officials put up notices on walls and trees saying that the new pope, in the exercise of his temporal power, had granted an amnesty to political prisoners. All persons imprisoned for political offences were to be released, on condition that they would promise to be good citizens in future. Exiles or others who had gone abroad for political reasons were to be allowed to return to the Papal States on giving notice at any time in the next twelve months. Existing criminal proceedings for political offences were to be dropped. There was no amnesty for ordinary crime.

There was nothing unusual in the grant of an amnesty on the accession of a new pope. But this amnesty was of particularly wide application, since it released more than a thousand prisoners and allowed hundreds of exiles to come home. The Romans were impressed and delighted. Crowds hurried to the Quirinal palace, where the pope came out on the balcony and blessed them. Two days later, on his return from a service at Monte Citorio, a hundred young men 'of good families' took the horses out of his coach and dragged it with their own hands back to the Quirinal. In a month Pius IX had become one of the most popular popes in the history of Rome.[3]

In Vienna Metternich viewed the Roman excitement with some scepticism. His dispatches and other published documents disprove the often repeated statements that he had tried to bar Pius IX's election to the papacy and that he bitterly resented the July amnesty. In fact, he was quite satisfied with the election, though he felt some qualms when he began to see the trends of Pius's policy.[4] ('We were prepared for everything but a liberal pope,' he said, 'and now that we have one, who can tell what may happen?'[5]) He regarded the amnesty as 'indispensable', though at the same time he perceived its dangers. 'With a few exceptions,' he wrote gloomily to the Austrian representative in Turin, 'the men pardoned will be the incorrigible promoters of the movement whose aim it is to overthrow all order legally existing.'[6] This foreboding was fully justified, for the returning exiles included Mazzinians and other revolutionaries who helped to shape the events of 1848–9.

The amnesty was only the beginning. A new era seemed to be opening for the Papal States. Public enthusiasm grew as Pius IX went on with his modest programme of reform, in which he was helped and advised by Cardinal Gizzi, his secretary of state.

For the most part Pius was only making up for time lost by his predecessors. A commission on railway-building, gas-lighting in the streets of Rome, a telegraph system, an agricultural institute, changes in criminal law, provision for prison inspection, improvements in public education – all these were welcome, but overdue, administrative changes or innovations. Perhaps the most truly liberal gesture was the lifting of strict press censorship. Newspapers' freedom was not complete. They were still watched over by a board of five censors, but four of these were lay and only one an ecclesiastic. This was a big step forward, and scores of small newspapers began to be published, particularly in Rome.

Apart from the effects of the new press law, civil rights were hardly affected by these reforms, but hopes of at least some shadowy form of representative government were raised in April 1847 when the pope set up a council of state and began discussions about the establishment of a consultative assembly. The council of state consisted of one representative of each province, chosen by the pope from a list of names submitted by the cardinal legate or prelate in charge; its function was to advise the government on departmental reforms, the constitution of municipalities and other public affairs. The edict announcing the council's formation 'was hailed', states Farini, 'with great satisfaction ... The journalists extolled it to the skies.'[7]

The public was as delighted as the journalists. A French visitor to Rome wrote a description of the torchlight procession from the Piazza del Popolo to the Quirinal on the evening when the council's formation was announced. 'It opened', he stated, 'by lines of men with lighted torches; then came the circular of Cardinal Gizzi, printed on white linen and carried aloft like a large banner; then a band of military music; then a dense column of men holding torches to the number, it is estimated, of about six thousand. Nothing is more striking than the order which reigned in the impromptu army, and nothing was more touching than to see walking side by side, in the same ranks, men of the highest classes, workmen in blouses, priests in their soutane, many of them with white hair, and all united in the same feeling, expressed in the same cry, *Viva Pio Nono! Viva Gizzi!*'[8]

The cries of '*Viva Gizzi*' were not to be heard much longer. The cardinal, who felt that his master was making concessions too easily, resigned in July. In a letter to a friend he said bitterly that it was quite impossible for a man of sense and upright intentions to work harmoniously with a person like Pius IX.[9]

The immediate cause of Gizzi's resignation was Pius's consent to the formation of a civic guard. This had been mentioned in the Rimini manifesto, which asked 'that a civic guard be instituted, to which shall be entrusted the maintenance of public order and the custody of the laws', and similar demands were made in other Italian states at this stage of the Risorgimento. A civic guard – a sort of armed special constabulary – was useful in the social conditions of the time, when the ordinary police were inefficient and malefactors abounded, but sovereigns who conceded the guard were undoubtedly giving hostages to fortune. Law-abiding citizens genuinely wanted a civic guard to protect them, but the revolutionaries saw it as a potential weapon to be turned against the authorities when occasion offered.

As established in Rome in July 1847 the civic guard was recruited from citizens between the ages of twenty-one and sixty. Priests, soldiers and certain tradesmen were exempted from service, and the new force became in effect a people's army. One of its leaders was Angelo Brunetti, a successful wine-carter and local politician from the Trastevere, who was always known as Ciceruacchio (little Cicero), a nickname given to him either because of his eloquence or because of his rotundity. As a one-time Carbonaro, a member of Young Italy since 1833 and an experienced Mazzinian agent he seemed hardly the right man to share responsibility for an armed force established to preserve existing law and order.

3

This first year of reform in the Papal States was watched with great interest by the rest of Italy. In Piedmont it was warmly approved by the liberals, and particularly by those who favoured the neo-Guelf theory, since they felt that the pope had taken to heart the lessons of Gioberti's *Primato*. Charles Albert began reluctantly to consider the possibility of more reforms in Piedmont, but they were not introduced until the autumn of 1847.

Lombard liberals also welcomed the news from Rome. The Austrian viceroys of Lombardy-Venetia had done their best to suppress political agitation in their territory, and to make Milan a peaceful cultural centre, famous for its opera, ballet and charming ballet-girls. But much was stirring under the surface, and the young Lombards made the papal reforms an excuse for displaying their anti-Austrian feelings. They followed the viceroy to his summer residence on the shores of Lake Como, where they rowed up and down the lake, singing a popular 'Hymn to Pius IX', or carved on trees the words *Viva Pio Nono*. Anti-Austrian fervour also inspired the great demonstrations on the occasions of Confalonieri's funeral and the appointment of an Italian to succeed the Austrian archbishop of Milan.

Tuscan liberals were encouraged by the pope's actions to press for internal reforms and a civic guard; thousands of petitions were presented to the grand duke, who agreed in September 1847 that a guard should be established. There was no hope of such a concession in the kingdom of the Two Sicilies, where progress was barred by the rigours of Bourbon absolutism, but in 1847 liberals found some consolation in the publication of Luigi

Settembrini's *La protesta del popolo delle due Sicilie*. The protest was a scathing indictment of bureaucratic oppression and King Ferdinand II's personal share in it; it was thus an effective reply to Ferdinand's own claim that his kingdom's laws were better than those of any part of Italy.[10]

Settembrini was a teacher and literary critic who had been sentenced to four years' imprisonment for taking part in a conspiracy in 1839. His pamphlet exaggerated the king's wickedness and stupidity, but it was a document of the first importance, since it began the trial of the Bourbon dynasty of Naples before the court of world opinion and set the pattern of polemic anti-Bourbon writing which W. E. Gladstone was to follow a few years later.[11] The pamphlet was published anonymously, but its authorship was soon discovered and Settembrini discreetly withdrew into voluntary exile.

The general stir of excitement in the Italian states was repugnant to Metternich, who remained convinced that Austrian predominance in Italy was essential for the maintenance of an ordered European society. He blamed Rome for the Italian unrest, and he felt that Pius had gone much too far by relaxing press censorship and arming the townspeople as members of the civic guard. He decided that the moment had come to teach Pius a lesson.

Though it was hardly a good time for pressing Austrian claims, since the empire was on the verge of breakdown under the weak rule of Emperor Ferdinand, Metternich was resolved that some action must be taken to strengthen the Austrian hold on Italy. He took it at Ferrara on 16 July 1847.

According to the treaty of Vienna, Austria was allowed to maintain a small garrison in the citadel of Ferrara, in the Papal States. The garrison was now reinforced, and Austrian troops occupied the city of Ferrara itself. Metternich later explained his action by saying that Austrian soldiers had been attacked by a mob on returning to the citadel. This explanation was never accepted by the pope, who strongly protested against Austria's seizure of a papal city.[12]

Metternich had lost more than he had gained. The occupation of Ferrara was regarded as a direct attempt to intimidate the pope into abandoning his reforms. Charles Albert, who was still angry about the salt dispute, ordered the publication in the *Gazzetta Piemontese* of a statement expressing his sympathy with the Papal States. It declared: 'To see the city in the hands of the Austrians and to be able to do nothing to set it free is a torment that every Italian heart can understand.' Fearing further Austrian insults to the papacy, he offered to send a warship to Civita Vecchia to bring Pius IX to safety in Piedmont. The offer, though doubtless well meant, was slightly ludicrous in the existing circumstances and was not accepted.

Pius refused to be intimidated by Metternich. He prepared to go further still with his programme of administrative reforms, and he had also a plan for linking the Italian states in an Italian League.

The scheme that Pius IX had in mind was a long way short of the federation proposed by Gioberti. He was thinking only of a unified customs system and a co-ordinated programme of political reforms, which would be the same in each state. In the month in which the Austrians occupied Ferrara one of the pope's trusted advisers, Monsignor Corboli Bussi, was given the assignment of going round Italy to explain the idea to sovereigns and governments.[13]

The envoy's instructions were to visit Florence, Modena, Turin and Naples, but after some rather difficult negotiations a joint declaration signed in November was between only three states – Piedmont, Tuscany and the Papal States. Modena and Naples were not interested. The terms, too, were less than the pope's original proposals: it was agreed to appoint special commissioners to work out the details of a customs union, but political reforms were not mentioned. In its limited way this agreement was a tiny step towards the unification of Italy on a federal basis, but without the support of Modena and the Two Sicilies the proposed alliance could not be called a genuinely Italian League. Whatever significance it possessed was to be swept away in the tumultuous events of the next two years.

4

The pope's reforms made a good impression on English liberals, whose enthusiasm was a little too much for Mazzini. 'I am furious against your countrymen!' he wrote to his friend Eliza Ashurst, who was visiting Manchester, in September 1846. 'I cannot meet with any one of my English acquaintances by the street, without being complimented, congratulated with – guess – the pope! The pope has *forgiven*! The pope has lowered the duties on cotton and raw silk! Therefore go and feel happy! The bright days of Italian Regeneration have begun – and so forth in newspaper style. As if we could clothe our soul with cotton and the forgiveness of other people's sins!'[14] Mazzini was sceptical, too, and was amused by rumours that he himself had been summoned to Piedmont to advise the king. 'The Piedmontese day-dreams are bordering on delirium,' he wrote to Lamberti. His private opinion of Charles Albert was given epigrammatically in a letter to his mother: 'They can do and say what they like, but no one can change a rabbit into a lion.'[15]

At this time Mazzini was enlisting some of his liberal friends as founder-members of a People's International League, which was intended to continue the work of Young Europe; he was in constant touch with his agents in Italy and all over the world; and from South America he was receiving enthralling news of the fighting exploits of Giuseppe Garibaldi, which he was publishing in his own *Apostolato Popolare* and was also passing on to the general press.

For Garibaldi, the one-time second-class seaman in the royal Piedmontese navy, had begun a new phase of his career in South America as a soldier and sailor of fortune. On his arrival in Brazil at the end of 1835 he had first become captain of a small schooner engaged in the coastal trade; but when the province of Rio Grande do Sol revolted against the Brazilian government he and some other Italian exiles supported the rebels at sea until their ships were destroyed by more powerful enemy forces. After the collapse of the revolt he settled in Uruguay with his Creole wife, Anita, but in 1843 he returned to active service by supporting the Uruguayans against an attack by their powerful neighbour,

Argentina. He became commander of the Italian Legion, formed from the many Italian exiles in Montevideo, and it was here that he created the great Garibaldian symbol by dressing his legionaries in red shirts which were 'frustrated exports' intended for Argentina. The legion's part in three years' defence of Montevideo, and particularly its victory over an enemy force four times as large at Salto Sant'Antonio in February 1846, made splendid news stories for Mazzini's paper. The reports went from London to Italy, and Garibaldi was already a national hero in his own country before he returned to Piedmont in 1848. In him the Risorgimento had found its greatest man of action, of whom it was said that he had 'the heart of a lion and the mind of an ox'; this natural and republican fervour was a tremendous asset to the Italian cause, but added little or nothing to the political and philosophical thinking of the revolutionary movement.

By the summer of 1847 Mazzini knew that he could not afford to ignore Pius IX. The pope, more liberal than any of his predecessors, was an important factor in the Italian situation. After the first year of reforms Mazzini felt obliged to take up an attitude towards him, and he did so in one of the 'open letters' he was so fond of writing. Once again, as with the similar letter to Charles Albert in 1831, he was later to declare that he had not really meant what it said.

The letter was written in September, and its words give the impression that Mazzini shared the contemporary illusion that Pius IX might help Italy to find unity. God, he declared, had given the pope the mission of leading the world to the practice of religious truth; 'but for this, to accomplish the mission which God entrusts to you, two things are necessary: to be a believer and to unify Italy.' (It seems strange to find Mazzini telling the head of the Roman Catholic Church to be a believer, but perhaps, as Salvatorelli suggests, he really meant: 'Leave politics alone and trust in God and the inspiration of your heart.'[16]) The pope, he said, had important duties in Europe: he could make Italy into one great state, based on the people and justice and religion, and end 'the absurd divorce between the spiritual and temporal powers'. He was not, he explained, asking the pope to lead an army: 'You will not be called upon to act, but merely to bless

The Glorious Five Days of Milan, 1848

French troops marching on Rome, 1849

Giuseppe Mazzini

Pope Pius IX

Count Camillo di Cavour

Giuseppe Garibaldi

those who act for you and in your name.' But the task, said Mazzini, was one that must be accomplished. 'The unity of Italy is of God. It will be achieved without you, if not with you.'

Mazzini's later explanation of this letter was that it was meant to say to Italians, 'This is what the pope must do if he is to regenerate and create Italy. Do you think he will do it?' Yet it reads as if he really believed that Pius was capable of doing what was asked of him, and a letter to Lamberti at the same time shows that he had, in fact, 'a sincere impulse of hope'. It should be noted that he was not offering to follow the pope; on the contrary, as Salvemini points out, he was asking Pius IX to become a Mazzinian. He may well have believed that the pope would take his advice. If so, his letter was much more sincere than he subsequently suggested.[17]

It is uncertain whether the pope ever read the letter. Mazzini wrote to his mother that it had been thrown into Pius's carriage by one of his agents, apparently in November, but there is no mention of such an incident in the Roman press, and it may be that Mazzini simply assumed that his orders had been carried out. The pope's reference to 'Utopians' in his speech at the opening of the council of state does not prove that he had read Mazzini's letter, though he might have been thinking of it when he made his often-quoted remark, 'My God, they want me to be a Napoleon, and I am only a poor country parson.'[18] After waiting in vain for an answer or public acknowledgement Mazzini published the letter at the end of the year.

5

A slightly bizarre episode in the mid-century history of the Risorgimento was the mission which Lord Minto, a staunch British whig, undertook to Italy in the autumn of 1847.

It was apparently the pope himself who inspired the mission by asking for a British envoy to be sent to Rome. Lord Palmerston who was then foreign secretary told Queen Victoria that Pius IX had found that he was thwarted by opposing influences when he was seeking to make reforms, 'and he conveyed to your Majesty's government by several channels, but especially through Lord Shrewsbury and Dr Wiseman, his earnest request that he might

receive countenance and support from Great Britain and that
for this purpose some agent of the British government might be
sent to Rome'.[19]

The pope had good reason for seeking advice, for the Papal
States were unsettled after more than a year of reforms. The first
fever of enthusiasm was subsiding and was giving way to a
dangerous alignment of political parties. The Sanfedisti, as the
extreme reactionaries, were strongly opposed to the pope's
reforms, and there were many rumours of a plot between
Austrians, Jesuits and Sanfedisti with the object of provoking an
Austrian invasion and overturning the whole reform programme.
The occupation of Ferrara could possibly be seen as an unsuccessful attempt to put this kind of plot into action. At the
other extreme the radicals and revolutionaries were finding that
the much-vaunted reforms did not amount to a great deal, and
were showing signs of unrest. Thus the moderate liberals who
still supported the pope were caught between two fires, and as
months went by the unruliness of the extremist parties made it
difficult to preserve public order. The situation was bad in Rome
but even worse in Romagna, where political rivalries were
producing their usual crop of assassinations. Pius IX needed
wise counsel urgently if he were to continue safely along his
chosen path of administrative reform.

The British government agreed to grant the pope's request.
Lord Minto, the lord privy seal, was on the point of going to Italy
for a short time with his family. He was asked to make his holiday
a political mission, not only to Rome, but to other Italian
capitals.*

Lord Minto went to Turin, Florence, Rome and Naples, with
the general intention of guiding the sovereigns along the path of
liberal reform and promising them the good-will and support of
England if they took his advice. It seems to have been a well

---

* The prince consort thought that Lord Minto undertook the mission
for financial reasons. Some years later, in a marginal note on his copy of a
magazine article on Palmerston, Prince Albert wrote: 'The mission of
Lord Minto arose, in fact, out of his desire to see his daughter, Lady Mary
Abercromby, sister to Lady John Russell, and who was going to be confined
at Turin, without having to pay for the journey.' (Brian Connell, *Regina v.
Palmerston*, p. 141.)

meant and largely ineffective mission, though Palmerston claimed in the following July that 'the successful exertions of the earl of Minto at Turin and Florence were among the principal causes which have saved these capitals from serious convulsion during the past few months.'[20]

During his stay in Turin Lord Minto discussed the threats of an Austrian invasion if Piedmont introduced liberal reforms. He said that Britain regarded these threats as 'inexcusable', but his words made little impression on Solaro della Margarita, who rightly surmised that England would do nothing if a time came for action.[21]

The British envoy gave the same kind of non-committal encouragement in Rome, where he declared that 'her Majesty's government would not see with indifference any aggression committed upon the Roman territories with a view to preventing the papal government from carrying into effect those internal improvements which it may think proper to adopt.'[22] He saw Roman progressive leaders as well as members of the government, and it has been said that he 'encouraged some of the most dangerous revolutionaries in Rome, being evidently under the impression that they were good liberals of the English variety.'[23] He went to Naples at Ferdinand II's request, but had no success in his efforts to improve the king's relations with the people of Sicily. He was able, at all events, to return to England with the comforting knowledge that he had expounded whig views in most parts of the Italian peninsula.

6

Piedmont was in a state of considerable excitement at the time of Lord Minto's visit. Charles Albert, who had recently been given the nickname of *Il re tentenna* (the wobbling king), had surprised his subjects by a sudden display of determination.

It was an agricultural congress which gave Charles Albert a platform for an important statement on his warlike intentions towards Austria. It was attended by some three hundred members of the Sub-Alpine Agrarian Association, including delegates from Milan, Parma and Piacenza, and was opened at Casale on 30 August in the presence of Count Castagnetto, one of the king's close friends and confidants.

On 3 September Castagnetto asked for the congress's permission to read a letter from his royal master. Permission was granted, and the congress heard a statement which left no doubt of the king's warlike hopes. Though it seemed to have little relevance to agricultural matters, Charles Albert told the delegates that if ever God should allow them to undertake a war of independence, it would be he alone who would command the army. 'Let us hope on,' the letter ended. 'Ah, the great day when we shall be able to raise the cry of national independence!'[24]

This was a stirring call, which aroused hopes in Piedmont that Charles Albert was preparing to make war on Austria to avenge the occupation of Ferrara. This was not so. It was officially explained that the statement meant only that Piedmont intended to preserve its independence against any foreign aggression.

Charles Albert's letter had spoken of religion, war and independence, and had made no mention of the grant of more liberal laws. But Piedmont was still exhilarated by the news of the Roman and Tuscan reforms. The girls of Turin wore ribbons in the papal colours of white and yellow on their hats and dresses; the men wore papal cravats; and young people sang the 'Hymn to Pius IX' on the ramparts every evening. On the king's birthday crowds surged through the streets, crying *'Viva il re! Viva Pio Nono! Viva l'Italia!'* and became so unruly that police and military were called in to disperse them. It was becoming clear that Piedmont would not be satisfied without some kind of action on papal lines.

But in 1847 the king was still temporizing. At the end of October he produced a series of modest reforms, which included a relaxation of press censorship and the transfer of provincial administration to new provincial councils. There was nothing wildly democratic about these reforms, but they were enough to alarm Austria and to arouse the eighty-year-old Marshal Radetzky, commander of the Austrian forces in Italy, who had fought in seventeen campaigns, had been wounded seven times and had had nine horses shot under him. In a letter to his daughter Radetzky, showed that he regarded the reforms as a warning. 'The king of Piedmont has thrown off the mask and put himself at the head of the revolution,' he wrote. 'For this reason I believe that I must get ready for war and be prepared to fight before the gates of Milan at the beginning of spring.'[25]

In fact, the reforms were less significant than they seemed to Radetzky. They were only a half-measure, which did not fully meet the liberals' demands and left untouched the principle of absolute rule. That was as far as Charles Albert wanted to go. He did not mean his reforms to be a stepping-stone to constitutional government.

They had one immediate and important effect. Thanks to the changed censorship rules three new newspapers were started in Piedmont at the end of the year. One had the bold and prophetic title of *Il Risorgimento*, and was edited by Count Cavour (who became its principal writer) and Cesare Balbo. It called for independence, reform and a league of Italian princes, and it attacked both Metternich's Italy and the France of Louis-Philippe. It was not only a Piedmontese newspaper. Its policy was definitely Italian, as it showed when it called on the king of Naples to grant a constitution to his people. (But Ferdinand II, who in September had suppressed a double rising in Sicily and Calabria which was intended to force him to grant constitutional rule, paid no attention to *Il Risorgimento*'s advice.)

In this same year a statesman who was to play an important part in the resurgence of Italy made his first appearance in public life. Baron Bettino Ricasoli was a thirty-eight-year-old landowner whose family dominated the Chianti country between Siena and the Arno and was the most ancient noble house in Tuscany. The unsettled condition of his native state, where the liberals were not satisfied with Leopold II's concessions and the extreme radicalism of Guerrazzi and his followers was a constant menace to public order, impelled him to leave his family estate at Brolio and go to Florence, where he lectured the grand duke's chief minister on the government's shortcomings, especially its lack of leadership and the inefficiency of the administrative machine. Ricasoli's biographer comments that this unexpected intervention by the Tuscan count was subsequently 'considered by contemporaries looking back on two years of revolution as an event of great historical importance'.[26]

7

Charles Albert's militant attitude and his promise to lead the army in a war of independence had considerable effect on Lombardy-Venetia, where there was no abatement of anti-Austrian feeling and the desire for freedom. In Venice the Austrian censorship was denounced by Niccolo Tommaseo, a prominent man of letters, in a lecture at the Athenaeum, and six hundred notable people signed a petition supporting him. Whenever *Macbeth* was sung at the Fenice theatre Venetian opera-goers were loud in their applause of the song, *La patria tradita*.[27]

In Lombardy the Milanese began to hope that they would soon throw off the Austrian yoke and reassert their Italian nationality, though some, like Cattaneo, saw little advantage in freeing themselves from Austria to come under Piedmont's domination. An ingenious way of annoying the Austrians was put into practice on 1 January 1848, when all the citizens of Milan gave up smoking and stopped taking part in state lotteries. Since Austria drew substantial revenue from Lombardy by taxes on cigars (4,000,000 lire a year) and gambling (1,500,000 lire), the Milanese boycott was a serious blow to its finances.

On Radetzky's orders the military authorities took a curious form of reprisal. They realized that the Milanese must be suffering much personal hardship through suddenly giving up smoking, and they promptly distributed large quantities of cigars to the troops, both officers and men, who walked up and down the streets insolently puffing smoke into the citizens' faces. Feelings ran high. The Milanese infuriated the Austrians by calling them *porchi tedeschi* (German pigs). On 3 January the inevitable rioting occurred. Stones were thrown at the troops, who retaliated with swords and bayonets. Before the 'tobacco riots' were over five Milanese civilians had been killed and fifty-nine wounded.

Almost certainly the troops had exceeded their instructions. Their orders were to clear the streets, not to cut down civilians. But the harm had been done. The Lombards were confirmed in their determination to drive out the hated Austrians as soon as they could. The first lives had been lost in a year of war and revolt throughout the Italian peninsula.

THE QUARANTOTTO

Revolt in Sicily   Constitutions   The Glorious Five Days
The first war of independence   The pope's allocution
Naples, Messina, Leghorn, Rome

'IF I am not greatly mistaken,' Metternich wrote to the king of
Prussia on 1 January 1848, 'the year of 1848 will bring to light
quite a number of things which last year were hidden under a
cloud.'¹ It was an accurate prophecy. The Milan tobacco riots
were only the first of the many dramatic, inspiring and tragic
happenings of the year of European liberal revolution which
Italy remembers as 'the forty-eight' – the Quarantotto – the
year in which Piedmont challenged Austria in the first war of
independence and all the Italian states had to face revolts or
insistent pressure for freer forms of government.

Spellanzon describes the Quarantotto as 'the decisive year of
the history of our Risorgimento', the year in which the Italian
nation found 'consciousness of itself'.² Yet the first big rising
of the year could almost be described as an anti-Italian rising.

Amid all the talk of unity and federation Sicily was again in
quest of self-government and freedom from Neapolitan rule.
Under cover of the celebrations of the king's birthday Palermo
rose in revolt on 12 January. The radicals, who promoted the
rising, were seeking either Sicilian autonomy or entry with a
liberal constitution into an Italian federation, but they were soon
joined by peasants and mountain folk, who were rising for social
betterment, regular work and land. Mack Smith observes that
'many of the insurgents, even those waving tricolour flags, can
only have had the haziest notion, if any, of what Italy was, or a
constitution.'³ The rising was also supported by bands of brigands, led by prominent men in Sicily's underworld, the forerunners of the Mafia.

This was a formidable insurrection. Though bombarded from the forts by Bourbon soldiers and from the sea by guns of Bourbon ships, the rebels held out so courageously for seventeen days that the king's garrison felt obliged to leave the city on 30 January. By this time Messina, Catania and the greater part of the island had joined the rising, calling as usual for the constitution of 1812.

Since there were menacing signs of revolt in Naples also, Ferdinand thought it wisest to give way, though the constitution of 1812 was too much for him to swallow. Instead he offered both parts of his kingdom a liberal constitution on the lines of the French charter, which had been introduced when Louis-Philippe became king of the French, and added a scheme of self-government for Sicily.

The Neapolitan liberals accepted the new constitution, which provided for limited franchise, two-chamber government and the retention of ample power by the crown, and it was proclaimed in Naples on 10 February; but the Sicilians rejected it and asked for a different constitution which would have minimized the royal power and left Ferdinand with only a nominal sovereignty. When Ferdinand would not agree the old Sicilian parliament was revived and conservatives joined radicals in establishing a provisional coalition government.

So for a few months Sicily kept its independence, and because of its own preoccupations it was able to send only a hundred men to help the Italian cause when war broke out in the north. This was an unfortunate but characteristic result of Sicily's permanent 'municipalism'. Rosario Romeo pertinently remarks that 'the absence of Sicily from the field of decisive battles – and not only in the military sense – of the Risorgimento is significant as an expression of the incapacity of the Sicilian bourgeoisie to develop a national function and to say its word on the country's fundamental problems.'[4] Liberals in other parts of Italy felt that Sicily was more of a hindrance than a help in the attempt to form an Italian union.[5]

2

Soon after the successful Sicilian rising liberals demanded constitutions in other parts of Italy. In one way or another the sovereigns were obliged to follow Ferdinand II's example. The grand duke of Tuscany also took the French Charter as his model for a Tuscan constitution, which was granted on 11 February, and the same charter was the basis of Piedmont's statute, which Charles Albert reluctantly conceded in March. He was not converted to liberalism, but the recent revolution in Paris, which led to Louis-Philippe's abdication and the proclamation of the second republic, had warned him of the dangers involved in continuing to resist liberal pressure.

The statute which gave Piedmont a constitution in 1848 was retained as Italy's basic law until 1946. It provided that the Catholic religion should be the religion of the state; that there should be two chambers, of which the senate should be nominated and the chamber of deputies elected, and that these chambers would share legislative power with the king; that executive power would be entrusted to responsible ministers, but the promulgation of laws would be reserved to the crown; that individual liberty should be guaranteed and that there should be a free press and a permanent magistrature.

In a sense this was the end of absolute monarchy in Piedmont, though behind the façade of representative government the king still retained much of the real power. In changing the basis of the monarchy Charles Albert had broken the oath he had taken in 1823 under pressure from Metternich and Charles Felix. As a man of strong religious feelings he did not promulgate the statute until he had been given release from his oath by the archbishop of Vercelli.[6]

Simultaneously with the granting of the statute, war fever and hatred of Austria were increasing in Piedmont. One consequence of these emotions was that public anger was vented on the Jesuits, who were suspected of being in collusion with Austria. Even the king, who had been greatly under their influence, could not protect them now. Early in March they were expelled from Piedmont.

Pressure for war with Austria and internal reforms was becoming stronger in the Papal States, where the pope had caused some misunderstanding in February by concluding a proclamation with the words: 'Bless, then, Italy, O great God, and preserve for her ever this gift, the choicest of all, her Faith.'[7] The earlier part of the proclamation showed that the pope was only emphasizing his desire for peace and his unwillingness to join any warlike alliance; but the magic words 'Bless Italy' were taken out of their context, and liberals, both in Rome and in Piedmont, wrongly believed that the pope was offering his support for a war against Austria. This was far from Pius IX's mind, but in March he yielded to the popular demand for a constitution. It was only a palliative, since there were many Romans who were less interested in reforms granted by the sovereign than in the prospect of a revolution imposed by the people.[8]

The Roman constitution, as set up by a statute issued on 14 March, was less liberal than those of the other Italian states. In theory it established two-chamber government, but the members of the upper house – the high council – were nominated by the pope, and those of the lower house – the council of deputies – were elected by a greatly restricted number of voters. The councils were not allowed to propose laws dealing with ecclesiastical matters, and though they could propose, discuss and vote on laws concerned with general political and administrative affairs, they were always liable to be overruled by the cardinals' consistory court. The ecclesiastics retained a big share in the control of financial affairs, but they were now a minority in the ministry, in which laymen were included for the first time. This was an important innovation, which appeared to be marking the end of the purely theocratic state. In the first ministry Marco Minghetti was minister for public works, Count Giuseppe Pasolini (Pius's old friend of his Imola days) minister of commerce and Luigi Carlo Farini (who was to write the history of the Roman state and to become for a short time the prime minister of united Italy) minister-substitute for the interior. Ecclesiastics still held the key ministries of finance and instruction, and the redoubtable Cardinal Antonelli was president of the council of ministers.

Antonelli, who was Pius IX's chief minister for many years, was a shrewd politician whose special claim to distinction is that he managed to maintain the pope's temporal power long after its faults and incongruity had been clearly revealed. In his personal conduct he was quite unscrupulous. He used his high position to build up an immense private fortune and to find profitable jobs for his brothers. He was known to be a fluent liar, although, as a British diplomat once commented after a meeting with Antonelli, he was 'so charming and amiable and affectionate that one cannot be angry with him even when he tells lies'. His many illegitimate children were the fruit of a thoroughly disreputable sex-life.* In later years he was hated by everyone in Rome – the clergy, the aristocracy, the people.[9]

In contrast with the tobacco riots in Milan and the revolt in Sicily, the peaceful introduction of constitutional government in Tuscany, Piedmont and the Papal States might have seemed to suggest that Italy was entering a period of calm development along moderate lines. In fact the anti-Austrian sentiments of northern Italy were on the point of explosion.

3

The signal for action was the news from Vienna that the people had risen against the government in the capital and in other parts of the Austrian empire. Metternich had fled the country, and was never to return.

The great chancellor's day was over. Throughout a long and distinguished career he had tried with much success to hold at bay the forces of liberalism and revolution. Now his regime was dying. The national finances were in deficit, the administration

---

* Edmond About, the French author, discusses Antonelli with great candour in his book, *La Question Romaine* (Brussels, 1859), published while the cardinal was still at the helm of Roman affairs. About sees the great cardinal as little more than a lecherous peasant: 'When he stops in a salon near a pretty woman, when he stands close to speak to her, stroking her shoulders and looking deeply into her corsage, you recognize the man of the woods and you tremble as you think of post-chaises overturned at the side of a road.' (p. 145.) The comments of a British woman who spent many years in Rome are also pertinent. 'Even in his lifetime, surrounded by the halo of a sainted master, whispers about him were rife,' states Frances Elliot in *Roman Gossip* (London, 1894). 'Woe to the fair dame who, beguiled by his smooth tongue and fascinating manners, permitted herself to be *affichée*; innocent or guilty, her social fate was sealed.' But perhaps the society beauties were not in such great danger, after all, for Mrs Elliot delicately adds that 'it was not in these aristocratic circles that Antonelli found the ladies whom he most affected.' (*op. cit.*, p. 91.)

had lost its grip and the subject-nations were in ferment. The collapse of his system was partly due to the excitement aroused by the new French revolution, and partly to his own failure to march with the times. As one of his biographers observes, he 'had remained at the first stage of the maxim which summarizes the programme of every conservative statesman – to preserve what is old, but he ignored the second stage – to reconstruct.'[10]

Milan heard the news from Vienna on 17 March, and the Milanese at once realized that this was the moment for extorting concessions from the Austrians. The time seemed opportune both to Carlo Cattaneo, the republican federalist, and to Casati, the mildly liberal head of Milan's municipal council. Both the viceroy of Lombardy-Venetia and the governor of Milan had left the city when Radetzky, the army commander, had warned them that trouble was brewing, and it was O'Donnell, the vice-governor, who received the citizens' demands from Casati on 18 March.

Cattaneo favoured peaceful persuasion, but was against the idea of insurrection, which had been discussed ever since the tobacco riots. He told his friends that no rising could succeed without the support of thousands of well-armed men; and when he was assured that 40,000 rifles had been sent from Piedmont, he pointedly asked if anyone had seen them.[11] But Milan was in no mood for caution. When Casati's demands were refused the mob which had followed him to the viceregal palace took matters into its own hands. The palace guards were disarmed, the vice-governor was arrested, barricades were put up in the streets, the first shots were exchanged. Radetzky, after raiding the town hall and finding that Casati and the other municipal leaders had made their headquarters elsewhere, withdrew with part of the garrison to a fortified castle just outside the city, though leaving enough troops behind to hold the city gates and other key points.

The Milanese insurrection, to be known with pride as the Glorious Five Days, had begun. The whole populace, rich and poor, moderate liberals and republican democrats, joined in the task of evicting the Austrians. Though poorly armed and lacking the mythical 40,000 Piedmontese rifles they were able to hold the garrison at bay by determination and force of numbers.

Milan was ideally planned for the kind of street-fighting practised by its citizens. The streets were crooked and narrow, and were very suitable for the erection of barricades. For five days the excited populace held the city against all Austrian attempts to recapture it. Even girls took part in the fighting; a woman called Luisa Battistotti was said to have put on a fusilier's uniform and to have kept her rifle in her hands for the whole of the five days.[12] In the meantime a council of war was set up, and messages calling for help were tied to small balloons and sent out to the surrounding countryside.

It was a grim struggle. Most of the Austrian soldiers were Croats, who fought without regard for any rules of war. They were said to have burnt whole families alive, and a woman's hand covered with rings was found in the pocket of a dead Croat soldier.[13] At the beginning the Milanese were hampered by lack of ammunition, and two of Cattaneo's friends, who were fighting side by side, were careful never to fire at the same time for fear of wasting two bullets on the same Croat; but the shortage of bullets was later remedied by the capture of a number of Austrian arms stores.[14]

The Austrians were beaten. On the fifth day the Milanese captured the city gates, and Radetzky felt that his only course was to withdraw his troops from Milan and seek safety in what was known as the Quadrilateral – the four fortresses of Peschiera, Verona, Legnago and Mantua. These were the key to upper Italy and gave their possessors mastery of the river Po.

'It is the most frightful decision,' he reported to the Austrian government, 'but I can no longer hold Milan. The whole country is in revolt; I am pressed in the rear by the Piedmontese ... I shall withdraw towards Lodi to avoid the large towns and while the countryside is still open.'[15] (The Piedmontese were not, in fact, at Radetzky's rear in any military sense, but he had no reason to know that their army was coming to Milan's aid so slowly.)

Radetzky announced his withdrawal on 22 March. The Glorious Five Days were over. Milan and the surrounding countryside were free. So too was the much less warlike Venice, where the Austrian garrison made little attempt to resist the seizure of power by a menacing mob.

In Venice, as in Milan, the news of the revolution in Vienna was the signal for revolt. Crowds hurried to the governor's house and demanded the release of Daniele Manin and Niccolo Tommaseo, two leading republicans who had been arrested in January and kept in prison in spite of being acquitted of conspiracy. The governor gave way to the mob's demands, and the freeing of Venice then proceeded without violence or bloodshed.

Manin's first action on his release was to form a civic guard. A few days later the small Austrian garrison discreetly left the city, which quickly turned itself into a republic with Manin as president and virtual dictator. The other districts of Venetia also rose and evicted their Austrian masters. Thus the whole of Lombardy-Venetia was free of the Austrians, with the important exceptions of the forces inside the Quadrilateral and Radetzky's army marching across the Lombard plain to join them.

4

Ever since Milan had risen Italy had been waiting for action by Piedmont. Surely this was Charles Albert's hour; what the Milanese had begun the 'sword of Italy' must complete by driving the Austrians out of every corner of Lombardy-Venetia.

In Milan itself there was uncertainty about the terms on which Charles Albert's help should be accepted. The moderates were quite prepared for the annexation of Lombardy-Venetia by Piedmont; the democrats, and particularly Cattaneo, had no wish to come under Piedmont's domination. They felt, too, that a war of independence against Austria should be a national war, and they were afraid that the fusion of Lombardy-Venetia with Piedmont would be coldly received by other Italian states and would stop them from sending assistance.

Uncertainty in Milan was matched by hesitation in Turin. But one man's mind was clear. On the morning of 22 March the front page of *Il Risorgimento* carried a forthright article by Cavour.

'The supreme hour has sounded for the Sardinian monarchy', he wrote, 'the hour on which the fates of empires and peoples depend. In face of the events in Lombardy and Vienna, hesitation, doubt, dilatoriness are no longer possible, they would be the most disastrous kind of politics ... One way alone is open for the nation, for the government, for the king. War! Immediate war without delays ... We are in a position in which audacity is the true prudence, in which recklessness is wiser than restraint.'[16]

Cavour was right. If Italy were ever to expel the Austrians without the help of a foreign power, it could be only at a time when Vienna was shaken by revolution, Austrian government was in a state of chaos and Austrian armies could not hope for reinforcements from home. But Charles Albert was a prey to the very hesitation, doubt and dilatoriness that Cavour had condemned.

He had several reasons for holding back. For one thing, he was suspicious about the influence of the republican democrats in Milan. 'So I am to go to Milan to proclaim the republic?' he ironically asked a Milanese envoy who came to see him on 19 March. 'The republic will certainly be proclaimed if your Majesty does not go', was the tart reply. His ministers, too, were dubious about going to war: they were afraid that Piedmont might find itself in isolation, and they felt that the period of transition from absolute rule to government by statute was not an appropriate time for beginning military operations.

But pressure from Milan continued. A provisional government, containing both moderates and republicans, had been set up as soon as the Austrians withdrew. Envoys from this government came to Charles Albert on 23 March and asked directly for Piedmont's intervention in Lombardy.

This time the king agreed. In consultation with his council of ministers he drew up a proclamation to be published in the *Gazzetta Piemontese* on the following day. It announced that the Piedmontese were going to the aid of their brothers in Lombardy and Venetia, but made no mention of war with Austria. Foreign diplomats in Turin were told that the real motive of Piedmont's action was to prevent the establishment of a republic in Milan, but this was only partly true. Help to Lombardy meant war with Austria. Charles Albert had at last put himself at the head of the movement for national independence.

But precious days had been lost. The proclamation ought to have been made four days earlier, and the Piedmontese army should have been ready to march at once. It was not ready. On 25 March the nearest available battery, which was stationed at Novara, could not be moved because the horses needed rest, and a Piedmontese column which entered Lombardy on 26 March had no orders about its future movements. And every day was bringing Radetzky nearer to the safety of the Quadrilateral. The chance of overtaking his retreat was lost, and it was not until 8 April – a fortnight after the final liberation of Milan – that the first shots were exchanged between Piedmontese and Austrian troops.

The unpreparedness of the Piedmontese army at this critical moment goes far to disprove the theory that Charles Albert had been secretly planning war against Austria for many years. If this had really been so, he would surely have had his army ready in March 1848, since Lombardy had been in a state of unrest for weeks before the Glorious Five Days. It is true that the king's statements to Azeglio on his return from Romagna and to the Casale congress show that he romantically pictured himself as the leader in a war of Italian independence, but he had done little or nothing to make this dream come true. When war broke out the Piedmontese general staff did not possess a single military map of Lombardy.[17]

Charles Albert's proclamation was greeted with much public rejoicing in the Papal States and the duchies. In Rome crowds cheered the Piedmontese minister, cardinals and princes offered horses for the Piedmontese army, women gave ornaments and jewellery to be sold for the war, and a girl in Bologna, who had no such finery, presented (as Farini engagingly tells us) 'the treasure of her beautiful head of hair'.[18] General Durando, a Piedmontese officer who had been appointed by the pope to reorganize his armed forces, set off for the Lombard frontier with the advance guard of the papal army, which was soon reinforced by thousands of volunteers. His orders were only to defend the legations against a possible invasion, but he privately hoped to be able to cross the Po and join his countrymen at war. In spite of the papal government's disapproval he entered Lombardy on 21 April.

The proclamation had an immediate effect in the duchies, from which Austrian garrisons were withdrawn to join the main armies. The duke of Parma was forced to grant a constitution and subsequently left the country. The duke of Modena also fled with the retreating Austrians, but Tuscany entered the war on Piedmont's side and Leopold II, the grand duke, declared that 'The hour of Italy's resurrection has struck.'[19]

Tuscany sent both regular troops and volunteers to assist in the war of independence. These Tuscan forces remained in the field throughout the campaign, but a body of 16,000 Neapolitan regular soldiers, which was sent to the war in March under the command of General Guglielmo Pepe, was recalled by Ferdinand II in April.

These contingents were more important symbolically than materially. The presence of Roman, Tuscan and Neapolitan soldiers in northern Italy was significant because it showed that the war was a national one, but in the early stages they were not needed because the Piedmontese army was numerically superior to the Austrian. Many of the Italian conscripts serving in the Austrian army had deserted, and the sixty-one Austrian infantry battalions in Lombardy-Venetia had been reduced to about forty-one, each with an average strength of a thousand men. Since the Piedmontese were able to mobilize 70,000 men they began the war with a great advantage, but their dilatoriness, strategical incompetence and failure to follow up local successes gave Radetzky time to receive reinforcements, which were at last available as the ferment in the Austrian empire subsided.[20]

Charles Albert kept to his promise that he would lead his armies into war, but he had little capacity for high military command, and none of his generals, apart from Bava and the duke of Genoa (the king's second son), had much experience or technical skill. With such leadership the war was lost at the start. A swift advance would have allowed the Piedmontese to cut off at least a part of Radetzky's army before it had reached the Quadrilateral; instead, they followed him slowly across the Lombard plain and joined battle only in the Quadrilateral itself.

The Piedmontese reached the Mincio without opposition, and after crossing it, moved north, with the intention of capturing Peschiera. They fought their first battle of the campaign at

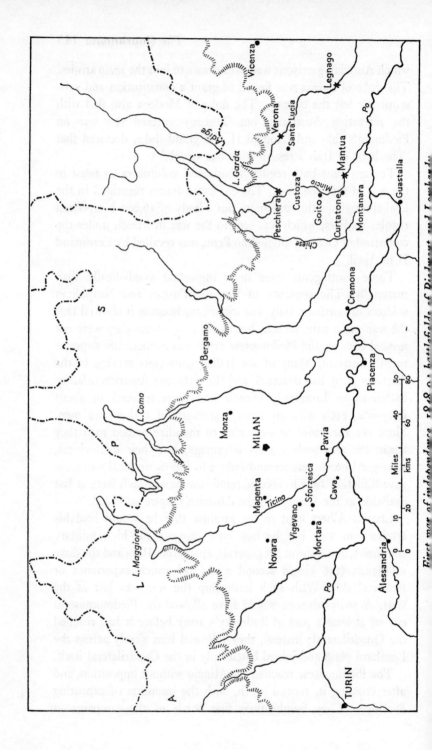

First map of independence 1848-9: battlefields of Piedmont and Lombardy

Pastrengo, between Peschiera and Verona, on 28 April, winning an inconclusive victory and not seriously shaking the Austrian positions. This modest success seemed to open the way to Verona, in the north-east of the Quadrilateral, but the Austrians checked their advance at Santa Lucia, where the Piedmontese suffered their heaviest defeat of the war. Their losses were 110 dead and 776 wounded, while the Austrian casualties were considerably lighter – 72 dead, 190 wounded and 87 taken prisoner.[21]

The battle of Santa Lucia was on 6 May. All hope of profiting from the Austrian army's temporary depletion had vanished, and strong reinforcements under General Nugent were coming to Radetzky's assistance. Charles Albert had missed his chance. Though the Piedmontese continued to make resolute attempts to take Peschiera the initiative of the war had passed to the Austrians.

At the end of May Radetzky moved in force from Verona towards Peschiera, and defeated the Piedmontese and their Tuscan allies at Montanara and Curtatone; but on the next day the Austrians were themselves defeated at Goito and Peschiera surrendered. For the moment it seemed as though Piedmont were on the way to victory. Charles Albert's soldiers acclaimed him as king of Italy.

But the wily old Radetzky was not disposed of so easily. His army was still in good shape after his defeat at Goito, and he decided to turn on General Durando, who had seized Vicenza with his papal regulars and volunteers. On 9 June Vicenza was attacked by a strong Austrian force, and after a desperate conflict, in which almost two thousand men were killed or wounded, Durando was obliged to surrender. By agreement with the victors he withdrew with the papal army south of the Po and gave his word that it would take no further part in the war for three months.

A lull in activities followed the fall of Vicenza – a lull which was all to Austria's advantage, since the situation in the Austrian empire was still improving and the generals were assured of a steady flow of reinforcements and supplies. It was at this time that Charles Albert had an unexpected visitor. Garibaldi had come back from South America with some of his comrades of the

Italian Legion and was hoping to be given a command in the Piedmontese army. The king greeted the ex-rebel coldly and passed him to the war minister at Turin with a private note saying it would be 'dishonouring to the army' to make such a man a general.[22] After an equally unprofitable interview at the ministry of war Garibaldi went to Milan and was given a command by the Milanese provisional government. He then built up a small force from local volunteers and the men who had come with him from Montevideo.

After their welcome rest the Austrians were now ready to deal with Charles Albert. The Piedmontese had taken up a position at Custoza, in the middle of the Quadrilateral, and it was here that they suffered their final and decisive defeat in the first phase of the war of independence. After a fierce three days' battle, which began on 23 July, they were driven back and forced to retire to Goito.

The campaign was nearly over. Charles Albert realized that he would never subdue the Quadrilateral, and he decided to fall back to Milan, at first with the intention of facing the enemy there; but Radetzky was hard on his heels, and the king rashly allowed himself to be pushed back into the city, which was indefensible, instead of establishing a strong defence line in front of it. His position was now hopeless. On 4 August the king and his generals unanimously agreed to ask for an armistice.

Radetzky was happy to agree to a cease-fire, on condition that the Piedmontese withdrew across the Ticino to their own territory; an armistice, always to be known as the Salasco armistice, was signed by General Salasco on behalf of the Piedmontese army. With no regular troops to support them, the Milanese knew that this time they were no match for the Austrians. The war, which had begun so gloriously and hopefully with Milan's five days' fight for freedom, ended with the return of Lombardy to Austrian rule, though further east the gallant defenders of Venice still held out against their former masters.

The first phase of the war appeared to have ended in disaster, but the efforts spent on it had not been entirely wasted. In spite of their poor leadership the Piedmontese troops had shown that they could fight well and bravely, and the co-operation of Roman and Tuscan contingents had at least given the war the semblance of a national struggle for independence. Moreover, the armies had fought under the national tricolour flag, which Charles Albert had agreed to carry into action. Certainly Piedmont seemed to have gained nothing as the Austrians swept back into Lombardy. But a retreat on honourable terms is very different from a crushing defeat. Charles Albert had not yet finished with Austria.

Piedmont's defeat in 1848 has sometimes been ascribed to Charles Albert's absorption in Lombard politics at a time when his whole attention should have been given to military strategy. The question of whether or not Lombardy should be fused with Piedmont was thrashed out while the war was being fought, and Cattaneo coined the biting epigram, 'While Charles Albert was collecting votes, Radetzky was collecting men.' But shortage of manpower was not the reason why Charles Albert failed. What was lacking was military expertise in the high command. Radetzky was a far better strategist than Charles Albert or any of his generals.

The Lombard political controversy of 1848 had no lasting effect on the Risorgimento, but it is interesting because it exemplifies the clash between republican federalism and monarchical union-by-fusion. The younger and poorer sections of the population wanted a Lombard republic; the aristocrats and the wealthier members of the middle class wanted union with Piedmont. On 12 May the Milanese provisional government asked the people to vote in favour of union.

This was not to the liking of Mazzini, who had come from London to Milan when it seemed as though Italy were within reach of independence. Though at first he kept his republicanism in the background, he was stirred to action when the government itself supported union with Piedmont. He started a paper, *Italia del Popolo*, which opposed the government's advice, but by this time the idea of fusion with Piedmont was widely favoured and Mazzini found himself hated by his fellow-countrymen. 'I am here disliked, dreaded, suspected, calumniated, threatened more than ever; and my writings are burnt in my native town, Genoa, almost under the eyes of my mother,' he wrote to Emilie Hawkes.

'I cannot deny my feeling entirely an exile in my own country.'[23]

The fusionists had their way, Lombardy was annexed to Piedmont; early in August royal commissioners arrived from Turin to take control in Milan. It was too late. Charles Albert was already falling back on the city, which he was soon to abandon. Annexation was a dead letter. As the Austrians came back to Milan, Mazzini joined Garibaldi, who kept his volunteer force in being and for a short time carried on a single-handed war against the Austrians. But Mazzini gave up hope and returned to London even before Garibaldi disbanded his volunteers and went to Nice, suffering from fever.

This small campaign of Garibaldi's showed that the experience he had gained in South America would serve him well in Italy. He seized a number of paddle-steamers on Lake Maggiore and used them for raids on Austrian territory, and for the few days before his force began to dwindle away he fought with considerable success. His men moved quickly, and were able to surprise the Austrians by cutting lines of communication in places where their appearance was not expected. But even Garibaldi's enthusiasm could not keep his volunteers together when they knew that Piedmont had withdrawn from the war. Only thirty of his original thousand men were with him when he gave up the struggle.

Venice had been holding out with great resolution while Charles Albert was at grips with the Austrians in the Quadrilateral, though it was sadly handicapped at the outset by the lack of any trained military force. It might have been possible to keep some of the Italian soldiers serving in the former Austrian garrison, but there were no Italian officers to command them, and Manin had decided to let them go back to their homes. A volunteer force was raised, and Piedmont sent the veteran General Alberto La Marmora to take command of it; but a small encounter with the Austrians at Montebello showed that the volunteers were of little use against trained soldiers. Any offensive action was impossible. All they could do was to defend their city, and they did so with great courage for more than a year.

Manin's proclamation of a Venetian republic was ratified by a constituent assembly in June, but a month later the newly-established chamber of deputies voted for union with Piedmont. The Salasco armistice put an end to all ideas of Piedmontese aggrandizement; Austrian Lombardy again interposed between Piedmont and Venetia. The Venetian republic was re-established, and Manin resumed his dictatorship, first as one member of a triumvirate and later on his own.

5

An important political event of the Quarantotto was Pope Pius IX's allocution of 29 April. His frank statement of his attitude towards the war of independence finally disposed of the neo-Guelf dream of an Italian federation under the pope's presidency.

Surprising as it may seem to a generation which knows how the Vatican reacted to two world wars, there was widespread expectation in Italy that the pope would join in the national war against Austria. Pellegrino Rossi, one of Rome's leading politicians, declared: 'The national sentiment, and its ardour for war, are a sword, a weapon, a mighty force; either Pius IX must take it resolutely in hand, or the factions hostile to him will seize it, and turn it against him, and against the popedom.'[24] Gabrio Casati, president of the provisional government of Milan, wrote to his friend Giuseppe Pasolini: 'What can the pope be afraid of? Is it not the cause of humanity, religion and the Gospel which we are defending?'[25] Even the pope's own ministers addressed a remonstrance to him on 25 April, urging him to allow his subjects to make war on Austria.

Pius IX had his own view on the matter. In an allocution to a meeting of the cardinals' consistory court on 29 April, he clearly explained why, as pope, he could not make war on the Austrian Catholics or the people of any other nation, though he also said that he would not try to prevent volunteers from taking part in the present war. These are the crucial sentences in the allocution:

> Seeing that some at present desire that We too, along with the other princes of Italy and their subjects, should engage in war against the Austrians, we have thought it convenient to proclaim clearly and openly, in this our solemn assembly, that such a measure is altogether alien from our counsels, inasmuch as We, albeit unworthy, are upon earth the viceregent of Him

that is the Author of Peace and the Lover of Charity, and, conformably to the function of our supreme Apostolate, we reach to embrace all kindreds, peoples and nations with equal solicitude of paternal affection. But, if, notwithstanding, there are not wanting among our subjects those who allow themselves to be carried away by the example of the rest of the Italians, in what manner could We possibly curb their ardour?[26]

This was really the only statement that Pius IX could have been expected to make. How, indeed, could the head of the Roman Catholic Church have taken part in a war between Catholic countries? As Spellanzon says, the statement could not cause surprise except to those who had formed a mental picture of an unreal Pius IX, a Pius IX who was promoter and animator of the Italian revolution, a Pius IX who was liberal and an enemy of Austria. But none of the pope's words had at any time given colour to such suppositions; his allocution was in keeping with his character, his religious faith and his political attitude. The mythical radical and nationalist Pius IX had never existed.[27]

Yet many people, both high and low, had formed this fanciful picture and were deeply disappointed by his words. His ministers resigned. There were angry demonstrations in the streets of Rome. Indignation against Pius IX was expressed all over Italy. He tried to appease hostile opinion by appointing a new government under Count Mamiani, a liberal whom some regarded as an extremist, but the unrest in Rome continued and was viewed with alarm in other countries. In August the British government offered to take the pope to safety; H.M.S. *Bulldog* was sent to Civita Vecchia, and its commander was ordered to place his ship at the pope's disposal for conveyance to any part of the Mediterranean coast. But at this time Pius IX was still resolved to stay in Rome.

Though the neo-Guelf theory, which envisaged a fighting pope at the head of an Italian federation, had now gone by the board, the project for some kind of a league between the Papal States, Piedmont and Tuscany was revived in the summer of 1848. No satisfactory agreement could be reached.

6

The pope's allocution of 29 April gave Ferdinand II of Naples an excuse for recalling the army he had sent to the northern war. It was not, it appeared, a national war, so why should Naples be concerned with it? But General Pepe disobeyed the king's orders. He led two thousand of the Neapolitan troops across the Po and eventually took them to reinforce the defenders of Venice.

At this time Naples was anxiously awaiting the opening of the first parliament under the new constitution. The king's actions were being watched with suspicion, and a dispute over the words of the oath to be taken by deputies led to an insurrection in the capital. Barricades were thrown up in the streets, and on 15 May, the day when parliament was due to meet, there was a fierce battle in the streets between the demonstrators and the royal troops. The insurrection collapsed after long and bloody fighting, which Ferdinand watched from the balcony of the palace with his second wife. When 'victory' was announced, he kissed her and said cynically, '*My* demonstration is as good as all theirs!'[28]

The suppression of the 15 May rising was the first step on the way back to reaction in the Two Sicilies. Naples kept its constitution, but the ministers paid little attention to parliament. It was not consulted in September, when Ferdinand mounted a full-scale military and naval expedition to suppress the revolt in Sicily.

The operation was successful. The Sicilians had no chance against such a preponderance of armed strength. The ruthless bombardment of Messina earned Ferdinand his grim nickname of 'King Bomba': a dispatch from Admiral Sir William Parker, British commander-in-chief in the Mediterranean, speaks of the Neapolitans' 'savage barbarity' and says that no excuse could be found for their cruelty in continuing to fire on the town 'with unabated fury' for eight hours after all resistance had ceased.[29] But their brutality achieved its object. The Bourbon soldiers were able to land safely and to suppress the revolt in all parts of the island.

Though this was a shattering defeat for the Sicilian radicals, there were mixed feelings among the conservatives; even some who had supported the revolution had come to fear the possible establishment of a people's government more than a return to Ferdinand's rule. Jealousy of Palermo was another reason why many welcomed the restoration of the king's authority. Sicilian nobles and civic administrations presented addresses to the king thanking him for freeing them from 'the Palermitan yoke'.[30]

This summer something like civil war broke out in Tuscany. The trouble centre was Leghorn, a port with a mixed population drawn from all parts of Italy. In August it rose in open revolt against rule by Florence. Troops sent to restore order were attacked by the mob and forced to take refuge in the fortress.

This was Guerrazzi's opportunity to show that he was an administrator as well as an agitator. He offered his services to the government, and by sheer force of character and personality he was able to quell the Leghorn riots in three days. In October he became minister of the interior in a new Tuscan government formed by Montanelli, the part-author of the *Manifesto di Rimini*. The grand duke accepted the former agitator as minister with some misgivings.

But the greatest unrest in this uneasy autumn was in Rome, where the republicans were getting ready to strike. Mamiani won no public confidence as prime minister; he resigned in August, and after six weeks of a stop-gap ministry Pellegrino Rossi agreed to form a government.

Rossi was an able politician and diplomat, who had spent some years in France and had represented King Louis-Philippe at the papal court. He was hesitant to lead the government, for he had a Protestant wife and he knew that the republicans disliked him; but on becoming chief minister he threw himself whole-heartedly into a massive programme of reforms which increased the number of his enemies. His taxes on ecclesiastical property antagonized the clergy; judges, lawyers and all the hangers-on of the legal system were hostile to his efforts to reform the law by sweeping away the many antiquated courts; even more dangerously, the political clubs were opposed to him and he was bitterly attacked in the press. Given time, Rossi might well have achieved some notable reforms in the papal system of government. But he was not given time.

Violent articles in the press on the morning of 15 November inflamed the republican rabble who disliked the uncompromising chief minister. About noon on that day Rossi left his carriage in the courtyard of the parliament house and walked towards a staircase. A crowd pressed round him and abused him; a dagger flashed, and he fell to the ground, fatally wounded. His fellow deputies were so terrified of the mob that not one of them dared to denounce the crime when parliament met.

Rossi's murder was the signal for revolution. A petition calling for a democratic ministry and a constituent assembly was drawn up after a public meeting and presented to the pope. In despair he appointed two democrats as ministers in place of Rossi, but the mob was still unruly, and it was soon clear that the pope himself was in danger. In the evening of 25 November Pius IX left the Quirinal in the disguise of an ordinary priest and was driven to Gaeta, in Neapolitan territory.

The Quarantotto was ending in confusion. The pope was in voluntary exile, but Bourbon rule was re-established in the Two Sicilies; Piedmont remained under constitutional government, and its people still resented an armistice which had taken them by surprise. Yet the events of the year had provided, as Salvatorelli observes, the most genuine revolution of the Risorgimento up to that time – the only one which had been accompanied by popular self-determination. The Quarantotto and the catastrophes of 1849 marked the dramatic end of the insurrectionary period and the beginning of the era of evolution and compromise.[31]

THE GREAT DEFEATS

The roman Republic   *Novara*   *The assault on Rome*
            Venice surrenders

NOTHING was finally settled by the Quarantotto, though in that
year all the issues of the Risorgimento were raised in one way or
another. The year 1849 was more decisive, for it was then that the
unity of Italy was born from three military defeats. Salvatorelli
believes that these defeats can rightly be acclaimed as victories,
'for they were affirmations of the peoples' will to gain their
rightful place in the world'.[1]

But in Rome at the beginning of 1849 there was no reason for
thinking of defeat. After the pointless violence of Rossi's murder
a new era seemed to have opened. The pope had gone. Theocracy
had given way to democracy. A constituent assembly was to
decide the future form of the state. The already legendary
Garibaldi had been elected to the assembly and was dividing his
time between Rome and the northern provinces of the Papal
States, where he was building up a new Italian Legion, consisting
of twenty-two Italians and two South Americans who had
sailed with him from Montevideo, volunteers from the universities and the commercial and artisan classes, a few ex-convicts
and forty-two lancers from Bologna under the separate command
of Angelo Masina.[2] The only shadow came from a French threat
to send an army to Civita Vecchia, ostensibly to protect the
departed pope.

The constituent assembly met on 5 February. Its decisions
were prejudged by the prince of Canino, a notorious and garru-
lous demagogue connected with the Bonaparte family, who cried,
'Long live the republic!' when answering the roll-call, and by
Garibaldi, who asked, 'What use to lose time in vain formalities?
The delay even of a minute is a crime. Long live the republic!'[3]

The trend of the debate confirmed their republican enthusiasm. When it ended after three days the president of the assembly read a decree announcing that the pope's temporal power had ended, that he would be guaranteed all necessary independence in the exercise of his spiritual power, and that the Roman state's form of government should be a pure democracy, with 'the glorious appellation of the republic of Rome'. On the following day the republic was formally proclaimed from the Capitol.

The formation of the republic brought a sharp reaction from Gaeta. On 18 February Pius IX called for armed assistance from the Catholic powers of Austria, France, Spain and Naples. His note to these 'daughters of the Church' observed that they were geographically placed 'so that they can repair promptly to the dominions of the Holy See to re-establish the public order overthrown by a horde of sectaries'.[4]

Meanwhile the new Roman republic awaited its destined leader. This was Mazzini's hour. He had been elected to the assembly. He had been made a citizen of Rome. He had recommended the summoning of the constituent assembly and the establishment of republican government. But he was in Florence, not in Rome, when the decisive events took place. He stayed there till 2 March.

Mazzini had two reasons for delaying his journey to Rome. The first was political. The new Tuscan government had shown itself to be too liberal for Grand Duke Leopold II, who decided to leave Florence and await developments outside the Tuscan boundaries. When Leopold had gone Mazzini tried to persuade the government, which was then a triumvirate of Guerrazzi, Montanelli and Manzoni, to unite with the Roman republic; but the triumvirs were not ready to adopt republican government, and Mazzini's efforts failed. His second reason for being in no hurry to leave Florence was a personal one. Throughout his stay there he was the guest of his former mistress, Giuditta Sidoli, whom he had not seen since they parted in Switzerland in 1833. 'To see her once more', he wrote to Lamberti, 'has given me more joy than I am able to express.'[5]

At last, when he realized that he had no hope of making Tuscany a republic, Mazzini went to Rome, which he entered on a mild March evening 'with a sense of deep awe, almost of worship'. His unique place in the new republic was at once recognized. When he went to the assembly for the first time he was invited to sit next to the president, and he was soon developing his favourite theme of 'the third Rome'. Rome, he said, had been always a kind of talisman for him: 'Following the Rome which wrought by military conquest, following the Rome which wrought by conquest of persuasion, will come, I whispered to myself, will come the Rome that shall work by the energy of example; following the Rome of the Emperors, the Rome of the Popes, will come the Rome of the People. And the Rome of the People has arisen.'[6]

A few days after Mazzini had spoken news came from Turin that Charles Albert had denounced the Salasco armistice and was resuming war with Austria.

2

Charles Albert was fully entitled to denounce the armistice, for its terms provided that either Piedmont or Austria could annul it on eight days' notice, and though Britain and France had tried to mediate between the two countries there seemed little hope of converting the armistice into a peace treaty.

Piedmont had been uneasy throughout the autumn and winter. Ministries came and went; one was headed by Gioberti, who came back from exile and was acclaimed as the democrats' leader. Before forming his government he had attacked the previous ministries for wanting to make peace with Austria, but the warlike policy he had advocated in opposition looked very different to him when he reached the seat of power. He then understood that Piedmont should have allies before resuming the war, and he began to make plans for restoring the pope and bringing both the Papal States and Tuscany into the war on Piedmont's side.

This was an attempt to graft the neo-Guelf idea on to democratic politics. It brought Gioberti the unexpected support of Cavour, but his own ministry would have nothing to do with it, and he had to resign. This was his last appearance in active politics, since he was no longer in tune with the policies of any party; but he was still to serve his country as a political writer. The prime minister who succeeded him, Urbano Rattazzi, had to follow the wishes of king and people and lead Piedmont back to war.

Charles Albert had always meant to go on with the war. At the time of the armistice he had told his generals and the head of the Milanese government that his only reason for staying on the throne was to reorganize the army and resume the struggle for Italian independence. But who should lead the army now? Charles Albert had shown his incapacity for high command, and none of the Piedmontese generals had won any great reputation. Efforts to find a suitable general in France were unsuccessful, and the ultimate choice fell on a Pole, Albert Chrzanowsky, a competent soldier who had fought in the Napoleonic wars and had led the revolutionary forces in the Polish insurrection of 1830. Though ready to accept the supreme command, he felt that Charles Albert's prestige had a good effect on the troops; at his new general's request, the king remained the nominal commander-in-chief, while Chrzanowsky took the humbler title of chief of staff.

The appointment of this small but energetic general, whose stature was in striking contrast with Charles Albert's tall figure, was followed by another which was more surprising. The Genoese General Ramorino, who had won no glory from his involvement in the abortive 'invasion of Savoy' in 1834, was chosen to command the Lombard division. This was a political move: the division threatened to mutiny unless the command were transferred from the aristocratic General Olivieri to the notoriously democratic Ramorino, and the king felt obliged to make the appointment. (After Ramorino had made a blinding error which helped to lose the war, Charles Albert said: 'I was expecting it. I never wanted him and I held out, but in the end I had to give way.')[7]

Charles Albert had said that he would use the armistice to reorganize his forces, but the army which was put under Chrzanowsky's command left much to be desired. Though on paper it numbered about 150,000 men, the actual fighting strength was more like 55,000, and there was a great shortage of efficient officers.[8] A German historian writing soon after the war commented on the Piedmontese army's low morale and general feeling of defeatism: 'The army counted in its ranks not less than 30,000 married men, most of whom were averse to war. Almost all the generals and all the older officers disapproved of it, and anticipated an evil issue; the newly-appointed officers alone were confident of an easy and brilliant success, counting on the expected defection of Italian and Hungarian soldiers in the Austrian ranks.'[9] These deficiencies were obvious to Chrzanowsky's experienced eye, and after the war he was asked why he did not resign his command when he saw that the troops were not ready and defeat was inevitable. He explained that his resignation would have encouraged the enemy and further demoralized the army, and in any case he could not betray the king's trust.

Why did Charles Albert resume the war? Because he feared a republican rising if he did not do so, because he was still obsessed by his dream of winning Italy's independence and because Lombard exiles painted glowing pictures of popular insurrections all over Lombardy if a Piedmontese army of liberation crossed the Ticino. The exiles were wrong. The Lombards were in no mood to repeat the Glorious Five Days. When the Piedmontese entered Lombardy there was no sign of local uprisings to support them.

Viewed as a military exercise, Piedmontese tactics in this second stage of the war were almost entirely deplorable. Chrzanowsky spread out his forces in a long line from Lake Maggiore to the Po. He and the king were with the main striking force at Novara, to the north of the line, and when the armistice formally ended at noon on 20 March this force moved east to the Ticino and prepared to cross into Lombardy. At the south of the line Ramorino and the Lombard division were stationed at Cava, almost midway between the Ticino and the Po, with orders to hold up any Austrian advance into Piedmont.

The campaign began with a characteristic gesture by Charles Albert. Chrzanowsky expected the Austrians to advance towards Novara, and he therefore decided to cross the Ticino and meet them in Lombardy, possibly near Magenta. At half past one the duke of Genoa, the king's second son, who commanded the fourth division, was ordered to advance on Magenta, and a company of bersaglieri made ready to cross the bridge over the river. They were stopped by Charles Albert, who put himself at their head and rode first over the bridge into Lombardy. After a moment's suspense, in which onlookers feared that the bridge might be mined or that hidden Austrian snipers might fire on the vanguard, the crossing was safely completed, and the troops loudly cheered their king's arrival on Lombard soil.[10]

But the Austrians were not there. The Piedmontese intelligence services were of little value. Radetzky was not going anywhere near Magenta. The bulk of his army was massed on Pavia and was approaching Piedmont by way of Cava, where Ramorino had been stationed to stop any Austrian advance.

If Ramorino had obeyed Chrzanowsky's orders the Austrians' victory might at least have been delayed. But he had wrongly formed the impression that the enemy would be advancing from the south, and without consulting his commander-in-chief he had moved away from Cava with most of his force and taken up a position on the other side of the Po. Cava was now only weakly held, and the gate was virtually open for the entrance of the Austrian armies. They poured through the gap and turned north towards Mortara and Novara.

In the meantime Chrzanowsky had recrossed the Ticino, but it was too late for him to establish positions for stopping the Austrians. In three actions at Borgo San Siro, Gambolo and Sforzesca, which together formed the battle of Sforzesca, the Piedmontese fought stubbornly and well under Chrzanowsky's own command. The numbers were slightly in Austria's favour— 9000 Austrians against 8500 Piedmontese, but losses were rather heavier on the Austrian side – 25 killed and 180 wounded, against Piedmont's 21 killed and 94 wounded. Honours were even, since each side gained a limited objective; the Austrians kept open the route from Pavia to Mortara, and the Piedmontese barred the approach to Vigevano. The battle had no effect on the issue of the war, but it showed that, in spite of its low morale, the new Piedmontese army had fighting qualities which were not inferior to the Austrians'.[11]

But Ramorino's fatal blunder had ruined Chrzanowsky's strategy. From Sforzesca the Austrians moved up the Mortara road, and a bitter fight for Mortara ended with the complete rout of the Piedmontese, who fell back on Novara. The end was near.

Chrzanowsky had 50,000 men at Novara, where the Austrian general, D'Aspre, attacked with inferior numbers. The crucial battle was at the outlying township of Bicocca, which changed hands several times before it was finally taken by D'Aspre. Then further Austrian troops arrived, and the Piedmontese position at Novara was seen to be untenable. During the fighting Charles Albert had moved recklessly among the bullets, refusing to take cover and deliberately seeking death; but he survived to ask Radetzky for an armistice on 23 March. 'Even death has cast me off,' he said sadly.

Severe terms, including the military occupation of Alessandria and the surrender of the king's eldest son, the Duke of Savoy, as a hostage, were proposed by the Austrian general, Hess, as conditions for an armistice. When Charles Albert heard them he at once decided to abdicate in favour of Victor Emmanuel, duke of Savoy, in the hope that his son would be able to get better terms from the Austrians. He called his generals together and told them of his decision. 'I perceive,' he said, 'that my person is now the sole obstacle to a peace become inevitable, and moreover I could never reconcile myself to signing peace. Since I have not succeeded in finding death I must accomplish one last sacrifice for my people. I resign my crown, and abdicate in favour of my son.'[12]

His reign ended, Charles Albert passed through the Austrian lines and journeyed through France and Spain to Oporto, where he died in July, only four months after the battle of Novara.

The armistice terms conceded to the new king, Victor Emmanuel II, were certainly more favourable than those offered to Charles. This was not, as was once thought, because Victor Emmanuel stood out against Austrian bullying, but because he conciliated Radetzky by promising to crush the left wing revolutionary party in the Piedmontese parliament.* The new terms

* The old legend of Victor Emmanuel's heroic resistance to Austrian pressure is disproved by Radetzky's own account of their meeting, which shows that the king had volunteered his promise *before the armistice terms were drawn up*. (Howard McGaw Smyth, 'The Armistice of Novara', *Journal of Modern History*, 1935, pp. 177–8; Mack Smith, *Il Risorgimento*, pp. 319–20.) Rosario Romeo points out that it would not have been in Austria's interest to discredit the Piedmontese monarchy when it seemed to be on the point of settling with the forces of revolution once and for all. (*Dal Piemonte sabaudo all'Italia liberale*, p. 123.)

provided for the reduction of the Piedmontese army to its peace-time strength, the payment of an indemnity of 230,000,000 lire (later reduced to 75,000,000 lire) and the occupation of parts of Piedmont by 20,000 Austrian troops until a formal peace treaty was signed.[13]

Charles Albert had lost a war, but he had gained a reputation that was to have great significance for Italy's future. The last days of his reign had given him a new 'image'. His equivocal position in the conspiracy of 1821, his stern punishment of the abortive rebellion of 1833, his years of absolute rule and resistance to liberal influences, his inept generalship in 1848 which led to the surrender of Milan – all these phases of his career were forgotten or overlooked; he had become, and was long to remain, the patriot king who had risked and lost all in the attempt to free Italy from foreign domination. A talented contemporary, the Marchioness Costanza d'Azeglio, said of him: 'What can be said with truth is that if all had sacrificed themselves as he did, the cause would not be lost. There are moments which redeem a whole life and he has touched a chord which vibrates in all hearts – nationality.'[14] However incredible such a culmination would have seemed for the greater part of Charles Albert's reign, by his last campaign, abdication, exile and death he became one of the heroes of the first stage of the Risorgimento.

But Charles Albert's new 'image' was not the only benefit which Italy gained from an apparent defeat. As Omodeo observes, 'Novara engulfed him, but consolidated the dynasty.'[15] The position of the house of Savoy was now enhanced. It had become the acknowledged leader in the struggle for Italy's independence.

Though the war was over, Lombardy and Piedmont were not entirely at peace. In Lombardy the city of Brescia had gallantly risen in support of the war of liberation. It held out against the Austrians for several days after Novara, but was at last subdued and savagely punished by the notorious General Haynau – the 'General Hyena' who had such rough treatment from the draymen of Barclays' brewery when he visited London a year or two later. In Piedmont, too, there was trouble at Genoa, which resented the armistice and rose in revolt to continue the war on its own. The Piedmontese government regarded Genoa's action as a revolt against its own authority, and with Austrian approval Piedmontese troops were sent to suppress the insurrection.

Novara also had its effect on neighbouring Tuscany, where Guerrazzi realized that the return of the grand duke would be the only way of averting Austrian intervention. He began to negotiate for Leopold II's return, but the Austrians were too quick for him. At the end of April General D'Aspre entered Tuscany with 18,000 men, and announced that he had come to safeguard the grand duke's rights. Leopold II came back, but the Austrians stayed and were still in Florence a month later, when an American visitor noted that Austrian officers in white coats with purple facings filled every café and went jingling everywhere through the streets.[16]

3

News of the renewal of war in northern Italy had been given a mixed reception in the new Roman republic. Some of the extreme republicans sneered at 'the king's war', but the true nationalists felt at once that aid should be sent to Piedmont. After considerable debate a proclamation was issued on 22 March, announcing: 'The battalions of the republic will combat side by side with those of the sub-Alpine and other Italian states ... From the Alps to the sea there is no real independence, no freedom, as long as this consecrated land is trampled by the Austrian ... To arms! and life to Italy!'[17]

Even when the defeat at Novara became known at Rome the assembly refused to believe that the cause was irretrievably lost, and there was still talk of sending Roman troops to Piedmont. But none were sent.

The executive power of the republic was now concentrated in the hands of a triumvirate, consisting of Mazzini, Staffi and Armellini. Only one triumvir mattered. Mazzini was dictator of Rome, and for a few weeks had the opportunity of showing his abilities as an administrator. He worked from a small office in the Quirinal, was accessible to all callers, dined each day at a cheap restaurant and gave his small monthly salary of thirty-two lire to charity. Yet from this modest and unostentatious background he was able to exercise a moral ascendancy which allowed him to take the first steps towards establishing reforms affecting the whole life of the Papal States.

His reforms were both ecclesiastical and social. He began a re-adjustment of ecclesiastical funds which gave a fairer share to the poorer priests, he abolished the death penalty, he removed taxes which oppressed the lower classes, he introduced universal suffrage and freedom of the press, he abolished salt and tobacco monopolies. As far as was possible he suppressed acts of anti-clerical violence and vandalism.

Though republican in name, this was liberal government in the grand manner, and it won the approval of English liberals. Palmerston declared that 'Mazzini's government of Rome was far better than any the Romans had had for centuries.' *Punch* praised him in rhapsodic stanzas, of which one concluded:

> And Rome's old heroes from their spheres
> Shout, chiming in with British cheers,
> Bravo, Mazzini.[18]

But Mazzini was not concerned only with the government of Rome. He was anxious to preserve order all over the territory of the Papal States, which were now regarded as part of the Roman republic. When he heard that republican extremists were attacking Catholics and generally terrorizing Ancona and its neighbourhood, he declared that a man of action and decision must be sent there to stop the terrorism. He chose for this task the young conspirator, Felice Orsini, who had been released from prison by the pope's amnesty and in 1848 had fought in Durando's army in the northern war. In 1849 he was elected a deputy of the Roman assembly, and the good impression he made there was the cause of his being selected for the pacification of Ancona.

Mazzini had chosen wisely. Orsini's resolute actions settled the rebellion, and he was warmly praised by Mazzini when he returned to Rome early in May. Since Orsini is usually remembered as a conspirator and would-be assassin, it is noteworthy that he too, like Mazzini, had considerable gifts for administrative action when the opportunity offered.

This period of concentration on domestic affairs was cut short by ominous news from France. General Cavaignac, who had been dictator of France after the fall of Louis-Philippe, had pledged his country to send aid to the pope. Cavaignac had now fallen from power. Prince Louis Napoleon, the former participant in an anti-papal revolution, was the newly elected president of the second French republic. He decided to carry out Cavaignac's pledge, and a French expeditionary force was prepared for the occupation of Rome.

Looking back on his decision twelve years later, Louis Napoleon, who was then Emperor Napoleon III, told two British diplomats that the consent he gave to the expedition of 1849 was the greatest political mistake he had ever committed.[19] Certainly it created grave and lasting tensions by involving France in the continued occupation of Rome, but in the circumstances of 1849 Louis Napoleon could hardly have rejected the pope's plea. There was no question of his hand being forced by some clerical plot. France was still a Catholic country, and all Catholics were indignant at the Romans' treatment of the pope. But the anti-clerical element also favoured a military expedition, since it feared that Austria might win a permanent ascendancy in Rome if France took no action. Intervention was thus desired by the whole country. Mistake though it was, Louis Napoleon was politically compelled to make it.

To the Roman republicans, and to Italian liberals generally, the French intervention seemed an act of black treachery. France was again a republic and was, in fact, the mother of all republics. It was remembered how, as a young man, its president had taken up arms against papal misgovernment. The Roman republic felt that it had the right to expect help, not opposition, from republican France. But this feeling took no account of the French people's strong Catholic sentiments, or of the fact that France, as a whole, did not like the republican form of government.* It had chosen a Bonaparte as president with a huge majority over his nearest rival, the devotedly republican General Cavaignac. It was about to elect a new assembly which was largely anti-

---

* Commander A. C. Key, R.N., who bivouacked with the French expeditionary force for a week in May, wrote in a private letter: 'Strange to say, I have not found *one* republican in the French army or navy.' (Colomb, *Memoirs of Admiral Sir Astley Cooper Key*, p. 206.)

republican. The France of 1849 was clearly in no mood to support a Roman republic.

The French expeditionary force set sail for Italy under the command of General Oudinot, son of one of Napoleon I's marshals. The first detachment of some 8000 to 10,000 men landed at Civita Vecchia, about forty miles north-west of Rome, on 25 April. Oudinot believed that his mission was to free Rome from an unpopular and detested government which had unscrupulously seized power. He expected to be hailed as a liberator, and he did not imagine that he would encounter any serious resistance.

Other Catholic powers were also moving against Rome. An Austrian force was moving south through Romagna and the Marches, a Neapolitan army was on its way north and it was reported that Spain was preparing an expeditionary force to fight for the pope. But the French, above all, were seen as the immediate danger to the Roman republic.

Rome was getting ready to defend itself. Two days after Oudinot's landing Garibaldi rode into the city at the head of his bronzed legionaries and was greeted by excited crowds, crying 'He has come, he has come!' Ramparts, earth-mounds and stockades were being built at Porta Angelica and Porta Cavalleggieri, on either side of the Piazza di San Pietro, which was regarded as a likely area for a French attack; but after some thirty hours' work on them an American resident was shocked to see that 'the labourers were leaning picturesquely on their spades, doing nothing, and everything was going on as leisurely as if the enemy were in France instead of at a few hours' march of the city.'[20] The big question of the hour was whether the civic guard would join in the city's defence. It was answered on 28 April, when the guard were assembled in the Piazza Santi Apostoli and Sterbini, a leading deputy, asked them if they were ready to fight for Rome. Their rousing shout of *'Guerra !'* left no doubt of their apparent determination, though the same American noted drily that 'the enthusiasm did not seem of the right stuff – it was rather a *festa* demonstration.'[21]

The defenders of Rome were a mixed bag. Some 2500 were regulars – papal troops of the line and carabinieri who had gladly joined the revolt against the papal government. Garibaldi's legion, enlarged by artists and other volunteers who had joined it in Rome, numbered nearly 1300, and there was another volunteer body of 300 *finanzieri* (custom house officers) under the command of the disreputable Callimaco Zambianchi. Volunteers who had taken part in the Lombard campaign added another 1400, there were 1000 civic guards, and some 300 students and several hundred other citizens were giving active help outside the military and paramilitary formations. At the last moment the defence was greatly strengthened by the arrival of 600 Lombard bersaglieri, under the command of Luciano Manara, a young Milanese nobleman who had fought valiantly during his city's Glorious Five Days. But even with this useful addition the total strength of the defence was not much more than 7000.[22]

The defenders were soon in action. Oudinot had decided to march on Rome without delay, and on 29 April his army bivouacked a dozen miles from the city. He was so confident of being welcomed by the Romans that he took no precautions to protect his troops.

Since he was approaching from the north-west it was clear that the danger areas were the Janiculan and Vatican hills. Garibaldi, with his own legion and some 1200 volunteers, was defending the Janiculum, while the walls round the Vatican were held by papal troops and the civic guard. Since the Villa Corsini, which was outside the walls opposite Porta San Pancrazio, was on ground as high as the defences, Garibaldi set up his headquarters on its terrace, from which he could watch the approach of the French army.

Oudinot's misunderstanding of the situation greatly simplified the defenders' task in this first encounter of the siege of Rome. The French general had brought neither scaling-ladders nor siege-guns. His troops advanced in column, and it was only when two cannons opened fire on them that Oudinot realized that Rome would be seriously defended. Unprepared for the ensuing battle, the French were overcome by a sudden assault by Garibaldi's legion and Masina's lancers. In spite of the French troops' great superiority in numbers they had no chance of reaching the city gates, and though for a time they held both the

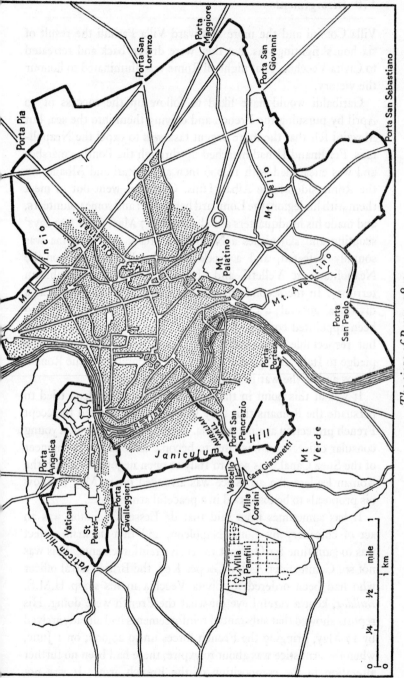

The siege of Rome, 1849

Villa Corsini and the more westward Villa Pamfili the result of six hours' fighting was that they were driven back and retreated to Civita Vecchia. That night all Rome was illuminated to honour the victory.

Garibaldi would have liked to follow up the success of 30 April by pursuing the French and driving them into the sea, but Mazzini felt that the more urgent task was to expel the Neapolitans. Ferdinand II had marched up through the Pontine marshes and was encamped with 10,000 men at Frascati and Albano, on the Rome side of the Alban Hills. Garibaldi went out to meet them with his legion, the Lombard bersaglieri and some volunteers, and made his headquarters at Palestrina on 7 May. After two days' scouting and skirmishes a Neapolitan attack on Palestrina was soundly defeated, and a week later the Romans fell on the Neapolitans at Velletri and drove them out of republican territory. In the second engagement Garibaldi was serving as a divisional general; a regular officer, General Pietro Roselli, had been appointed commander-in-chief. The choice of such a dull but respectable commander was meant, says Trevelyan, 'as a pledge to Italy and Europe of the regular character of the Roman troops and of the war in which they were engaged.'[23]

It was at this point in the siege that Louis Napoleon tried to persuade the Romans that they would be well advised to accept French protection against Austria. Ferdinand de Lesseps, a young consular officer who was later to become famous as the engineer of the Suez Canal, was sent to Italy to open negotiations with the Roman leaders. An armistice was arranged on 17 May to allow his proposals to be discussed in a peaceful atmosphere.

It has sometimes been said that de Lesseps' mission was an act of chicanery by Louis Napoleon, and that its main object was to gain time for Oudinot to receive reinforcements. This was not so. Commander Astley Cooper Key, the British naval officer who had been ordered to Civita Vecchia in his sloop H.M.S. *Bulldog*, kept a careful eye on what the French were doing. His reports showed that substantial reinforcements had already arrived by 17 May, bringing the French forces up to 20,000; on 1 June, when the armistice was about to expire, there had been no further alteration in the composition of the French army. It was not until 21 June that he reported the arrival of fresh reinforcements, bringing the numbers up to 30,000, with thirty heavy siege-guns and forty pieces of field artillery.[24]

This evidence shows that Louis Napoleon was genuinely seeking a way to avoid unnecessary fighting; but the mission was a failure. The only workable agreement that de Lesseps could make with the triumvirs was unacceptable to his own government. On 1 June Oudinot denounced the armistice and threatened the early resumption of hostilities.

A charge of chicanery can be better sustained against Oudinot than against Louis Napoleon, though it is not completely certain that his much disputed letter to the Roman commander-in-chief was written in bad faith. This letter denounced the armistice from the time it was written – 5 p.m. on 1 June – and stated that he had informed the Italian advanced posts that fighting could now be resumed by either side. It also said that, in order to give French residents time to leave Rome, he would not attack '*la place*' until 4 June.[25]

The Romans maintained afterwards that this was a promise not to attack at all until 4 June, but Oudinot retorted that '*la place*' obviously meant the city's own fortifications and did not refer to any advanced posts outside the boundaries. His explanation is plausible and may be correct. In any case the specific mention of the Italian advanced posts in his letter was a clear warning that these posts should be on their guard.

Whatever verdict is passed on Oudinot's conduct, nothing can excuse the stupidity of the Roman high command, which allowed the whole of 2 June to go by without taking steps to reinforce and strengthen the crucial advanced posts at the Villa Pamfili and the Villa Corsini. Even if nothing was expected to happen until 4 June, every hour was precious if the outlying villas were to be properly defended. But Roselli left the Villa Pamfili in the hands of the 400 men who had guarded it during the armistice, and even visited them on the evening of 2 June to tell them that there was no need for special vigilance until 4 June. It was this stupidity, rather than Oudinot's ambiguity, which caused the defence of Rome to collapse so quickly.

The affair of 30 April had shaken French faith in Oudinot's

generalship, and the distinguished engineer-general Vaillant had been sent out to assist in the siege and if necessary to take over the command. He had decided, as the Romans had always expected, that the Janiculum area was the best objective for an entry into Rome, but to enable his siege batteries to be properly mounted it was essential to seize and hold the high positions of the two villas. The vital part of this operation was completed in a few hours in the early morning of 3 June. Two French columns approached the Villa Pamfili at 3 a.m.; one blew a breach in the boundary wall, the other found a gate of the park left open. The 400 Italian defenders, convinced that no attack was possible, were taken completely by surprise, and within a short time the French were not only masters of the Villa Pamfili but had also driven the Italians out of the Villa Corsini. The French were now in a position from which they could take the city at their leisure.

For the rest of that fatal 3 June the defenders of Rome made gallant but futile efforts to recapture the lost villas. This was virtually impossible, since units leaving the city gates came at once under enemy fire and had little freedom of movement. The various assaults, some of them temporarily successful, on the Villa Corsini are memorable only because of the heroism of the Roman volunteers, but have no military significance. Militarily, the most striking feature of the day was the failure of Garibaldi's generalship. This was not his kind of battle. For all his personal bravery his record on 3 June was that of a general who sent men to their death by ordering attacks which had no chance of success. [26]

The key to Rome was in French hands, but Garibaldi's legion, the papal troops and the volunteers showed great courage and endurance in guarding the walls and gates for many days, while a number of outposts continued to harry the French by making it difficult for Vaillant's siege works to be placed exactly where he wanted them. Even after 22 June, when the French had actually established themselves on the city walls in the Janiculum area, another line of defence was improvised and held for eight days along the Aurelian Wall.

Towards the end of the siege Garibaldi was unexpectedly joined by his wife Anita. She had been in Nice when she heard of the defeat of 3 June; though she was pregnant she felt that her place was at her husband's side. By the time she reached Rome, the end was already inevitable. The whole city was exposed to shell-fire; the remaining Janiculan defences were breaking up; the line of the Aurelian Wall was crumbling. Yet one odd touch of glamour marked the final stage of the siege. Up till that time only Garibaldi and his staff had worn the red shirts which the Italian Legion had made famous in its South American campaigns. Garibaldi now decided that it would be good for his legionaries' morale if they all had red shirts, and on 28 June they duly appeared in the new uniform which was to be associated with all Garibaldi's future exploits.

By 30 June systematic defence was no longer possible. On that day the assembly heard Mazzini say that three courses were open – to surrender, to fight in the streets or to go to the mountains and continue the struggle from there. At the deputies' request Garibaldi left the firing line to give them his advice. It was simple. Street fighting would no longer be practicable; the right course was to go out into the wilderness. '*Dovunque saremo, colà sarà Roma.*' ('Wherever we are, there will be Rome.') That, he said, was what he was going to do, and he would take any volunteers who wished to go with him.[27]

Mazzini agreed with Garibaldi, but most of the deputies thought differently. They decided to stay in Rome, and the siege ended with an assembly resolution which stated: 'In the name of God and the People – the constituent assembly of Rome ceases from a defence that has become impossible and remains at its post.'

Two days later Garibaldi left the city with some 4000 volunteers, to whom he had made his moving appeal: 'I am going out from Rome. Let those who wish to continue the war against the stranger come with me. I offer neither pay nor quarters nor provisions; I offer hunger, thirst, forced marches, battle and death. Let him who loves his country in his heart, and not with his lips only, follow me.'[28] So began an amazing march in which Garibaldi evaded the pursuit of three enemy armies, while his 4000 volunteers dwindled to a small band of faithful followers, whom he led at last to San Marino. There the remaining volunteers were disbanded, while Garibaldi set off for Venice with his wife and his closest companions. But Anita died in his arms and Venice was

falling. After eight weeks of heroic endurance Garibaldi knew
that he could do no more. He made his way across Italy and
briefly returned to Nice before sailing for the United States.

Rome was now occupied by the French, who were preparing to
hand it back to the pope. Mazzini had left the city and was soon
to return to England. Italian nationalism seemed to have suffered
another crushing defeat.

Yet the brief life of the Roman republic was a great event in
the Risorgimento. It had shown, indeed, that Mazzini's dream of
simultaneously conducting an internal revolution and a war
against foreign armies was quite impracticable; but it had also
shown the world how bravely Italians could fight and die for
their independence. Piedmont had led the way. Rome followed.
The message of Novara was repeated on the Janiculum.

4

With the fall of Rome, only Venice upheld the cause of Italian
freedom. The rest of Lombardy-Venetia was again under
Austrian domination, but Venice itself, under Manin's leadership, kept up the fight against the foreigner.

It was again a republic. The Salasco armistice had ended the
brief honeymoon of fusion with Piedmont. In the summer of
1848 the city's defence had been strengthened by the arrival
of the Neapolitan general, Guglielmo Pepe, with a number of
followers, and some 20,000 men were ready to resist the Austrians.

Though Venice was cut off from all contact with the mainland
by an Austrian cordon, the general morale was high, and when
two months passed after the Salasco armistice without any military
action, the Venetian leaders felt that the time had come for a
sortie in strength. On 27 October a raiding party set out from the
Marghera fort to attack the Austrians at Mestre, and scored a
tactical success. The Austrians lost 150 dead, 150 were wounded,
6 cannons were captured and 587 prisoners taken; the Italian
casualties were only 87 dead and 163 wounded. But after this
small demonstration of the defenders' strength the rest of the
winter of 1848–9 was mainly devoted to the task of getting
enough food to keep the inhabitants alive.

The spring of 1849 brought the battle of Novara and the

realization that Venice was now entirely alone against the Austrians in northern Italy. Yet there was still no weakening in the spirit of resistance. On 2 April the assembly decreed that Venice would resist the Austrians at all costs and that Manin should remain in possession of unlimited powers. It was a fine gesture, which showed how greatly the Venetians prized their independence.

After Novara the Austrians attacked Venice more vigorously. The prolonged battle in May for the Marghera fort, which was captured by the Austrians, was the beginning of the end. The city was now within reach of Austrian cannon-fire. Much damage was done by incendiary shells, but the Venetians were only amused by an Austrian attempt to anticipate twentieth-century air warfare by dropping bombs on the city from a fleet of balloons.[29] As summer went on, the firing on Venice gew heavier and the inhabitants suffered severely from food shortage and cholera. Internal conditions as well as military pressure made surrender inevitable. At the end of August, Manin, Tommaseo, Pepe and other leaders left the city, and Venice surrendered to the Austrians.

This was the third of the great defeats of 1849. Yet it was also a victory, for Venice had defied the Austrians for seventeen months and its capacity for both self-defence and self-government had won the admiration of all Italy.

Superficially it might have seemed in the autumn of 1849 that all the labours of the Quarantotto had gone for nothing. Piedmont's bid to liberate Italy had failed, Lombardy-Venetia was again an Austrian province, papal government was restored at Rome, constitutions had been quashed and absolute rule re-established in all Italian states except Piedmont. But in fact the apparently fruitless endeavours of 1848–9 had brought Italy to the point of no return. The memories of Charles Albert at Novara, of Mazzini and Garibaldi in Rome, of Manin in Venice, no less than of all the Italians who had given their lives in a vain fight for freedom, were too potent ever to be effaced. A nation which had given so much evidence of its determination and capacity to control its own destinies could not be kept indefinitely under foreign domination and influence.

CAVOUR

Victor Emmanuel's Piedmont   Mazzini and Lombardy
The Crimean War   Congress of Paris   Pisacane

FROM 1849 Piedmont had a unique place in the history of the Risorgimento. It was the only Italian state in which constitutional government was still preserved.

Elsewhere in Italy the upheavals of the Quarantotto were followed by reaction. Constitutions were torn up, jails were filled with political prisoners. Pius IX went back to Rome, but judged it safer to live in the Vatican rather than the Quirinal palace in the heart of the city; the Papal States were again under theocratic rule, backed by Austrians in the provinces and French in the capital, where in 1853 an Englishwoman found that 'the streets were as full of French soldiers as if it had been a besieged town'.[1] In Tuscany Grand Duke Leopold tried to restore the amiable despotism which had once made him a well-loved father-figure; but economic difficulties, Austrian soldiers in Florence, the trial of Guerrazzi (whose great services to his state were rewarded by exile), the abolition of the liberal constitution and the restoration of the death penalty caused a permanent breach between ruler and ruled. Modena and Parma also returned to absolute rule under Austrian protection; the duke of Parma had 300 of his subjects whipped in four years, and when he was assassinated in 1854 the police never succeeded in finding the murderer.

Nowhere was reaction more emphatic than in the kingdom of the Two Sicilies, where Ferdinand II resumed his absolute power and the Bourbon army acted as a domestic police force; many of the most intelligent men in the country had to spend long years in Bourbon jails – those squalid jails that W. E. Gladstone briefly visited in 1851 and thereafter described in his *Letter to Lord*

Aberdeen, which denounced the government of Naples as 'the negation of God'. Austrian rule in Lombardy was reasserted with great sternness. Men and even young women were publicly flogged for disrespect to their Austrian masters.* There were 961 political executions in twelve months, and Palmerston said that the Austrian ruling classes were 'the greatest brutes that ever called themselves by the undeserved name of civilised men'.[2]

The one exception to this sorry record of oppression and autocratic rule was to be found in Piedmont – no longer the Piedmont of Charles Albert but now the Piedmont of Victor Emmanuel II, Azeglio and Cavour. The contrast between the late king and the son who succeeded him was, as Valsecchi points out, a sign of the opposed character of two generations, of two historical periods. The tall, deathly pale Charles Albert was a hero of romantic legend, the mystical king of an Italy which existed only in dreams; Victor Emmanuel, short, sturdy, bushy-moustached, fiery and warlike, with a passion for hunting and an insatiable appetite for food and women, belonged to the prosaic world of reality.[3] But the new king's interest in pursuing various kinds of quarry did not distract his mind from affairs of state. He was a shrewd politician and a loyal Catholic who aroused an almost paternal affection in Pope Pius IX. He was also, as time was to show, a true Italian patriot.

Victor Emmanuel had a chance to show his political interests soon after he came to the throne. The Piedmontese chamber of deputies was dissolved and a new one was elected in May 1849; but only a third of the limited electorate went to the polls, and owing to the apathy of the moderate voters the new chamber had a revolutionary majority which did not reflect the feelings of the country at large. It was against the peace treaty and in favour of continuing the war, though renewed hostilities could have brought nothing but ruin to Piedmont. Victor Emmanuel seized his opportunity. He had promised Radetzky that he would crush the revolutionary left, and he was now able to do so. He again

* When a Milanese crowd hissed a prostitute who showed the Austrian colours on her balcony, 'Radetzky flogged fifteen persons for the crime – two of whom were young girls, singers of opera, aged twenty and seventeen.' (Hinkley, *Mazzini*, p. 134.)

dissolved the chamber, and before the election issued a proclamation from Moncalieri, sharply rebuking the deputies and calling on all electors to do their duty by going to the polls.

This was bringing the crown directly into politics. If it was not a *coup d'état*, it was certainly an ultimatum.[4] But the bold throw succeeded. A new election, in which 80,000 people voted, compared with 30,000 in May, left the democrats in the minority, while the docile majority consisted largely of civil servants, military men and ecclesiastics. It was the kind of chamber which would do the king's bidding, and it obediently approved of the peace treaty with Austria.

The proclamation of Moncalieri was given a constitutional veneer by bearing the prime minister's signature as well as the king's. In this first phase of his reign Victor Emmanuel owed much to the loyalty and guidance of Massimo d'Azeglio, who became prime minister when Rattazzi resigned after Novara. Azeglio was twenty years older than the king. He had taken up politics only after the publication of his book, *Degli ultimi casi nella Romagna*, but as a staunchly conservative prime minister he stood firm against the rampant democracy of the left wing minority, led by Valerio, Brofferio and (in the left centre) Rattazzi. Azeglio's wisdom upheld the prestige of the house of Savoy and preserved it for greater tasks; he also helped to win popularity for Victor Emmanuel himself, whose adherence to the Piedmontese statute, while his fellow sovereigns were tearing up their constitutions, earned him the affectionate nickname of *Il re galantuomo*, the honest king.*

Azeglio was prime minister for some three and a half years before making way for Cavour. His work in those years was of great importance to Piedmont, for he began the process of modernization which was necessary to equip the country for its future role.

His first objective was to reduce the power of the Church,

---

* But it is going too far to say, as Gwilym O. Griffith, for example, suggests in *Mazzini: Prophet of Modern Europe* (p. 236), that Victor Emmanuel had 'an honest and undissuadable devotion to constitutional government'. He kept the statute because it was expedient to do so, but he gave more than one indication that he would rather have ignored parliament and governed with a cabinet of his own men.

which was still strongly entrenched in Piedmont. It controlled all secondary and most elementary education, it had its own courts for ecclesiastics, it had the monopoly of marriage (since there was neither civil marriage nor civil divorce), it had the right to censor religious books, it insisted on Protestants and Jews being kept in an inferior position. Azeglio was determined to free the state from clerical bondage, and he entrusted Siccardi, the keeper of the seals, with the task of introducing an ecclesiastical reform bill.

Siccardi's draft bill, introduced in January 1850, was a comprehensive one, including provision for civil marriages and many other drastic changes. At the chamber's request it was reduced to three clauses, dealing respectively with the abolition of ecclesiastical courts and the Church's right of asylum, with the existing power to enforce penalties for non-observance of religious festivals and with property owned by religious orders. Many of Azeglio's conservative supporters deserted him during the debate on Siccardi's bill, but it was duly passed with the consent of the left.

Then the storm broke. Franzoni, archbishop of Turin, told his clergy to protest against the violation of clerical immunity if they were summoned before a lay court. He was ordered to leave Turin on the grounds that he was menacing public order; when he refused to go he was summoned to appear before a lay court. He declined to attend, and he was then arrested in his palace and later sentenced to a month's imprisonment and a fine. His imprisonment was not very rigorous, since he was lodged in the commandant's house at the Turin citadel; but it was a striking sign of the breach between Church and state. Fransoni widened the breach by forbidding extreme unction to be given to one of Azeglio's ministers on his death-bed, unless he withdrew his adherence to the Siccardi laws. The minister would not withdraw, and died without the Church's blessing.*

The minister who was thus penalized for the Siccardi laws was Pietro Santarosa, minister of agriculture. The vacancy caused by his death was filled in October by Count Camillo Benso di Cavour who became minister of marine, commerce and

* The refusal of extreme unction was, in fact, a decision of the whole clergy synod of Turin, but Fransoni was held to be personally responsible for it. (Marshall, *Massimo d'Azeglio*, p. 191.)

agriculture. The man who was soon to become the political and diplomatic architect of the Risorgimento had come at last to the corridors of power.

Cavour was forty years old at the time of his first ministerial appointment. Members of his family had moved in court circles in Turin for many years, and Cavour was the godchild of Prince Camillo Borghese, the provincial governor under the French administration, and his wife, Princess Pauline, one of Napoleon I's sisters, whose entrancing statue by Canova is one of the treasures of the Borghese gallery in Rome.* The family remained at court after the restoration; Cavour himself was given a post as one of Prince Charles Albert's pages. But he hated having to dress up in scarlet uniform 'like a lackey', and his ostentatious satisfaction when he wore it for the last time greatly offended his royal master. This incident was the seed of his unwillingness to take any part in state affairs while Charles Albert was on the throne.[5] After a few years in the army, in which he had little interest, Cavour resigned his commission and later took over the management of the family estates at Leri. Besides being a keen and progressive agriculturist, and a founder of the Sub-Alpine Agricultural Association, he paid many visits to France and England, where he gave close attention to new agricultural methods and to social, political and economic affairs. These studies were a good foundation for his work as editor of *Il Risorgimento* and his subsequent entry into Piedmontese politics.

While Cavour was serving his ministerial apprenticeship Gioberti wrote *Il Rinnovamento*, the last of the important books which played a part in shaping Italy's destiny. It was published in 1851; its subject-matter was Piedmont, Italy and Europe.

Gioberti's advice to Piedmont was that it should give up 'municipalism' – the local patriotism which tended to keep Piedmontese development separate from the rest of Italy's. He urged that Piedmont should take up the Italian cause without reserve, and that Victor Emmanuel should be ready to lead the Italian national movement.

---

* Princess Pauline gave her godson a christening present of 1,000 Roman scudi, with which in 1836 he was able to buy a house and grounds at Grinzane for 1,300 lire. (Romeo, *Cavour e Il Suo Tempo. 1810–1842*, p. 1, n. 2.)

This policy meant the abandonment of the neo-Guelf ideal that Gioberti had previously advocated. He now saw that Piedmontese hegemony was more practicable than any federation under the pope's presidency. But it also implied, in Gioberti's view, the alignment of Piedmont with European democracy. Writing before Louis Napoleon's *coup d'état*, which began the conversion of the second French republic into the Second Empire, Gioberti thought that democracy was becoming firmly established in western Europe, and that Piedmont should therefore follow the prevailing trend. Victor Emmanuel, he maintained, should accept the liberal-democratic premise and should work with liberal allies for the renewal of Italy.

The particular significance of the *Rinnovamento* is that Victor Emmanuel read it carefully. He did not often read books, but he realized that this one was important. It must have been a powerful influence in convincing an essentially conservative king that it was necessary for him to co-operate with liberal ministers.[6]

The king had accepted Cavour's appointment as minister with some amusement. He knew the count, and he shrewdly observed to Azeglio: 'You want me to nominate Cavour? I shall be pleased to, but be sure that before long he will take all your portfolios from you!'[7] It was a good forecast, for Cavour quickly made his mark as a cabinet minister and was soon concerned with the whole range of government business. In April 1851 the minister of finance resigned, and Cavour added the finance portfolio to those he already held. By this time he was recognized as the real leader of Azeglio's ministry. His achievements in his first two years included important measures of economic and financial reorganization, but his administrative duties still left him time to be actively involved in the work of the chamber of deputies. It was in this work that he made an audacious political gesture by instituting, in February 1852, the new party alliance which became known as the *connubio* (marriage).

The origin of the *connubio* was Prince Louis Napoleon's *coup d'état* of December 1851, which gave him a ten years' tenure of the presidency of the second French republic and so paved the way for the establishment of the Second Empire. This *coup* was interpreted throughout Europe as a triumph for reaction, and in all countries the extreme right wings were given new heart for their attacks on socialism, liberalism and democracy. Piedmont was no exception; since Azeglio himself was a right-wing politician the forces of reaction seemed to be in the ascendancy. Cavour, whose own personality and early political studies had combined to make him an inflexible liberal, felt that something must be done to save liberalism. As a member of the right centre party he decided that safety lay in alliance between his own group and the democratic left centre, led by Urbano Rattazzi.

No doubt Cavour's desire for power played some part in the reaching of this decision; but its real object was to erect a barrier which the forces of reaction could not overcome.[8] Its success helped to consolidate the parliamentary regime, which was still a novelty in Piedmont and might well have been overthrown by a reactionary *coup*. Cavour said later that the *connubio* was the finest act of his political career.

A single interview with Rattazzi in January 1852 was enough for arranging the marriage. In the following month, during a debate on a new and reactionary press law, Cavour openly accepted Rattazzi's offer of co-operation and established a single liberal front. Azeglio, though amazed at this anti-governmental action by one of his own ministers, stayed in office. It was Pinelli, the veteran president of the chamber, who gave the new alliance the name of *connubio*.[9]

In this way Cavour, by breaking with his old aristocratic friends on the extreme right, formed a centre party which commanded a substantial majority in the chamber of deputies. Later in the year, on Pinelli's death, he again affronted Azeglio by supporting Rattazzi as a candidate for the presidency of the chamber. Rattazzi was elected. Cavour acknowledged the protests of the extreme right by resigning from the ministry.

He was not in the wilderness for long. Azeglio was soon in trouble over a further measure of ecclesiastical reform. This was the bill for relaxing the Church's hold on marriage: it provided for optional civil marriage ceremonies for people to whom a religious ceremony might be denied, and decreed that a marriage would be recognized by the state only if it had been registered with the state registrars. The chamber passed the bill in July by 94 votes to 35, but when the pope wrote to Victor Emmanuel saying that he could not accept such a measure, the king told the cabinet that his conscience would not allow him to assent to it. Azeglio resigned, and after Balbo had tried to form a ministry and failed, the king was obliged to send for Cavour. On 4 November 1852 he took office with a cabinet consisting mainly of ministers who had served under Azeglio.

For the next nine years, except for short intervals, Cavour was prime minister of Piedmont. They were significant years for Italy, since Piedmont's experiment in free government was 'a central and integrating part of the Risorgimento'. It gave proof of the Italians' capacity for self-government, and showed too that a small Italian state, situated on the borders of the Austrian empire, could maintain liberty and constitutional rule under wise leadership.[10]

The pattern of the Risorgimento was becoming more sharply defined. The prophets had made their prophecies, the conspirators had staged their plots and their revolutions. These were the forerunners. The next advance would be made at a higher level. Victor Emmanuel, the king, and Cavour, the statesman, were taking over the leadership.

2

It has been said of Mazzini that 'his political action was finished in 1848; then it was time for him to begin to do something which could preserve his memory in the history of science or literature.'[11] Such a judgment does less than justice to Mazzini's work after his short-lived but substantial success as chief triumvir of the Roman republic. It is true that he made no other substantial contribution to the Risorgimento. His plots were failures, his dream of freeing Italy by armed insurrections was no longer regarded as realistic. Yet his function as the prophet of the new Italy remained of the utmost importance. He was always the ominous figure in the background, warning that revolution would come if action were not taken.

After the fall of Rome Mazzini escaped from the Papal States by sea, made a short stay in Geneva and a longer one in Lausanne, and then returned to London and his English friends. 'Italy is my country, but England is my real home, if I have any,'[12] he said as he resumed his old activities of writing articles and pamphlets and raising funds for various causes.

The Ashursts and their circle, Jane Carlyle and all his old friends were delighted at his safe return. A new acquaintance he made about this time was Elizabeth Barrett Browning who remarked on his 'pale, spiritual face, his intense eyes full of melancholy illusions'.[13] One of his early tasks was to found a new society, the Friends of Italy, with the object of enlightening English people about Italian politics and the national movement.

Many famous English writers, including Leigh Hunt, Walter Savage Landor and George Henry Lewes, were on the council of the new society, which held its first public meeting in 1851. For a couple of years it did useful propagandist work by holding meetings, publishing pamphlets and presenting petitions to parliament, but after 1853 public interest was diverted to eastern Europe and the Friends of Italy were dissolved in 1855. In view of its earlier success it would be unfair to regard this Anglo-Italian venture as yet another of Mazzini's failures. Indeed, Emilia Morelli claims that 'among so many societies which were started in England at that time, in the name of the universal brotherhood of peoples, that of the Friends of Italy was the only one which had a clear and precise programme'.[14]

Throughout his later years in England and during his occasional visits to Switzerland Mazzini kept up his contacts with Italian revolutionaries. He found many adherents in Lombardy-Venetia, which still cherished the memory of Milan's Glorious Five Days. Among them were the members of an active group in Mantua who spread their net all over the province.

Their devotion to the revolutionary cause and Mazzini's fondness for letter-writing led to their undoing. Some of his letters calling for a national loan, to be paid back when freedom was won, fell into the hands of the Austrian police in 1852. A register of subscribers to the loan was found, and more than a hundred men were arrested. Of these, fifty were pardoned, forty-seven were imprisoned and nine, chosen from different social classes and different cities, were hanged in a pit at Belfiore, near

Mantua, at various times between December 1852 and March 1853.

The 'massacre of Belfiore' caused great indignation in Lombardy. Even before the last hangings had taken place a large group of Milanese workmen had decided to carry into effect an insurrectionary plot they had been hatching for some time. The plotters made contact with Mazzini and asked him to lead their rising, which was to start on Shrove Tuesday, 6 February, with the slaughter of the Austrian general staff as they sat at dinner in the castle. Though he declined their invitation he agreed to go to Lugano, on the Swiss-Italian border, and be ready to join the revolutionaries if their attempt was successful; but he was not happy about the details of the project. He was told that some 2000 workmen were in the plot, but he felt that it could not succeed without middle-class leadership and support. He therefore sent two of his agents to Milan – one to negotiate with middle-class citizens, the other to get more workmen into the movement.

Their mission was unsuccessful. The Milanese middle class was apathetic, and the leaders of the insurrection decided to call it off. Their counter-orders did not reach all the conspirators in time. On the appointed day some attacked Austrian soldiers in the streets, others made a weak attempt to raid the castle, and the rising was quickly and ruthlessly suppressed. Twelve men were executed.

Though Mazzini was not responsible for the Milanese plot, he was blamed for it both inside and outside Italy. His presence at Lugano looked like damning evidence that he had inspired it, and he was savagely attacked in the Piedmontese press. Some of the exiles who had followed him faithfully now began to desert him. Many of them regarded Manin, who had been living in Paris since the fall of Venice, as their true leader and the chief representative of the Italian national movement outside the peninsula.

Even in this hour of failure Mazzini remained a formidable figure. He still personified the ideals for which he had always striven – freedom, unity and independence for Italy. In spite of his blunders he would always be a force to be reckoned with until these ideals were achieved.

And even his blunders – and the blunders of others – were by no means irrelevant to the Italian struggle. The martyrs of Belfiore and the Milanese workmen may seem to have given their lives without reason and advantage, but such tragic events had their meaning for the Risorgimento. Cavour's work in the later part of the 1850s was made easier because of the hotheads who had kept the Italian question alive.[15]

3

The statesman who was now guiding the destinies of Piedmont was no orator. He spoke monotonously and had no great mastery of language, yet because of his clear mind he was always heard with great attention. In appearance he was a caricaturist's dream. Edward Dicey's charming word-picture puts him clearly before us:

> The squat – and I know no better term – pot-bellied form; the small, stumpy legs; the short, round arms, with the hands stuck constantly in the trousers' pockets; the thick neck, in which you could see the veins swelling; the scant, thin hair; the blurred, blotched face; and the sharp grey eyes, covered by the goggle spectacles ... The dress itself seemed a part and property of the man. The snuff-coloured tail-coat; the grey, creased and wrinkled trousers; the black silk double tie, seeming, loose as it was, a world too tight for the swollen neck it was fastened around; the crumpled shirt, the brown satin single-breasted waistcoat, half unbuttoned, as though the wearer wanted breath, with a short, massive gold chain hanging down in front, seemed all to be in keeping with that quaint world-known figure.[16]

This mild exterior was deceptive. The man who almost looked as though he had slept in his clothes was a statesman of high intelligence, great daring, much personal charm and – when necessary – complete unscrupulousness. Like the monarch he served, he was a true patriot. The deceit and sharp practices for which he has often been criticized can be excused, though not justified, by the high aims for which he was working.

Though Cavour dominated both ministry and chamber throughout his years in office it would be wrong to suggest that he was in any way a dictator. He governed by law, not by edict;

he did not try to suppress opposition; he upheld both the authority of parliament and the prestige of the monarchy; and he gave full liberty to the press.[17] Undoubtedly he was a skilful manager of the parliamentary system. He once confessed in a letter to the Comtesse de Circourt: 'I have no confidence in dictatorships, above all non-military dictatorships, and I think that parliament enables one to do many things which would be impossible for an absolutist ruler ... I have never felt so weak as when parliament was shut.'[18] It is true that he often dealt with vital diplomatic issues behind the assembly's back, but he never sought to discredit parliamentary government. It was thus on a genuinely liberal basis that he began his work as prime minister.

His first problem was the contentious civil marriage bill, which had been passed by the chamber of deputies. Here the senate saved him by prudently rejecting the bill and thus averting an open breach between king and parliament. Cavour announced that a new bill would soon be introduced to take its place, but he had been dead for several years before the government of united Italy took up the marriage question again.

Ecclesiastical reform, however, remained in the government's programme, since the Church had an excessive place in Piedmont's national life. Even at this time there were more than 10,000 priests in Piedmont (one for every 200 inhabitants) and over 600 monastic houses with more than 8000 friars and monks; and conditions were much the same in Sardinia.[19] It was over a measure for dissolving the monasteries that a grave constitutional crisis arose in 1855, when the king supported the bishops against the government and Cavour resigned. Since no other minister could form a government the king was obliged to give way and recall Cavour, who compromised by accepting amendments which reduced the number of monastic houses affected by the measure.

In general, Cavour's policies were directed towards strengthening Piedmont's economic, business and financial life, but he kept a watchful eye on those international affairs which might be turned to Piedmont's advantage. One of these was the Crimean war, in which Britain was allied to France for the protection of

Turkey against Russia after a dispute between those countries over the custody of Christian shrines in Jerusalem. Austria, which was greatly in Russia's debt, declined to help its former friend and preferred, in the words of one of its statesmen, 'to astonish the world by its ingratitude'. This was a crucial decision. In the opinion of H. A. L. Fisher, 'By smashing the strong links which bound Austria to Russia the Crimean war created the conditions which led to the liberation of the German and Italian nations.'[20] In Italy's case the process was greatly assisted by Piedmont's entry into the war as the ally of England and France.

This was an unexpected alliance, since Piedmont was bound by no treaty and appeared to have no direct concern in the quarrel between the great powers. Yet Piedmont's own interests and the wishes of one of the western allies sent Italian troops to fight Russia in the Crimea.

Much argument has been devoted to the question of who was responsible for Piedmont's entry into the war. It has been variously described as a diplomatic master-stroke by Cavour and a plot between Victor Emmanuel and the French ambassador. But it hardly matters who thought of it first, since the question of participation in the war became a live issue in the Piedmontese press almost as soon as the eastern crisis began. Everyone was talking about it. The only question was whether the decisive step would actually be taken.[21]

Piedmont's interest in a remote war becomes more understandable when we remember that in 1853 the Crimean war was not expected to remain a localized conflict involving only three major powers. Both in England and on the continent many people saw it as the opening phase of a general European war, into which other countries would soon be drawn. An ambitious and militarily-minded country like Piedmont, which had gained much from earlier European struggles, was bound to weigh the pros and cons of joining one side or the other.

There could be no question of supporting Russia. The autocratic rulers of Russia, like those of Prussia and Austria, had always stood in the way of Italian progress and liberal development. But an alliance with England and France – even the France of the Second Empire – offered more attractions. Moreover, the western powers were trying to persuade Austria to join them. This was another reason for Piedmontese participation, for if Piedmont stayed out the war might produce a permanent Franco-Austrian alliance, which would hold Italy in a vice and destroy all hopes of ejecting Austria from the peninsula.

Victor Emmanuel II was all for war. He aspired to military glory, and he pictured war as a magnificent hunting-party, an agreeable holiday from the staid duties of constitutional government. He was obsessed with the idea of becoming a great general; he even offered to command all the allied forces in the Crimea, but his offer was not accepted.[22] Apart from his personal reasons for wanting to fight, he also saw the war as a means of redeeming the Piedmontese army from the stain of Novara.

Cavour at first regretted the war as an unfortunate interruption to trade. He then came to realize that it offered an opportunity for enhancing Piedmont's prestige, and by January 1854 he had made up his mind. 'Does it not seem to your Majesty,' he asked the king, 'that we ought to find a way of taking part in the war that the western powers are declaring on Russia?' The king agreed enthusiastically. 'If I cannot go myself, I shall send my brother,' he said.[23]

This was not a matter which could be settled in a month or two. Long negotiations were needed. In the first instance Piedmont's support was sought by the western powers as a guarantee to Austria that it would run no risk of being stabbed in the back by Italy if it joined the alliance. As time went on, Piedmont's aid was especially desired by Britain because the British forces had suffered heavy losses in the Crimea and there was a danger of the war being monopolized by France. Britain's first proposal was that the Piedmontese troops should serve as British mercenaries; this was rejected, but Piedmont accepted the offer of a British loan of £500,000 at three per cent every six months while the war lasted.[24] On these terms Piedmont signed a treaty of offensive and defensive alliance with Britain and France on 10 January 1855. Austria had joined the western allies a month earlier, but had made no promise of immediate military help.

Cavour knew that he was risking his political future by taking Piedmont into the war. 'I have taken a terrible responsibility on my head,' he wrote to a friend. 'No matter, come what may, my conscience tells me that I have undertaken a sacred duty.'[25] The expected opposition soon made itself heard. Both the extreme left and the extreme right attacked the treaty in the Piedmontese chamber. From the left Brofferio prophesied that the war would result in the loss of Piedmont's liberty, whichever side won, and another left-wing speaker denounced the treaty as inexpedient, impolitic, ruinous for the country and fatal to Italy. From the right Solaro della Margarita asked why Piedmont was the only minor power to enter the war, and warned the chamber that, if Austria changed sides, Italy might face an Austro-Russian invasion while Piedmont's army was far away in the Crimea. But Cavour held his ground. It was vital, he thought, for Italy to prove its military valour; the honours won by Italian soldiers in the distant east would do more for the future destiny of Italy than anything done by those who thought they could regenerate Italy by treaties and speeches. His arguments convinced the majority in the chamber, and the treaty of alliance was approved.

The Piedmontese troops did not, in fact, have much opportunity for proving their valour in the Crimean war. They fought in only one action. This was the battle of Chernaya on 16 August, when one Piedmontese division supported the French in resisting a Russian attempt to relieve Sebastopol. It fought well enough, but the extent of its contribution to the battle can be judged from the casualty list: 160 Italians were wounded and 28 killed, compared with 1500 French and 8000 Russian killed or wounded. The victory gave Cavour a chance to extol his countrymen's valour, but in England the prince consort grumbled that the Piedmontese expeditionary force 'has not done a day's work in the trenches, and but for the 16th would not have heard a shot fired'.[26] It had faced, however, a more deadly enemy in cholera, from which 2000 Piedmontese soldiers died.

The end of the Crimean war in December 1855 was doubly disappointing to Cavour. He had wanted the Piedmontese army to have more chances of winning military glory, and it was exasperating that Austria, by actively intervening on the allied side at the last minute, had supplied the final blow which knocked Russia out of the war. In this way Austria, which had taken no part in the years of bitter fighting, had won a place at the peace congress in Paris where its influence would outweigh Piedmont's. However, Cavour's policy had at least earned Piedmont the right to sit down with the great powers at the peacemaking congress in Paris. Its new status was also indicated by the visits paid by Victor Emmanuel, accompanied by Cavour, to Queen Victoria and Napoleon III at the end of 1855.

Cavour may have felt some qualms at introducing his coarse and licentious sovereign into the rarefied atmosphere of Windsor Castle. In Piedmont the king's infidelities were well known; he had even installed his principal mistress Rosina, a former waitress and daughter of a drum-major, in a royal residence in the palace grounds. Such conduct would not have amused Queen Victoria, but fortunately Victor Emmanuel was on his best behaviour in England, and the queen was quite pleased with him. It was different in Paris: the permissive *ambiance* of the Second Empire went to the king's head, and many stories were told of his outrageous behaviour.* The visit was useful politically, since it enabled Cavour and Napoleon III to meet for the first time. The war of 1859 was foreshadowed by the emperor's remark to Cavour 'Write confidentially to Walewski [the French foreign minister] what you think I can do for Piedmont and Italy.'[27]

4

Cavour was in Paris again for the peace congress in February and March 1856. He had not intended to go. Azeglio had at first

---

* Victor-Emmanuel's conduct in Paris was described in a letter from the aged Countess Damremont to the French ambassador in Turkey, which can be found in Paléologue's *Cavour* (Paris, 1929). At court: '*Un jour, au cercle de l'Impératrice, le Roi va droit à Mme. de Malaret, la dame du palais, et lui dit: "Bonjour, madame, j'aime beaucoup les Françaises et, depuis mon séjour à Paris, je me suis aperçu qu'elles ne portaient pas des pantalons comme ceux de Turin. C'est le paradis ouvert!" ... Le salon entier fut pris d'hilarité.*' (*op. cit.*, p. 64.) And at the opera house with Napoleon III: '*Victor-Emmanuel fixait depuis quelque temps une petite danseuse. Se penchant vers l'Empereur, il lui demande: "Sire, combien coûterait cette petite fille?" "Je ne sais," répond l'Empereur, "demandez à Bacciochi." Le Roi, se retournant: "Combien coûterait cette enfant?" Bacciochi répond: "Sire, pour votre Majesté, ce serait cinq mille francs." "Ah, diable! c'est bien cher!" reprend le Roi. Alors, l'Empereur, s'adressant à Bacciochi, "Vous mettrez cela sur mon compte."* ' (*Op. cit.*, p. 65.)

agreed to be Piedmont's plenipotentiary, but he had then withdrawn and Cavour was left as the only possible representative.
He grimly told his friends that this would finish his political
career,[28] and on his return to Turin he was duly reproached for
having won no territory for Piedmont as a reward for its war
effort. But he had achieved something of even greater value. He
had completed the task begun by the great defeats of 1849. He
had put the Italian problem squarely before the statesmen and
peoples of Europe.

The arrangement of peace terms with Russia gave no opening
for any discussion of Italian affairs. It was only after the treaty
was signed that a supplementary session was devoted to discussing
the general European situation, and Italy was at last in the
picture. The session was notable for a strong attack by Lord
Clarendon, the British representative, on the evils of Roman
theocracy (which he described as 'a European scandal') and the
misgovernment of Naples and other Italian states. Cavour expounded Italy's grievances with great moderation. He made the
congress understand that there was a risk of further revolutions
in Italy unless the governments of several states were drastically
reformed, and it was implicit that this would involve the end of
Austrian influence in Italy. The Austrian representative was
unco-operative. He opposed any enlargement of Piedmont's
territory, and he flatly rejected the idea that Austria should give
up Lombardy-Venetia in return for territorial compensation in
the near east. All the same it became clear that Austria was left
isolated in its reactionary attitude to European problems. Even
Victor Emmanuel, who had threatened Cavour with dire penalites
if he did not bring back at least the duchies from Paris, was
sufficiently mollified to reward him with the collar of the
Annunziata.

Cavour made one startling move at the end of the peace
congress. He privately suggested to Lord Clarendon that Britain
should join Piedmont in an immediate war on Austria.

The usual explanation of this proposal is that Cavour had been
misled by the tone of Lord Clarendon's fiery speech during the
congress; his suggestion of immediate war has been described as
'probably the gravest political error of his career'.[29] But was

Cavour really deluding himself, or had Clarendon given him reason to believe that the project was feasible? Omodeo thinks that in their private talks in Paris Lord Clarendon may have come for at least a moment under Cavour's spell. Possibly the heady atmosphere of the Second Empire, which had one kind of effect on Victor Emmanuel, may have had a different effect on the sober English statesman; in a city redolent of plots and intrigues he may well have dreamed of a war to rescue Italy which seemed utterly unthinkable in the staid surroundings of the British foreign office.[30] Whatever grounds Cavour may have had for thinking that England would help Italy against Austria, a brief visit to London convinced him that Palmerston would have nothing to do with such a plan.

Feminine influence played a curious part in Franco-Italian relations at this time. The dazzling countess of Castiglione, an eighteen-year-old, golden-haired Piedmontese who had been called 'the most beautiful woman in Europe', had come to Paris with her husband at the end of 1855 and was soon introduced into the court life of the Second Empire. By the end of January 1856 she had the distinction of being singled out for conversation with the emperor at a Tuileries ball.

The countess was a distant cousin of Cavour, who must have noticed her social success when he came to Paris for the peace congress. No doubt he had also heard that she had no objection to deceiving her husband. It occurred to him that if her friendship with the emperor could be developed, she would have many opportunities of asking him to help the Italian cause. He therefore gave her a diplomatic 'mission': she was to flirt with, and if necessary seduce, the emperor. On 25 February Cavour wrote to Cibrario, his deputy in the Piedmontese foreign office, saying that the countess had begun her mission discreetly at a Tuileries concert and that he had promised to get her father a post at the St Petersburg embassy if she succeeded.

Virginia Castiglione ('Nicchia' to her friends) did all that Cavour had asked. She became Napoleon's mistress and was a guest at his Compiègne house-party two years running. (Her will requested that she should be buried in her 'Compiègne nightdress of 1857'.) What is not known, and never will be, is how far the emperor's attitude towards Italy was influenced by his prolonged intimacy with this seductive Italian girl.*

Cavour's 'mission' for Virginia Castiglione was probably a diverting break in his Paris routine. A far more significant result of his visit was the contact he established with Daniele Manin, the leader of the Italian exiles in Paris and a close friend of Marquis Giorgio Pallavicino, an ardent Italian nationalist who lived in Turin. Cavour felt that he needed as much Italian support as possible for his future work. He knew that Mazzini was too staunchly republican to be a possible ally, but he hoped that the Parisian group, though largely Mazzinian in origin, might be willing to take a more pragmatic line for the good of Italy.

He had good grounds for his hope, since Manin had publicly stated that he was ready to waive his republican principles on condition that Italy would become one great united kingdom. This statement was made in his message to Victor Emmanuel II which appeared in the republican press on 19 September 1855. In formally announcing his conditional support of Piedmont, Manin then said: 'If regenerated Italy must have a king, there

---

* Italian historians tend to ignore this curious episode, or to dismiss it, like Franco Valsecchi, by saying that 'the affair with the beautiful Nicchia was nothing more for the emperor than *un'avventura d'alcova*'. This is surely underrating an affair which lasted the best part of two years. On the other hand, the French writer Alain Decaux, using the countess's private and revealing diary, has built it up into an elaborate plot by Cavour and Victor Emmanuel, who are supposed to have sent the girl to Paris expressly to become Napoleon's mistress. This seems unlikely, and is certainly not proved by the known fact that Victor Emmanuel visited the countess alone in her home on two occasions before she went to Paris. Cavour's involvement in the assignment is definitely established by his letter to Cibrario on 25 February 1856: '*Vi avverto che ho arruolato nelle file della diplomazia la bellissima contessa di Castiglione, invitandola a* coqueter *ed a sedurre, ove d'uopo, l'Imperatore; gli ho promesso che ove riesce avrei richiesto pel suo padre il posto del Segretario a San Pietroburgo. Essa ha cominciato discretamente la sua parte al concerto delle Tuileries d'ieri.*' ('I inform you that I have enrolled the very beautiful countess of Castiglione in the ranks of diplomacy, and have invited her to flirt with and seduce, if necessary, the emperor; I have promised her that if she succeeds I will ask for her father to be given the post of secretary at St Petersburg. She began her role discreetly at yesterday's Tuileries concert.') (Catalano, Moscati, Valsecchi: *L'Italia nel Risorgimento del 1789 al 1870*, p. 679; Decaux: *La Castiglione, Dame de Coeur de l'Europe*, chaps. V–X; Camillo di Cavour: *Cavour e l'Inghilterra*, II, p. 108.)

must be only one, and that one the king of Piedmont ... Convinced that before everything else we must make Italy, as that is the principal question, superior to all others, it [the republican party] says to the house of Savoy: "Make Italy and I am with you. If not, not." '[31]

Cavour was satisfied with his first approach to the exiles, though he found them a little Utopian. After a talk with Manin he wrote to Rattazzi, saying that Manin had spoken about '*l'unità d'Italia ed altre corbellerie*' (the unity of Italy and other nonsense). The phrase shows that at that time Cavour had little interest in Italian unification, and it thus contradicts a statement he is reported to have made later in the year to Giuseppe La Farina, a Sicilian who had formerly been Mazzini's agent in Paris and had joined forces with Manin and Pallavicino after the peace congress. In a newspaper article written in 1862 La Farina described an interview he claimed to have had with Cavour in Turin on 12 September 1856, and alleged that Cavour had said to him: '*Ho fede che l'Italia diventerà uno Stato solo, e che avrà Roma per sua capitale*' (I have faith that Italy will become a single state, and that it will have Rome for its capital).[32] But there are doubtful points about La Farina's assertion, and it is probably safer to rely on the letter to Rattazzi, which implies that Cavour had not yet advanced beyond the idea of a greater Piedmont which would include all northern and possibly part of central Italy.*

What is certain, however, is that from 1856 onwards the Italians in Paris and their collaborators in Italy became an integral part of Cavour's plans. In 1857 they formed themselves

---

* La Farina's statement is critically examined by Raymond Grew in *A Sterner Plan for National Unity: the Italian National Society in the Risorgimento* (Princeton, 1963). He points out that in September 1856 La Farina was not yet a prominent figure in the Manin–Pallavicino movement, and that the National Society, which was supposed to have been mentioned in the interview, was not founded until the following year. It seems unlikely that the two men met on the date given by La Farina; possibly they met in September 1857, but we have only La Farina's word for Cavour's remark about Italian unity. In Grew's opinion, 'What a writer of La Farina's skill writes about Cavour, six months after his death, in the effort to make a political point about something else, is inadequate evidence on which to interpret an important element in Cavour's policy.' (*Op. cit.*, p. 114.)

into the Italian National Society, with Pallavicino as president and La Farina, who had become their most prominent spokesman, as secretary. (Manin died in the same year.) The society's declared aims were unity and independence, but its outlook was entirely un-Mazzinian, since it saw the Risorgimento more as a political change than as a moral and social revolution. It was both a pressure group and an active political organization which included both monarchists and republicans; it became, says Omodeo, 'the secret instrument by which Cavour acted upon the different Italian states'.[33] A new and important member was Garibaldi, who had come back from the United States and had bought an estate on the small island of Caprera. He was elected vice-president in December 1857, and remained with the society (later as honorary president) until he resigned at the end of 1859 after quarrels with La Farina and others.

5

In some ways it seemed that the development of the Risorgimento had now passed entirely out of Mazzini's hands. Cavour had clearly become the architect of Italy's future, and Mazzini could hardly compete with one who controlled the military and financial affairs of a great Italian state. Yet Mazzini still counted in the making of Italy. Though he had nothing to do with the National Society it owed him nearly all its philosophy. His final conspiracies failed like the earlier ones, but they continued to warn Cavour that he must give Italy an acceptable alternative to revolution.

In the year which followed the Milan disaster of 1853 Mazzini induced Orsini to lead two attempted risings in Carrara – one in September 1853, the other in March 1854. The aim was to get the Carrarese to rise, and then extend the rising through Modena to the Papal States, as a first step to setting all Italy free. Both ventures failed through lack of local support. After the first attempt Orsini was taken prisoner, tried and sentenced to exile; on the second occasion he was able to escape capture.

By 1856 Mazzini had a new reason for fostering insurrection in Italy. He had grounds for believing that Napoleon III had his own plan for reshaping Italy and that this envisaged the division of the country into three kingdoms – upper Italy (an enlarged

Piedmont), central Italy (of which Prince Napoleon, son of the ex-king of Westphalia, would be king) and Naples and Sicily (where Lucien Murat, son of ex-king Joachim, would sit on the throne instead of the Bourbon Ferdinand II). The surviving Murattists warmly supported the emperor's plan, but Mazzini saw that it meant Italian subordination to France, so that there could never be a true rebirth of Italy. Mazzini decided to strike before Napoleon's plan could be put into operation.

In preparation for new revolutionary outbreaks he spent some time secretly in Genoa in the early summer of 1856, though he was still under sentence of death in Piedmont. One of his fellow-workers there was a young English girl, Jessie White, the red-haired daughter of a Gosport yacht-builder, who had thrown herself heart and soul into the Italian revolutionary cause and was more Mazzinian than Mazzini himself. ('She is very absolute in her opinions,' Mazzini once commented.)[34]

The plan which he had in mind was for simultaneous risings in Sicily, Genoa and Leghorn, with the object of foiling the plot for a Murattist restoration; and two enthusiasts were ready and eager to lead an insurrection in Sicily and the Neapolitan provinces. They were Carlo Pisacane, a Neapolitan duke who had been head of the war committee of the Roman republic, and Rosolino Pilo, a young Sicilian nobleman.

Naples, rather than Sicily, was finally chosen for Pisacane's landing, since Mazzini's chief Neapolitan agent had told him that the kingdom was ripe for revolution and an armed expedition from outside would be enough to start it. Mazzini, who had returned to London, passed on the news to Pisacane at Genoa, but it was not until June 1857 that the expedition was ready to set out. In the meantime Jessie White, who was again in Genoa, this time as foreign correspondent of the *Daily News*, had tried to persuade Garibaldi to lead it, but he had coolly replied that he was not the man to lead an expedition for which he saw no hope of success.*

---

* A further reason for Garibaldi's refusal may have been that he did not like Pisacane. They had had several clashes in the days of the Roman republic, when Garibaldi had favoured a military dictatorship and Pisacane had opposed it. (Gramsci, *Il Risorgimento*, p. 162.)

Garibaldi's assessment of the expedition's chances was correct. As Joachim Murat and the Bandiera brothers had found, Neapolitan peasantry were unwilling to rise in support of would-be liberators. Yet that was an essential part of the programme. 'We individuals, whatever we do, cannot create the insurrection of a people; we can only create the occasion for it,' Mazzini had written to Pisacane earlier in the year. But the people did not want the occasion. The agent's report that Naples was ripe for revolt had been no more than idle gossip.

Elaborate arrangements were made. Pisacane and twenty-five followers sailed from Genoa in the postal steamer *Cagliari*, which they hijacked an hour after it had left port. It was intended that they should join up with Pilo, who had gone ahead with boats bearing arms and ammunition; but they missed each other, and Pilo took no part in the landing. On his way to Calabria Pisacane put in at the island of Ponza, where he released some hundreds of political prisoners. Many of these joined the expedition, and he had more than 300 men when he landed at Sapri, on the Calabrian coast.

The Neapolitans made no response to their liberators' appearance, but Pisacane marched into the interior. At Padula he had his first encounter with Bourbon troops; thirty-five of his men were shot, about two-thirds deserted and he went on with only a hundred men. At Sanza they were set upon by militia and peasants who regarded them as brigands, and after a desperate battle all the invaders were killed or wounded and Pisacane shot himself. The survivors were tried at Salerno and sentenced to long terms of imprisonment.

Contemporary observers felt that this new disaster was another proof of the futility of Mazzini's tactics, but it had useful lessons which were noted by Garibaldi. In particular, it showed that no invasion was likely to succeed unless it had some kind of backing from Piedmont, even if this were no more than silent connivance.

Repercussions of the Pisacane affair were felt in England for several months. The crew of the *Cagliari*, the vessel that Pisacane hijacked, were arrested and imprisoned in Naples; among them were two British engineers, and in view of the curious circumstances of the whole episode the British government took no action to secure their release. The men were still in jail when the whig government went out of office in February 1858, and it was left to Lord Malmesbury, the new foreign secretary, to complete the arrangements for setting them free. It was a complicated business, since it could never be clearly established that the Neapolitan government had had no right to arrest the two men. Malmesbury grumbled in April that 'out of seven English lawyers, three say the capture was legal, four illegal'.[35]

Nothing was achieved by the rest of Mazzini's 1857 plot. The project for action at Leghorn was unsuccessful: several conspirators were arrested, but it was noticeable that the grand duke did not receive any demonstrations of loyalty, which were usually made when he suppressed a revolt. At Genoa Mazzini tried to countermand the rising when he learned that the government was aware of it, but a few of his supporters did not receive the new instructions, and hopefully began an attempt to seize the city on 29 June. There was a short skirmish between troops and revolutionaries at Fort Diamante, and thereafter the rising collapsed. Mazzini remained in hiding for a short time, and then returned to England. He was fortunate not to be caught, for the police began a thorough round-up of likely conspirators. Among those arrested on suspicion was the English girl Jessie White, who was kept in jail until she was tried and released in October.

There was a general feeling in Piedmont that such conspiracies should no longer be allowed to happen. Azeglio, who was temporarily out of politics, wrote to a friend: 'This silly and wicked scrimmage in Genoa has made everyone lose patience with those who made it and with those who should have foreseen and prevented it.'[36] Cavour was equally indignant, and wrote to Villamarina, the Piedmontese minister in Paris, saying that he would like to hang Mazzini; but since the letter was meant to be shown to the French government it may not have represented his real views.[37]

Once again Mazzini seemed to have made a sorry hash of things. He was depressed by his failure, and James Stansfeld, with whom he stayed at Hastings on his return to England, found him greatly changed. 'He has aged terribly, he is ill, inconsolable, on account of the death of Pisacane, whom we all loved,' Stansfeld wrote to Jessie White in her Genoa jail.[38]

Though Mazzinian methods were becoming more and more discredited in the eyes of the world, their justification was that they were helping to keep alive the spirit of popular initiative. In a letter written a few months after the Pisacane tragedy, Mazzini commented: 'The Piedmontese monarchy, even if it wished, could not assume the initiative. An established government, in league with others, dominated by monarchical traditions, cannot spontaneously and openly approve insurrection. Insurrection can come only from the people'.[39] This was true as far as it went, and all that Mazzini did to preserve the popular initiative was well worth while. What he did not foresee was the interplay between this initiative and government action which was soon to be a decisive factor in the Risorgimento.

THE FRENCH ALLIANCE

*Orsini and Napoleon   Meeting at Plombières   Prelude to
action   The second war of independence   Villafranca
Annexations*

SINCE the Crimean war and the Paris peace congress Cavour had
known that Napoleon III might be willing to help Piedmont to
drive the Austrians out of the Italian peninsula. At the beginning
of 1858 a violent incident brought the emperor closer to Italy.
This was Felice Orsini's attempt to assassinate him.

Orsini was the notorious conspirator who had done good
service to the Roman republic and had been involved in some of
Mazzini's plots. The project of an attempt on the emperor's life
had been suggested to him in London, probably at the end of 1856,
and he had kept it in mind throughout the following year.
Mazzini was not directly concerned with it, but he knew what
was afoot and gave it his general approval. 'The execution of the
attempt against Napoleon is a vital thing for the country,' he
wrote to one of his supporters. 'Almost the whole matter is bound
up with it.'[1]

The plot was held up for some months while Orsini offered
his services to Cavour for the task of driving foreign oppressors
out of Italy; but Cavour took no notice of the offer and Orsini
decided to go ahead with the assassination. It was arranged that
three other conspirators – Pieri, Gomez and Rudio – should go
to Paris with him and share the attempt. All four of them went
to France in January 1858, armed with five powerful bombs, four
pistols and a poniard. *The Times* said afterwards that they were
armed 'not so much for a murder as for a field-day'.[2]

It seems strange that Orsini, as a champion of Italian independence, should have sought to remove the very man whom
Cavour saw as a friend of Italy; but his republican sentiments

convinced him that independence could never be won by an alliance with imperial France. He believed, too, that the emperor had allied himself with Austria to destroy Italy, and he considered that Napoleon's death was necessary for Italy's salvation. As Orsini saw it, a people's government would take over in France if the emperor were removed; this government would bring home the French troops which had been in Rome since 1849, thus taking away one of the strongest props of the pope's temporal rule, and would send an army to Italy to assist in driving out the Austrians. This was the reasoning which led Orsini and his fellow-conspirators to hurl their bombs at the emperor's carriage as he arrived at the Paris opera house on 14 January for a performance of *William Tell*.

The explosions were massive, but the emperor and empress escaped unhurt. The police, the cavalry escort and the bystanders were less fortunate; casualties treated after the incident numbered 156, including thirteen out of the twenty-eight lancers and thirty-one policemen. No one was killed outright, but an American merchant and a boy of thirteen were among the eight people who died of their wounds. Orsini and two other conspirators were arrested. It was soon known that Orsini was the moving spirit of the attempt, and his trial was regarded as the great event of the year.

The proceedings were highly unorthodox. Orsini explained that he had resolved to kill Napoleon III because he had become convinced that the emperor would never do anything for Italy. He freely admitted his guilt, and his counsel, Jules Favre, confined his defence to a skilful attempt to win sympathy for the self-confessed criminal. Both court and public were taken aback when Favre read aloud a letter which Orsini had written in prison to Napoleon III. In this letter Orsini disclaimed all hope of pardon, but appealed for French help for Italy. 'Remember', it ended, 'that so long as Italy is not independent, the peace of Europe and your Majesty is but an empty dream. May your Majesty not reject the words of a patriot on the steps of the scaffold! Set my country free, and the blessings of twenty-five million people will follow you everywhere and for ever.'[3]

The origin and authorship of this astonishing letter, which

should never have been read in open court in a criminal case, are a matter of some interest. Its style suggests that Jules Favre had a big share in drafting it, but the encouragement to Orsini to write it seems to have come from the emperor himself, who sent the chief of police, Pietri, to see Orsini in prison. Probably Napoleon asked for it to be written as a kind of insurance against further attempts on his life by Italian revolutionaries. He may have thought that they would be more likely to leave him in peace if one of their leaders had publicly acclaimed him as a sovereign who might help Italy.

To make the point still clearer, Orsini, no doubt on Pietri's prompting, wrote a further letter to the emperor, saying explicitly: 'May my compatriots put far from their counsels all trust in assassination, and learn from the words of a dying patriot that their redemption must consist in their self-denial and unity, and in the practice of true virtue.' (To make sure that Italians read these letters, they were both published, at the emperor's request, in the *Gazzetta Piemontese*.)[4]

Even Favre's superb advocacy could not save Orsini from execution. Nor could the pleas of Napoleon's wife, the Empress Eugénie, who had been deeply moved by Orsini's dignity in court and now asked the emperor to pardon his would-be assassin. But Napoleon's ministers felt that mercy for Orsini would encourage revolutionaries in France, and pardon was refused.

Orsini's plot and execution had the important effect of strengthening Napoleon's wish to help Italy. The Empress Eugénie, looking back on the incident in her old age, said it was at this time that Napoleon 'resolved, in his innermost consciousness, on the Italian war'.[5]

Cavour used Orsini's attempt as a means of further discrediting Mazzini. In an address to the chamber on 16 April he called Mazzini 'the chief of the assassins', spoke of the use of 'the Mazzinian dagger' and raised fears of an imminent attack on Victor Emmanuel. The picture was over-lurid. Mazzini wrote a spirited answer, and roundly declared that regicide had no place in the programme of the republican party. This may have been literally true, but Mazzini's private approval of the attempt on Napoleon suggests that his official *démenti* was not entirely honest.

2

Orsini's appeal for help for Italy may have echoed in Napoleon's ears in July 1858 when he went to take the waters at the little spa of Plombières, in the Vosges. It was not only his health which had taken him there. He had also a rendezvous with Cavour.

Napoleon had several reasons for feeling that the time had come for him to take his part in an Italian war. In spite of his apparent *volte-face* when he opposed the Roman republic in 1849, he had never lost the old romantic attachment to Italy which led him to march with the Carbonari in 1831. He was afraid, too, that he was not yet free from the persecutions of the Mazzinians and other revolutionaries, and he hoped to disarm them by solving the Italian problem. Like Victor Emmanuel, he wanted military glory, and it gratified his vanity to think that he would be able to re-draw the map of Italy in accordance with his own wishes. Moreover, he had a political motive for needing a good war. A year earlier a Piedmontese special envoy in Paris had reported to Cavour: 'The emperor's prestige is getting lower every day . . . Unless I am completely mistaken, the emperor will be lost within two years if he cannot consolidate himself by a war which is popular in France.' War against Austria seemed the best possibility. It was an urgent matter for him to agree with Cavour on the right technique for starting it.

The idea of the rendezvous at Plombières was the emperor's. Cavour knew that this was a meeting he must keep secret, and he used a false passport for his journey to France. In two meetings on a hot summer day the emperor and the minister made plans for an Italian war of liberation and a reshaping of the map of Italy.

Their first problem was to find a way in which Piedmont could make war on Austria, and France could come to its assistance, without making it appear that Piedmont and France were the aggressors. Their solution was ingenious. In the first instance Cavour was to arrange secretly that the people of Massa, which was part of the Austrian-protected duchy of Modena, should make an appeal for annexation to Piedmont because of their hardships under Modenese rule. The Piedmontese government would very properly refuse the appeal, but at the same time it would warn the duke of Modena that he must reform the administration of Massa. The duke would certainly decline to do so; Piedmont would then occupy Massa at the inhabitants' request, Austria would back up Modena and declare war on Piedmont, and France would come to Piedmont's rescue. Thus the war of liberation would begin, with Austria clearly shown as the aggressor.

Assuming, as the two plotters were happy to assume, that France and Piedmont won the war, their next task was to plan the future of Italy. This would be a federation on lines recalling the proposals of Gioberti and Balbo. Austria would be expelled from the peninsula, which could then be reorganized as four states – a kingdom of upper Italy, including Piedmont, Lombardy-Venetia, Romagna and the legations, and the whole 'valley of the Po', which would take in the duchies of Parma and Modena; a kingdom of central Italy, consisting of Tuscany and the central provinces of the Papal States, to be ruled over (Cavour suggested) by the Bourbon duchess of Parma; the papal territory, now reduced to Rome itself and its surrounding province of Lazio; and while the kingdom of the Two Sicilies would not be immediately affected it was hoped that Ferdinand would retire to Austria before long, and then Napoleon could carry out his cherished plan of giving the throne of Naples to Lucien Murat. The whole plan was a long way short of genuine Italian unity, but at least it guaranteed Italy complete independence of Austrian rule.[6]

France, however, would expect its price for its help to Piedmont. Napoleon asked for the cession of Nice and Savoy. Cavour was hesitant. Savoy, on the French side of the Alps, was more French than Italian, in spite of its long connexion with Piedmont, and its cession seemed fairly reasonable. But Nice at that time was a completely Italian town, and was actually the birthplace of the national hero, Garibaldi. Its cession was harder to swallow, but in the end Cavour agreed that the price should be paid.

Another agreement reached by Napoleon and Cavour at Plombières was for the marriage of Princess Maria Clotilde, Victor Emmanuel's eldest daughter, to Napoleon III's rakish and middle-aged cousin, Prince Napoleon,* who was also a possible candidate for the central Italian throne. This would forge a pleasant dynastic link between Italy and France.

Clotilde was only fifteen. Later generations may be shocked at the callousness with which Napoleon and Cavour proposed to sacrifice a young girl's happiness for their own purposes, but marriages to repulsive husbands for reasons of state were still one of the occupational risks of princesses in the middle of the nineteenth century. In fact, the Piedmontese royal family was much distressed by Cavour's proposal, and Victor Emmanuel left the final decision to Clotilde herself, a religious, energetic, self-possessed and extremely attractive girl. After due reflection she felt that it was her duty to further her country's interests by marrying Prince Napoleon.

The marriage took place on 30 January 1859. It was the first part of the secret Plombières agreement to be carried into effect. Much of the general plan devised at Plombières was overtaken by the course of events, but the central understanding between Piedmont and France was firmly established. Cavour had found the foreign ally he needed for the liberation of Italy. Napoleon III was personally committed to the assistance of Piedmont in the war of liberation, though Cavour and King Victor Emmanuel were to have some black moments before the emperor could bring himself to honour his pledge.

3

The opening of 1859 gave public signs of how far the rulers of France and Piedmont had gone in their determination to solve the Italian problem through war with Austria. At the New Year's diplomatic reception in Paris Napoleon made a pregnant remark

* The prince, who was nicknamed Plon-plon, was very similar in appearance to Napoleon I, and for all his dubious past had a shrewd understanding of affairs of state. He had fought in the Crimean war with the rank of general, but his reputation suffered a severe blow when he withdrew from the campaign, allegedly on account of ill-health, at the beginning of winter. Thereafter the wits changed his nickname from Plon-plon to Craint-plomb. The famous actress Rachel had been one of his many mistresses, and it was at least a sign of constancy that he visited her on her death-bed. (F. A. Simpson, *Louis-Napoleon and Recovery*, pp. 270–1; Philip Guedalla, *The Second Empire*, p. 225.)

to the Austrian ambassador. 'I regret,' he said, 'that our relations with your government are not as good as they were in the past; but I pray you to tell the emperor that my personal feelings for him have not changed.' A few days later, in opening parliament at Turin on 10 January, Victor Emmanuel declared: 'While we respect treaties we cannot be insensible to the cry of anguish (*grido di dolore*) that comes to us from many parts of Italy.'

The implications of these two statements were clear. Early in February the French emperor's intentions were made still plainer in an anonymous pamphlet published in Paris under the title, *Napoleon III and Italy*. The pamphlet, which was understood to have been inspired by Napoleon himself, and was actually written by his friend Viscount de La Guéronnière, pictured a federal Italy without Austrian *immixtion*. One sentence was considered to have particular significance: 'Napoleon I thought he must conquer peoples to free them; Napoleon III wishes to free them without conquering them.'

It seemed at first that Napoleon had overplayed his hand in sponsoring this provocative pamphlet. In France it was condemned by both politicians and generals, and prices slumped on the Bourse. Walewski, the foreign minister, complained to the emperor: 'The effect of the brochure is detestable. The day when your Majesty lets it be known that your policy no longer rests on the maintenance of treaties, on that day you will have the whole world against you'.[7] In England Lord Malmesbury saw it as a virtual declaration of war. 'The truth is', he wrote in his journal, 'that he [Napoleon] is determined to go to war with Austria to propitiate the Italians and to save his own life from assassination.'[8]

Malmesbury was right, but he did not know all the facts. On 18 January – a fortnight before the offending pamphlet was published – Napoleon had made a secret politico-military treaty with Piedmont. It had been signed in Turin by Cavour and General Alfonso La Marmora, for Piedmont, and by General Niel and Prince Napoleon, who had come to Italy to make arrangements for his wedding, for France.

Yet even at this stage Napoleon's determination to make war was not as great as Cavour and Victor Emmanuel would have wished. A French marshal who saw Napoleon at the end of January noted afterwards: 'Our conversation would indicate that if the emperor has had the idea of making war, he is beginning to feel the necessity of renouncing his plan.' And in March, after news of his treaty with Piedmont had become known, a note was published in the official *Moniteur*, on the emperor's instructions, disclaiming the warlike intentions of which he was being accused. The note observed that Napoleon had done no more than promise the king of Piedmont to defend him against any Austrian aggression.

It was true that one purpose of the Plombières meeting was to find a way of provoking Austrian aggression, but Cavour was beginning to fear that the emperor might go back on his word. He knew that Walewski was against the war and appeared to be backed by French public opinion; other governments were alarmed, and there were rumours of an Anglo-Austrian-Prussian ultimatum to France. Yet if the emperor withdrew, Piedmont could not fight Austria alone, and the national disappointment would play into the hands of Mazzini and the revolutionaries. Victor Emmanuel was furious. 'That dog the emperor is laughing in our face,' he said. 'He is a swine.'[9]

But the preparations for war went on. The Piedmontese army was mobilized, and Garibaldi, whom Charles Albert had brushed aside in 1848, was summoned to Turin and invited to lead a brigade of *cacciatori delle Alpi* (hunters of the Alps). The invitation served a double purpose: besides enlisting Garibaldi's military talents in the coming war, it was a gesture of conciliation to the political left, and was thus a counterblast to a recent 'Declaration to the Italians', signed by Mazzini and a hundred others, which advised Italians to take no part in a war sponsored and directed by 'L. N. Bonaparte'. Garibaldi was given the rank of general in the Piedmontese army and was asked to have his men ready for action after only a few days' training. This was an outrageous request, but Garibaldi agreed to it, and boasted that he could make a soldier in a fortnight.[10] His boast was justified by his men's achievements.

Cavour's alliance with the National Society had useful results at this time. Through its agents in the various Italian states it encouraged volunteers to come to Piedmont and raised funds to pay their expenses. In three months it brought nearly 20,000 volunteers to Turin, and 5000 of these were accepted for the Piedmontese army.

The world could now see that Piedmont was getting ready to fight, and the governments of Britain, Prussia and Russia anxiously considered the calling of an international congress to deal with Italian problems. One of the conditions of holding a congress was to be the voluntary disarmament of Piedmont. Cavour was in despair. The powers' demand would have wrecked his plans. But at the very moment when there seemed no alternative to accepting it, Austria saved the situation for Piedmont. On 23 April an Austrian ultimatum, demanding Piedmontese disarmament within three days, was presented at Turin.

Cavour could have hoped for nothing better. The elaborate Plombières scheme involving Massa and the duke of Modena could go by the board. Austria had voluntarily taken up the role of aggressor. The Piedmontese cabinet had no hesitation in rejecting the ultimatum. Before meeting the Austrian envoys Cavour asked the chamber of deputies to grant full powers to the king. As he left the chamber he observed prophetically: 'I leave the last sitting of the Piedmontese parliament. The next I attend will be the parliament of the kingdom of Italy.'[11]

4

The second war of independence had important political effects on Piedmont's neighbours. Tuscany, indeed, was stirred to action even before the first Austrian soldier had crossed the Ticino, and the rebellion was so smooth and expeditious that an Englishwoman in Florence was able to comment: 'We have made at Florence a revolution with rose-water. Since yesterday a dynasty has been, *not* overturned, but calmly put aside; an entire change of national policy effected; a provisional government appointed.'[12]

This Tuscan revolution of 27 April, which peacefully ejected Grand Duke Leopold II by means of a liberal *coup d'état* and an army mutiny, had been planned for many months by Marquis Ferdinando Bartolommei, Tuscan representative of the National Society, in association with democratic leaders, though the

ground had really been prepared for forty years by Vieusseux
and others concerned with Tuscany's cultural development. Its
great significance was that Tuscany's new leaders were guided
by the vision of a single Italy in which Tuscany would be merged.
Napoleon III's idea of forming Italy into four states was thus
rejected before it could be tried, and Italian unity was made
virtually certain. Prompted by Carlo Boncompagni, the Piedmontese representative at Florence, the provisional government
decided to join Piedmont and France in the war against Austria.

On the day of the Tuscan revolution Massa rose against the
duke of Modena, thus spontaneously (but quite unnecessarily)
providing the *casus belli* that Napoleon had imagined at Plombières. The duke of Modena retained the rest of his duchy until
the defeat of the Austrians at Magenta produced further upheavals
in central Italy.

Austria's declaration of war had ended Napoleon's hesitations.
France was obliged to honour its treaty with Piedmont, and
preparations were made for sending one part of the French army
overland by the Mont Cenis route, while the other part went by
sea to Genoa. The French forces employed in the war numbered
120,000, but it was Piedmont's well-trained army of 60,000 men
which faced the Austrians alone until the French arrived.

This was a less onerous task than might have been feared. The
first Austrian troops crossed the Ticino on 29 April with the
intention of marching on Turin; but heavy rains held up their
advance, which was further hampered by dissension between the
Austrian commander and his chief of staff over their first objective.
Giulay, the commanding general, favoured Turin; Kuhn, the
chief of staff, wanted to cross the Po and deal first with the
defensive triangle formed by Alessandria, Valenza and Casale.
Several days were wasted in a reconnaissance of the Po position,
and it was only on 7 May that the Austrians really decided to
march on Turin. This lapse of ten days since the expiry of the
ultimatum on 27 April was of great value to Piedmont. By 9 May
four French army corps were already in Italy. The chance of a
triumphal Austrian entry into Turin had virtually disappeared.

On 12 May Napoleon landed at Genoa. Cannons boomed,
church bells pealed and excited crowds shouted their welcome as

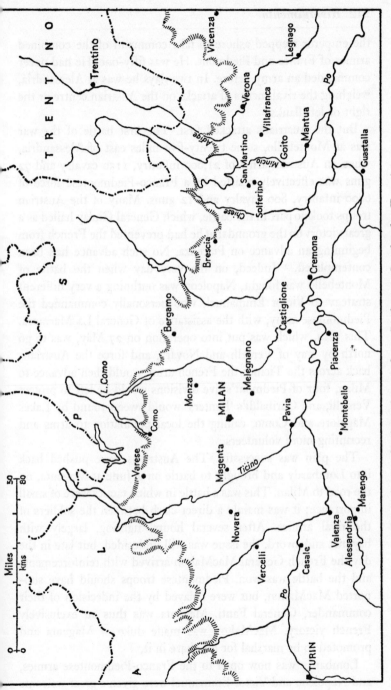

Second war of independence, 1859 : Piedmont, Lombardy, Trentino

the emperor stepped ashore to take command of the combined armies of France and Piedmont. He was fifty-one. He had never commanded an army before. In two days he was at Alessandria, weighing the rival merits of attacks on the Austrian centre or the right or left flanks.

But the Austrians attacked first. The first battle of the war was at Montebello, some twenty-five miles east of Alessandria, when an Austrian army of 21,000 infantry, 1150 cavalry and 72 guns was effectively resisted by a Franco-Piedmontese force of 6800 infantry, 800 cavalry and 12 guns. Many of the Austrian troops took no part in the battle, which General Giulay hailed as a great victory on the ground that he had prevented the French from beginning an advance on Piacenza. No such advance had been contemplated.[13] Indeed, on the very day when the battle of Montebello was fought, Napoleon was outlining a very different strategy to Victor Emmanuel, who personally commanded the Piedmontese army, with the assistance of General La Marmora. This plan, which was put into operation on 27 May, was to go north by way of Vercelli and Novara, and force the Austrians back across the Ticino; the French army would then advance to Milan, four of Piedmont's five divisions would be left to protect Vercelli, and Garibaldi's 'hunters' would sweep round by Lakes Maggiore and Como, calling the local population to arms and recruiting more volunteers.

The plan was successful. The Austrians were pushed back into Lombardy and brought to battle on 4 June at Magenta, on the road to Milan. This was a battle in which tactics were of small importance; it was mainly a direct clash between the soldiers of the rival armies. After several hours' fighting, largely with bayonet and sword, the issue was still undecided, but late in the day the French General MacMahon arrived with reinforcements and the battle was won. Piedmontese troops should have supported MacMahon, but were delayed by the indecision of their commander, General Fanti. Magenta was thus an exclusively French victory. MacMahon was made duke of Magenta and promoted to be marshal for his share in it.

Lombardy was now open to the Franco-Piedmontese armies, and Napoleon and Victor Emmanuel were given a great welcome when they entered Milan on 8 June. In a proclamation to the Milanese people Napoleon urged them to put themselves 'under the flag of Victor Emmanuel'.

On the same day the retreating Austrians were attacked by the French at Melegnano. This was a minor action, in which the Austrians sacrificed their rearguard to allow the rest of the army to retreat in safety.

While the main French force had been on its way to Magenta Garibaldi's *cacciatori delle Alpi* had been carrying out their northern diversionary action with much success. Their biggest clash with the Austrians was at Varese, midway between Lakes Maggiore and Como, on 26 May. Here Garibaldi won a classic victory by holding the enemy's centre and counter-attacking on both flanks – an interesting example of his intuitive sense of tactics and his quickness in summing up military situations.[14] Garibaldi then made his headquarters at Varese and liberated Como from the Austrians; but after Magenta the *cacciatori* ceased to act independently and became a unit of the main Franco-Piedmontese army, in which they were always placed on the left flank. They had done useful work in the north, but can hardly have affected the general progress of the campaign.*

The Austrian defeats at Magenta and Melegnano had immediate effects in the duchies of Modena and Parma. The duke of Modena knew that he could not keep his throne without

---

* It was on the eve of the battle of Varese that Garibaldi had a strange encounter which was to affect his personal life for twenty years. As he waited at Robarello, a young woman and a priest drove out from Como to see him. They asked him to liberate Como from the Austrians, and he promised to do so when he had finished his immediate operation. The young woman was Marchioness Giuseppina Raimondi. Garibaldi fell deeply in love with her, saw her again at Como and proposed marriage; she refused him because she was in love with an officer in the regular army. Towards the end of 1859 she changed her mind, and Garibaldi married her in the private chapel of the Raimondis' house at Fino on 24 January 1860. After the ceremony an anonymous note was put into his hand, saying that Giuseppina still loved another. Garibaldi challenged her, and she admitted that she had a lover. Garibaldi then left her for ever. In the 1870s he was desperately anxious to marry Francesca Armosino, by whom he had two children, Manlio and Clelia; but it was not until January 1880 that his marriage to Giuseppina Raimondi was annulled, leaving him free to marry Francesca at last. (Curatulo, *Garibaldi e Le Donne*, pp. 295–301.)

Austrian protection, which was now withdrawn; he appointed a regency to govern during his absence and left for Mantua. On 14 June a provisional government took over the powers of the regency and proclaimed the annexation of Modena to Piedmont. In view of Modena's Austrian connexions Victor Emmanuel agreed to assume control. Luigi Zini was sent to the former duchy as royal commissioner, and soon afterwards the resolute and experienced Luigi Carlo Farini was appointed governor.

The duchess of Parma, who had preserved an uneasy neutrality while war raged on Parma's borders, also withdrew from her duchy after the battle of Magenta. Here too a provisional government asked for annexation to Piedmont, and Piacenza followed the same course when the Austrian garrison left for the front.

Austrian troops were also withdrawn from Romagna, Umbria and the Marches, in spite of an urgent plea by Cardinal Antonelli to the young Austrian Emperor Francis Joseph that they should be allowed to stay there. Their departure was followed by risings in Bologna, Ravenna, Perugia and other towns, and the papal legates fled. Most of the risings were bloodless. An exception was Perugia, to which Antonelli sent a papal army of 4000 Swiss mercenaries, under the command of Colonel Schmidt, to suppress the rising.

The insurgents gave in to Colonel Schmidt after three hours' fighting, but his mercenaries' savage behaviour brought much discredit to the Papal States. Odo Russell, a British diplomat in close touch with the Vatican, wrote to Lord Malmesbury:

> I regret to inform your lordship that the papal soldiers after entering the town acted with cruel ferocity. They shot everyone they could find and entering private houses pillaged and murdered their peaceful inmates, including old men and helpless women, nine of whom were mothers ... A highly respectable American family (Mr Perkins of Boston with his wife, mother, sister and niece) were dining at the Hotel de France in Perugia at the time of the invasion and saw the innkeeper and a waiter murdered by the soldiers under their own eyes.[15]

Antonelli defended the papal troops on the ground that the Perugians had fired on them from the windows of houses, but few in Italy or elsewhere felt that this was a satisfactory excuse for the soldiery's brutal excesses. But Schmidt had done his job. Perugia was quiet, and all Umbria and the Marches remained under papal rule for more than a year.

The revolts in Romagna proved rather an embarrassment to Cavour and Victor Emmanuel. A central government for the four legations was formed in Bologna, and one of its first acts was to invite Victor Emmanuel to become dictator of Romagna. But the annexation of part of the Papal States at that time would have raised grave diplomatic difficulties. Victor Emmanuel preferred to temporize, and a Romagnol delegation was sent away without a definite answer.

In Lombardy the Austrians continued to retreat after the battle of Melegnano; their aim was to join up with the substantial reinforcements which were being massed in Venetia behind the Mincio, and then to counter-attack. By 15 June the entire Austrian army had crossed the Chiese, the last river before the Mincio. The French and Piedmontese, who were three days' march behind them, followed without excessive haste.

A French air reconnaissance preceded the resumption of action. M. Godard, a French balloonist, was sent by the emperor to Marshal MacMahon at Castiglione, in the hope that he would be able to provide useful information about the enemy's movements. M. Godard duly ascended, but there was nothing to be seen from the air except three Austrian horsemen near the village of Pozzolengo.* Even this scanty information seemed to be useful, for it confirmed MacMahon's belief that the enemy had retired behind the Mincio.

The Austrians had, indeed, crossed the Mincio, and had even considered a further retreat to the Adige. But their plans were changed, owing to a mistaken report that big French reinforcements were on their way by sea to the Adriatic. Fearing that he might be caught between two fires the Austrian General Hess decided to re-cross the Mincio and face the French and Piedmontese between the two rivers, Mincio and Chiese.

---

* This was not the first air reconnaissance in military history. Arrivabene says that a similar reconnaissance was made for the army of the Sambre-et-Meuse in the battle of Ligny in 1815. (*Italy under Victor Emmanuel*, I, p. 159.)

In joining battle on 24 June the French had no idea that the whole Austrian army had come back to meet them. They thought they would be dealing only with rearguard detachments which the Austrians might have left behind as a cover. They soon found that they were engaged in something very much bigger than a rearguard action.

The battle of Solferino was the biggest clash between armed forces since Napoleon I's defeat at Leipzig. In all, some 260,000 men were engaged in it, and the struggle for the two villages of Solferino and San Martino was conducted largely at bayonet-point, since the crack Austrian riflemen were repeatedly over-whelmed by the charging French infantry. '*Il semblait que le vent nous eût poussés*,' said a young French infantryman, to illustrate the enthusiasm with which he and his comrades had thrown themselves into the fight.[16]

Napoleon's plan of action was to pierce the Austrian centre and capture Solferino. The Austrians tried to break through the French right, while on their own right they were facing a sturdy Piedmontese attack (led by Victor Emmanuel himself) on San Martino. The French right stood firm, but the Austrian centre broke and let the French through. Heavy rains fell in the evening; when they ceased, the Austrians were seen to be in full retreat to the Mincio.

It was a humiliating defeat for them, for at first the French were not prepared for a full-scale battle, and the Austrians should have been able to take advantage of the poor deployment of the French forces. In the end they were lucky to be allowed to retreat without serious pursuit. This was because of the indecisive tactics of Marshal Canrobert, who threw away his chance of cutting off the retreat of the Austrian left.

If Solferino was a great victory for the French and Piedmontese, it was also a costly one. Casualties were heavy on both sides. The killed or wounded included 3 field-marshals, 9 generals, 1566 officers (630 Austrian, 936 Franco-Piedmontese) and 40,000 other ranks; and in the following days almost as many were laid low by typhus or died of fever. The battlefield told its own grim story on the morning after Solferino. The whole area was covered with dead bodies of men and horses; many of the corpses had already been robbed of their boots by Lombard peasants. Everywhere, too, were haggard and shattered wounded, still waiting for attention and suffering from hunger and thirst; owing to lack of transport it took three days before they could all be taken to Castiglione en route for improvised hospital accommodation at Brescia or Milan.

The terrible scenes of the battle and its aftermath made a deep impression on Napoleon III. They also horrified a young Swiss stretcher-bearer called Henry Dunant. It was the lack of proper care for the wounded at Solferino which led Dunant to take the initiative for the foundation of the Red Cross a few years later.

5

After Solferino there could be no doubt that France and Piedmont were winning the war. The Austrians had not been annihilated, but they were on the run. Piedmont could now look forward to the early liberation of Venetia, so that the whole of northern Italy would be free. Two days after the battle Cavour and Constantino Nigra, his friend and secretary, had a long talk with Napoleon and found him disgusted by the horrors of war but proud of the re-assertion of France's military glory. He said nothing to indicate that he had any intention of making peace before the Austrians were driven out of Italy.[17]

But many chastening influences were at work on Napoleon. His own health was suffering in the blazing Lombard summer; he was distressed by the heavy loss of French lives at Solferino and the many deaths caused by typhus. Moreover, the military situation was not so simple as it had seemed in the hour of triumph when the Austrians were retreating from Solferino. The enemy was now secure in the fortresses of the Quadrilateral; he calculated that he would need 300,000 men to attack or invest them, and after the army's losses he could not be sure of putting more than 100,000 men into the field.

He had also to think of French public opinion. At the moment France was delighted with his military success; the empress and her son, the prince imperial, were pelted with flowers when they drove back from Notre Dame after attending a Te Deum for Solferino, and the military bands could hardly be heard for the cheers of the excited crowds.[18] But would they still cheer if more lives were lost in costly attacks on well-guarded fortresses? Certainly his political opponents, both Catholic and republican, would be quick to take advantage of any military failure.

This was not all. Germany, and particularly Prussia, was watching the attack on Austria with some suspicion. The Frankfort diet had ordered the mobilization of 350,000 men; the French troops left in France numbered little more than 50,000. In Paris Empress Eugénie was alarmed. 'The language of Prussia and the armaments of the German confederation became so threatening,' she said in later years, 'that I begged my husband to think now only of France, and to make peace at once . . . We could not let France be overrun to satisfy the unbounded ambitions of the Italian people.'[19]

Finally, the realignment of Italy was disturbing. Napoleon had said that he would free Italy from the Alps to the Adriatic, but this had implied the formation of a kingdom of northern Italy as one of several Italian states. That was not how things were working out. The demands of Tuscany, Romagna, Modena and Parma for annexation to Piedmont were pointing towards the creation of one vast Italian state of north and central Italy, which might grow larger at the expense of the Papal States or the Two Sicilies.[20] Even Napoleon's romantic attachment to the Italians could not make him view with complacency the emergence of a new great power on the French frontier.

It is easy to understand how the arguments against continuing the war must have seemed overwhelming to Napoleon. Without informing his Piedmontese allies, he decided to demand an interview with Emperor Francis Joseph of Austria.

The two emperors met at Villafranca, half-way between Verona and Valeggio, on 11 July. Everything was settled in less than an hour. Francis Joseph agreed to give up Lombardy, apart from the two fortresses of Peschiera and Mantua; it would be handed over to France, who could then present it to Piedmont. Austria was to keep Venetia, and the rulers of Modena and Tuscany were to be restored to their thrones. The two emperors proposed that an Italian confederation should be created under the honorary presidency of the pope, and that Venetia, though an

Austrian province, should be one of the Italian federal states. They also decided to ask the pope to introduce reforms in the Papal States. No mention of Romagna or of Parma and Piacenza was made in the agreement, since neither emperor was directly concerned with these territories.[21]

The terms of the Villafranca agreement were very different from the plan which Cavour and Napoleon had devised at Plombières. The promise of independence was not fulfilled; Austria was still to occupy a substantial area of Italian territory. Cavour was furious when he read the text of the agreement; he advised Victor Emmanuel to reject it and continue the war. But the king saw things more clearly on this occasion. He realized that the peace must be accepted, since Piedmont could not fight Austria on its own.

Cavour was not convinced. It was widely reported that he was so offensive to the king that he was dismissed from the royal presence after a stormy two hours. In the end Cavour decided to resign his post of prime minister, rather than have any share in ratifying an agreement which had been drawn up without the knowledge or participation of himself or Victor Emmanuel. *'Torneremo a conspirare'* ('we shall go back to conspiracy'), he said bitterly to a friend.

Italian patriots shared Cavour's opinion that they had been betrayed by Napoleon. Ten years earlier he had destroyed the Roman republic. Now he had stabbed Piedmont in the back. Pictures of Orsini, Napoleon's would-be assassin, suddenly appeared in every shop window in Turin.[22] Posters giving the terms of the agreement were torn down from the walls in Florence; a whole edition of the Tuscan *Monitore*, in which the terms were published, was burnt by an angry mob.[23] Odo Russell reported from Rome that 'the announcement of peace has created a most painful impression on the minds of the Roman population. They think their cause abandoned by France.'[24]

This was the end of the second war of independence. Yet its results were not so unsatisfactory for Italy as they seemed at the time. Napoleon had not done all that he had promised, but it was thanks to his help that Piedmont had begun the expansion that was soon to lead to the establishment of the kingdom of Italy.

The first move was the annexation of Lombardy as Piedmont's spoils of war. There was no plebiscite, the Lombards were not invited to say what sort of government they wanted; their laws and administrative system were simply replaced by the Piedmontese laws and administrative system. At the same time Piedmontese royal commissioners stayed in Parma, Bologna and Florence.

Indeed, all the contemporary indignation at Napoleon's 'betrayal' cannot hide the fact that the Italian situation was greatly improved by the war of 1859 and the revolts which accompanied it. The Piedmontese monarchy was now directly involved in the work of Italian liberation. Even Mazzini felt obliged to assume 'an attitude of active, if mistrustful, co-operation'.[25]

This attitude was expressed on 20 September in an 'open letter' he addressed to Victor Emmanuel from Florence, where he stayed for a few months after the war. In this letter he reiterated his faith in the popular initiative, and he reproached Victor Emmanuel for not having made use of it. 'You have not made brothers of the people of Italy,' he wrote, 'nor have you asked them to make a brother of you . . . You have refused the arms of our people, and have called in . . . the arms of a foreign tyrant.' Yet he still believed that Victor Emmanuel might put himself at the head of a national revolution, and he appealed to the king to do so. 'You spoke of independence and Italy gave you 50,000 volunteers,' he wrote. 'Speak of liberty and unity and it will give you 500,000.' If the king would take this step Mazzini, republican though he was, was ready 'to cry with my brothers of the common fatherland, "President or king, God's blessing be upon you, and upon the nation for which you have dared and conquered." '[26]

6

Mazzini's stay in Florence coincided with the post-war crisis over the future government of central Italy. The territories which had revolted against their former rulers were still going their own ways. Yet the Villafranca agreement had declared that the grand duke of Tuscany and the duke of Modena should return to their thrones. It was already clear that this was unlikely to happen. The austere Baron Ricasoli had become the virtual dictator of Tuscany. He was pressing with all his strength for fusion with Piedmont, but only as a first step to membership of a new and united Italy. General La Marmora, who had succeeded Cavour as prime minister, was unwilling to annex Tuscany in contravention of the Villafranca agreement; but his advice to the Tuscans to bring back the grand duke on the best terms they could get was bluntly rejected by Ricasoli. 'Tell General La Marmora', he wrote to his brother, 'that I have torn his letter into a thousand pieces.'[27]

On 16 August the Tuscan assembly voted unanimously that the former dynasty was totally incapable of ruling in Tuscany. Four days later it asserted 'the firm intention of Tuscany to make part of a strong Italian kingdom under the constitutional sceptre of Victor Emmanuel'. But this vote was ineffective until the policy of union with Piedmont was accepted by Piedmont itself. Ricasoli was ready to wait, though rather impatiently, until that moment came.

Another strong man, Farini, was holding equally firm in Modena and Parma. His post of governor had been terminated, but he had returned to Modena as an ordinary citizen and had been appointed dictator by the unanimous vote of the Modenese parliament. Here too the Tuscan pattern was followed – unanimous votes for annexation to Piedmont and reluctance in Turin to accept the proffered territories. Bologna also had a dictator from Piedmont, General Cipriani, and its assembly passed a similarly ineffective measure in favour of annexation to Piedmont. In November the three areas – Romagna, Parma and Modena – were joined together under Farini's dictatorship with the territorial name of Emilia.

Though the union of northern and central Italy under King Victor Emmanuel was foreshadowed by these developments, the Piedmontese government was unwilling to take action in defiance of the great powers. The terms of the Villafranca agreement were confirmed in a treaty signed at Zürich, and any further annexations by Piedmont would have been contrary to the treaty. Napoleon had invited the powers to discuss Italy's problem at a congress, but it seemed unlikely that such a congress would sanction a partial unification of Italy.

Fortunately for Piedmont and Italy, the congress was never held, for Napoleon had begun to realize that he could get better results for France by direct negotiations with Piedmont. Since he had not freed Italy 'from the Alps to the Adriatic' he had not yet demanded the cession of Nice and Savoy, which was the agreed price for France's help in the war. He now felt it would be a fair bargain to offer Piedmont a free hand in central Italy in exchange for the two provinces. Since he had no hope that the other powers would agree to such a deal, he decided that in one way or another the congress must be called off.[28]

He returned to his old ploy of expressing his views in an anonymous pamphlet. This was *The Pope and the Congress*, published in December 1859 and written, like the previous pamphlets, by the Viscount de La Guéronnière. It was sympathetic towards Italian nationalism, but hostile to the pope's temporal power. It suggested that the pope should not only be ready to sacrifice Romagna, but should even surrender all the outlying papal provinces and confine his temporal power to Rome and its neighbourhood.

The pamphlet was well received in northern and central Italy. In Florence, where a couple of English girls were sent home at Christmas for distributing leaflets denouncing Ricasoli's government, another Englishwoman noted: 'The effect produced by the pamphlet on every class of Florentines has been well-nigh as broadly marked, even to the eye of a casual stroller through the city, as was that of the numbing fear-stroke of Villafranca in July last ... The whole town wears a certain jaunty, self-congratulating air.'[29]

In contrast, the pamphlet caused great indignation at the Vatican. Pius IX was unwilling to give up Romagna or any other part of the Papal States; he regarded them all as part of the Church's patrimony. He had already asked Victor Emmanuel to speak at the projected congress in favour of the return of the legations to papal rule, and he was angered at the French pamphlet's proposals. When he first read them he could not believe that they represented the emperor's opinions, and on New Year's Day he told the commander of the French garrison in Rome that he was sure the emperor would condemn the pamphlet.

A letter from Napoleon himself soon disillusioned the pope. 'If the Holy Father,' the emperor wrote, 'for the peace of Europe, will renounce his claim to these provinces, which for fifty years have caused embarrassment to his government, and in exchange demand from the powers a guarantee for the remainder, I do not doubt the immediate return of order.'[30] Napoleon had shown his hand. In his anger the pope threatened to excommunicate him, but was dissuaded by Cardinal Antonelli.[31] Instead he took the action that Napoleon had expected. He refused to be represented at the congress.

As a great Catholic power, Austria also took offence at the pamphlet, and asked for an assurance that the views expressed in it would not be proposed or supported by France. When Napoleon refused to give such an assurance, Austria also declined to attend the congress. In view of these two refusals the congress was cancelled. The field was clear for Napoleon's secret negotiations with Piedmont.

The handling of these negotiations was greatly simplified by Cavour's return to power. After resigning from the government he had gone to Switzerland and then to his estate at Leri, where he kept in close telegraphic contact with the men controlling events in central Italy. His temporary withdrawal from office was a sound tactical move, since it had shown him to be an uncompromising champion of Italian freedom. In his retirement he had come to understand that the peace of Villafranca was really a blessing in disguise, since its very imperfections opened the way to new and wider plans.

For some months Cavour made no move against General La Marmora's ministry, but towards the end of the year he became impatient with the hesitations of government policy and prepared to return to active politics. The threat was enough. Cavour's opposition in the chamber would have paralysed the government. La Marmora tactfully resigned.

It was a difficult moment for Victor Emmanuel. In spite of his long co-operation with Cavour he did not want him back as prime minister. They had not only quarrelled about Villafranca, but there was also a personal issue between them. In the winter of 1858–9, after his wife's death, the king had been anxious to marry his mistress Rosina. Cavour had strongly opposed the marriage, and had especially annoyed the king by suggesting that Rosina was unfaithful to him. The marriage did not take place, but the incident rankled with the king, even though Cavour had promised never to speak to him about Rosina again. This promise may have helped the king to overcome his rancour when his retiring ministers assured him that 'the current was running for Cavour'. Cavour was sent for, and on 20 January 1860 he was again president of the Piedmontese council.

His first task was to negotiate with Napoleon. It was agreed that Piedmont should annex Tuscany and Emilia (Modena, Parma and Romagna) in exchange for the cession of Nice and Savoy to France. Ricasoli, the Tuscan leader, argued that there was no need to hold plebiscites, since the respective assemblies had voted for annexation; but he was overruled, and plebiscites were held in both territories on 11–12 March. The results, which were announced on 15 March, gave huge majorities in favour of annexation to 'Victor Emmanuel's kingdom'. In Emilia there were 426,006 ayes against 1506 noes, and in Tuscany, out of 534,000 registered electors, 366,571 voted for annexation and 14,925 for a separate Tuscan state. No doubt the Tuscan abstentions included a number of people who still supported the grand duke, but a two-thirds majority of all on the electoral roll was quite enough to determine Tuscany's future. This was Ricasoli's greatest triumph, the outcome of many months of patient work for unity. The plebiscites as a whole had the effect of providing 'a popular investiture of the monarchy'.[32]

Now Napoleon's price had to be paid. The treaty for the cession of Nice and Savoy to France was signed on 24 March, and here too the people were asked to express their views in a plebiscite. Both areas realized that their most viable future lay with their French neighbours. In Nice there were 25,743 ayes, 260 noes and 4743 abstentions; in Savoy, 130,533 ayes, 235 noes and 4610 abstentions.

So the bargain with Napoleon was completed. The new parliament which was opened in Turin in April was, as Cavour had prophesied, an Italian parliament. Though there were bitter complaints about the loss of Piedmontese territory – not least

*Victor Emmanuel II, king of Piedmont, 1848–1861, king of
united Italy, 1861–1878*

Orsini's attempt to assassinate Napoleon III, 1858

Napoleon III visiting the wounded at Montebello, 1859

from Garibaldi, whose birthplace was now a French city – Cavour was able to convince the chamber that the advantages of uniting so large a part of Italy far outweighed the unfortunate territorial losses.

With his personal triumph in the Italian chamber of deputies Cavour had brilliantly completed the first stage of the making of Italy, and had done so without provoking any action by the great powers. Napoleon had tried till the last minute to delay the annexation of Tuscany, which he still envisaged as part of a central Italian kingdom, but he had acquiesced in face of the overwhelming popular vote, and there was no break between Piedmont and France. Because the alliance held, Austria too had to accept the annexations and to give up all hope of replacing the grand duke of Tuscany and the duke of Modena on their thrones. This was a sharp setback to Austrian policy: Tuscany, governed by a junior branch of the imperial dynasty, had been Austria's advanced post in Italy, and its fusion with Piedmont implied the virtual collapse of Austrian influence in the peninsula. Among other powers Britain had watched Italian developments with some disquiet. An Italian living in England noted in his diary: 'Lord John Russell is still very sore on the question of Nice and Savoy. He says it is now impossible to trust Cavour any longer.'[33] But these were personal feelings. There was no question of British intervention in Italy.

The era of change had begun, and the cession of Nice and Savoy was as significant for the history of Italy as the annexation of Tuscany and Emilia. This cession, as Rosario Romeo points out, brought the old Piedmont to an end. With its outposts surrendered, the vigorous sub-Alpine kingdom was no longer the guardian of the Alps, and Turin itself was militarily indefensible. A monarchist historian ruefully proclaimed in the chamber of deputies: '*Finis Pedemontii !*'[34]

The change in Piedmont's position was itself a reason why the building of a new Italy, preferably with Rome as its capital, was now essential. The first big move had been made by governmental initiative. It was now the turn of the revolutionaries. In mid-April 1860 Garibaldi and his Thousand were on their way to Sicily.

Part III

1860–1870

GARIBALDI

*The Sailing of the Thousand   The conquest of Sicily
Occupation of Naples Invasion of the Papal States King
and dictator*

ALEXANDRE DUMAS the elder tells a curious story of a visit he
paid to Garibaldi in Turin on 4 January 1860. Garibaldi admired
Dumas's novels, Dumas had written a book about the Italian
Legion's exploits in South America, but the two men had never
met before. If Dumas's account of their first meeting can be
believed, he asked Garibaldi to note the exact day and hour
of his visit, and then declared: 'Within a year you will be
dictator.'[1]

Dumas was not strictly correct. A year after their meeting
Garibaldi had been, but had ceased to be, a dictator. But if the
prophecy was really made it showed considerable insight on
Dumas' part, for at that time Garibaldi had no plans which were
likely to make it come true. He was, it is true, a national figure;
his beard, his red shirt and his imposing figure were known all
over the world; but his latest fighting had been in the service of
Victor Emmanuel and in the conventional blue uniform of a
Piedmontese general. There was little, apart from his flamboyant
character, to indicate that he might soon resume his career as a
soldier of fortune. Indeed, his private life may have seemed more
important to him than public affairs at the time of Dumas's visit,
for he was then awaiting his disastrous wedding to Giuseppina
Raimondi, which took place later in January.

The year 1859 had been an eventful one for him. The reputation
he had won in South America and in the defence of Rome had
been enhanced by his successful handling of his *cacciatori delle
Alpi* in the battle of Varese, and he had been chosen for further
duties in central Italy after the peace of Villafranca. In August he

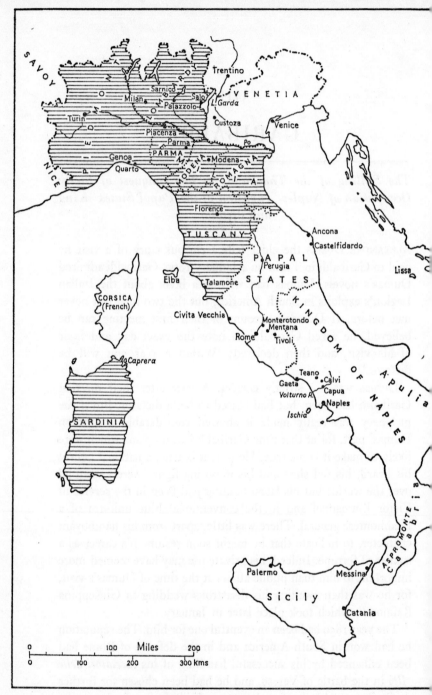

First annexations: 'Victor Emmanuel's kingdom' (shaded) in April 1860

went to Florence, where he was greeted with public demonstrations and cries of '*Viva Gallibardi*', which was as near as the Tuscan lower classes could get to his name. As second-in-command to General Fanti in the combined army of the central Italian states, he was expected to encourage the plan for the annexation of Tuscany to Piedmont, but Victor Emmanuel called him back to Turin when it was learnt that he was himself planning to invade Umbria, in the Papal States, in support of an expected rising. This would have been an entirely premature move, which neither Victor Emmanuel nor his ministers could have approved at that time.

After brief visits to his fiancée's family and his own home on the island of Caprera, Garibaldi returned to Turin at the end of the year, and was responsible for launching a Million Rifles Fund with government sanction. It was a fine patriotic gesture, and though the fund never reached its ambitious target it raised the quite considerable sum of 1,500,000 lire.

At this time Garibaldi had a long talk with Victor Emmanuel, who took a great liking to the frank and impetuous revolutionary. The king spoke without reserve, and his caustic remarks about Cavour may have given Garibaldi the dangerous impression that the king did not care overmuch about the niceties of diplomacy. Almost certainly Garibaldi came away from the interview with the mistaken belief that Victor Emmanuel would support him in any action for Italy's good, even if it involved the sacrifice of constitutional government.[2]

In the meantime others were making plans for which, in due course, they would look to Garibaldi for leadership. The so-called party of action was beginning to exert its influence on the course of political and military events.

The party of action was not a parliamentary party, and though most of its members were Mazzinians or ex-Mazzinians it had no direct link with Mazzini. It was a radical and revolutionary pressure group, which was prepared to accept the monarchy instead of a republic if Victor Emmanuel would take action for the making of a free and united Italy. Garibaldi was its nominal leader, but Francesco Crispi, Agostino Bertani and Nicola Fabrizi were its most active politicians and organizers.

The name of Crispi is significant. This future prime minister of Italy was then a man of forty. He was a Sicilian lawyer and journalist; in exile he had become one of Mazzini's closest friends, and the party of action was much influenced by his knowledge of southern Italian affairs. A secret visit to Sicily in 1859 in a disguise of mutton-chop whiskers and thick blue spectacles convinced him that there was real hope of a popular revolution there, and that the south was a more promising field of action than Rome or Venice. A further argument for early action in the south was the fear that, if nothing was done there, Napoleon III might go back to his old plan of putting Lucien Murat on the throne of Naples. A Murattist restoration would have complicated the whole Italian position.

While Crispi's influence was one of the decisive factors in the launching of Garibaldi's expedition, it should not be forgotten that the whole venture was inspired by Mazzini and that it was, in fact, 'Mazzini's gift to the party of action'. Though he was not a member of the party, his correspondence shows that the expedition was the culmination of his thirty years of conspiracy. He had visualized the whole affair, even down to the number of men needed, for Garibaldi's Thousand was roughly equivalent to the battalion suggested by Mazzini.[3] Traced to its source, the sailing of the Thousand was due to Mazzinian initiative, and is thus the conclusive answer to those who say that the great conspirator should have stopped plotting after the fall of the Roman republic.

In 1860 Sicily was certainly in the mood for insurrection. Opposition to Bourbon rule could be found at all levels of society. In the upper classes many were thinking seriously of Italian unity under the king of Piedmont; the younger aristocrats had borrowed from central Italy the ingenious toast of '*Viva Verdi!*' – an apparent tribute to the great composer which was a play on the letters in his name, so that it really meant '*Viva V(ittorio) E(manuele) R(e) D'I(talia)*.'[4] In Palermo much of the secret activity was directed by Baron Giovanni Riso, who allowed his house to be used as a store for arms and ammunition, but students and other radical elements were also showing signs of unrest. Finally, the peasantry and the working classes were dissatisfied with their miserable standard of living and were ready to support any movement that might bring them social betterment.[5] It was clearly a promising situation, if advantage could be taken of it.

The party of action's objective, which had also Mazzini's approval, was a popular rising in Sicily, which would be supported by an expeditionary force from the north, led by Garibaldi. Crispi and Rosolino Pilo, the Sicilian exile who had been involved in the Pisacane affair, were to be responsible for arousing the Sicilians. On 2 March Mazzini made his own contribution by sending a stirring message to Sicily. 'What are you waiting for?' he asked. 'Dare, and you will be followed. But dare in the name of national unity. Garibaldi is bound to come to your assistance.'[6]

Mazzini was speaking without authority. At that time Garibaldi had not decided to lead the expedition. He was deeply incensed at the cession of Nice and Savoy, and he was ready for violent action of one kind or another; but he had not yet accepted the Sicilian plan. While Garibaldi hesitated, volunteers for an expedition began to assemble near Genoa early in April. It was arranged that Pilo should go in advance to Sicily to promote an insurrection. But Palermo had risen before he arrived.

The Palermo rising on 4 April was intended to be both popular and aristocratic. Its popular wing was led by Francesco Riso, a plumber, while the aristocratic leader was the baron of the same surname. But the noblemen failed to rise at the appointed time; the insurrection was begun by Riso the plumber and seventeen other workmen, who found that troops were waiting for them as soon as they came out of Riso's workshop near La Gancia monastery. The rebels had no chance; it was all over in an hour or two; and those who were not killed in the skirmish were shot by a firing squad a few days later. But though the Bourbon troops were easily able to suppress the insurrection in Palermo itself, they could not check the many minor outbreaks which occurred in the countryside, and even as far away as Messina. These outbreaks were more of a peasant revolt than the politically inspired revolution desired by Mazzini, and the simultaneous activities of brigands and gang leaders were not inspired by any worthy ideal.

This was the explosive situation which met Rosolino Pilo when he landed near Messina on 10 April. He eagerly seized his chance of helping to keep the revolution alive, and he told all the villages on the way to Palermo that Garibaldi was coming. With this encouragement the rebels held fast and waited for their leader.

Pilo was taking a risk, for when he had left for Sicily Garibaldi had still not made up his mind. The news from Palermo turned the scale. When Crispi told him what had happened he went to see the king and asked to be given a brigade of the Piedmontese army to support the rising and liberate Sicily. Victor Emmanuel consulted Cavour, but the request was refused, partly, at least, because Cavour feared that Garibaldi might lead his men against the Papal States instead of Sicily, with disastrous consequences for Piedmont's foreign policy. It was at that moment that Garibaldi finally decided to go to Sicily with a volunteer expeditionary force.

The assembly of the volunteers at Quarto, about three miles from Genoa, was an open secret. Garibaldi's first plan was to go to Sicily as soon as he could with 200 men, but owing to delays in obtaining arms he waited until he had enrolled 1000 volunteers. Among them were 200 members of the other nationalist movement, the anti-Mazzinian National Society, whose secretary, La Farina, was in close touch with Cavour. The leader of this group of volunteers was Giuseppe La Masa, who had made several tentative plans for Sicilian expeditions in earlier years. He was actually intending to go to Sicily with his own followers in 1860 and La Farina had promised to give him arms, ammunition and transport; but it now seemed wiser to amalgamate La Masa's expedition with Garibaldi's. La Farina's offer of help was also transferred to Garibaldi, who was in great difficulty because Azeglio, then governor of Milan, refused to allow him to draw rifles from the store accumulated there by the Million Rifles Fund; so the thousand rifles and five cases of ammunition with which the expedition sailed were all provided by the National Society, which also contributed eight thousand lire in cash. The modesty of the cash subsidy suggests that it came from the society's own funds and was not a secret gift from the Piedmontese government.

Garibaldi's famous Thousand were actually more than that

number. They sailed from Quarto in two ships on the night of 5–6 May 1860, and a small party was detached to land in the Papal States; but there were still 1089 men who landed at Marsala, in Sicily, on 11 May. They were a cross-section of the Italian middle and lower classes. About half were workmen. There were also 150 lawyers, 100 doctors and a mixed lot of authors, journalists, artists, sculptors, civil servants, merchant navy captains, engineers, chemists, business men, university lecturers and students. Most of the volunteers came from the north, but there were 100 Sicilians and Neapolitans and 11 Romans. The only woman in either of the vessels was Crispi's mistress, who is said to have served as cook and washerwoman, presumably with some assistance from the male volunteers.

One of the hotly debated points about the sailing of the Thousand is that of Cavour's attitude to it. Officially he was against it, but it is sometimes suggested that this was only a façade. According to this view he secretly connived at Garibaldi's venture and should be given some of the credit for it. It is even claimed that by this time he had fully accepted the idea of Italian unification and was already planning his own invasion of the Papal States.

This theory, which is put forward in many studies of the Risorgimento, is not borne out by the facts.* There was no alliance, either open or secret, between Cavour and Garibaldi. La Farina helped the expedition on his own initiative as secretary of the National Society, and not as Cavour's secret agent. Cavour's personal correspondence shows that, in all the circumstances, he felt that the government's only course was to stand back and await events.

'Garibaldi has landed in Sicily,' he wrote to Ricasoli on 16 May. 'It is very lucky that he did not execute his intentions of

* The legend of Cavour's secret support of Garibaldi's venture and complete conversion to the idea of Italian unity is examined and refuted by Denis Mack Smith in his article, 'Cavour's Attitude to Garibaldi's Expedition to Sicily' (*Cambridge Historical Journal*, Vol. IX, 1949). Historical revision, he comments, is showing 'that among Cavour's objectives there did not figure the unification of Italy if the price to be paid for it included either upsetting the monarchy or ending the dominant position of Piedmont in the peninsula.' (*Op. cit.*, p. 361.)

attacking the pope. We cannot stop him from making war on the king of Naples. It may be a good thing or a bad thing, but it was inevitable. Had we tried to restrain Garibaldi, he would have become most dangerous within the country.'[7]

And again to Colonel Cugia in Bologna on 17 May: 'Garibaldi's expedition is a most serious matter. Nevertheless, I believe that we neither could nor should have prevented it. It was openly favoured by England and weakly opposed by France. Many of our most devoted friends supported it. Should I have put myself in opposition to them? It would have been a mistake which would have created the greatest difficulties in the country.'[8] He was slightly more positive when he wrote to the prince of Carignano on 18 May: 'We must help them without compromising ourselves', but it is clear that he had no intention of either actively supporting or hindering Garibaldi's expedition, and was simply keeping a watchful eye on its progress.

Cavour had also to bear in mind King Victor Emmanuel's affection for Garibaldi. The swashbuckling king was fascinated by the great adventurer's patriotism and audacity, and he was resolutely opposed to any action that might have held up the expedition. In its early stages the Piedmontese navy could have stopped it without difficulty, but Cavour's orders to Admiral Persano and other naval commanders were that they should interfere only if Garibaldi showed signs of departing from his original plan of landing in Sicily and threatened to attack the Papal States. Since the king approved of the expedition, Cavour could not openly oppose it, though he sent a number of private messengers to Quarto who tried to dissuade Garibaldi from sailing.

One reason why Cavour could not possibly have connived at Garibaldi's venture was that he had no wish at that time to involve Piedmont in war with Naples. He had no particular fondness for Francis II, who had succeeded to the throne of the Two Sicilies in 1859, for Francis had refused to join in the war against Austria and had ignored all suggestions that he should reform his government in the interests of national independence. But although his obduracy in these matters had lost him Piedmont's sympathy, Cavour thought that it would be unwise to

create a Neapolitan crisis before the recently annexed territories
had settled down under their new regime.

There did not, however, seem to be much danger of such a
crisis when the expedition set sail, for Cavour, as Bertani revealed
later, was quite certain that it would fail. He was more concerned
with arrangements for the forthcoming general election, on which
his political future depended, than with wild-cat schemes for the
invasion of Sicily.

2

The sailing of the Thousand opened a new phase in the history
of the Risorgimento. The campaign to expel the foreigner was
now succeeded by civil war among Italians. Unity was not to be
achieved merely by driving out the Austrians. The time had come
for military action in which Italians would fight their fellow-
countrymen in the cause of national unity.

Early in the voyage to Sicily Garibaldi told his volunteers
that their battle-cry would be 'Italy and Victor Emmanuel'.
Most of them were prepared to follow his lead in accepting the
monarchy; the handful of hard-bitten republicans, who were
unwilling to go to Sicily on such terms, were used for a small
diversionary expedition to the Papal States under the dubious
leadership of Colonel Zambianchi, who was notorious for his
organization of bloodthirsty attacks on priests during the brief
life of the Roman republic. Zambianchi went ashore at Talamone,
on the Tuscan coast, with sixty volunteers, and was joined by
seventy-eight Tuscans from Leghorn. They entered the Papal
States and were at once attacked by papal gendarmes and driven
back into Tuscany, where Tuscan gendarmes arrested and disarmed them. The diversion was over.

Failure in this minor raid was unimportant. What mattered
was to make a successful landing in Sicily. This was duly achieved
at Marsala on 11 May.

Luck was on Garibaldi's side. A strong body of Neapolitan
troops had recently been withdrawn from Marsala, and there
was no one to oppose the Thousand's landing. Two Neapolitan
warships approached during the disembarkation and fired a few
rounds at them; but the firing was ineffective, probably because

the commanders were afraid of hitting two British warships and some foreign merchant vessels which were then in the harbour.

From Marsala Garibaldi moved inland, and on 13 May, when most of the island still stretched before him, he proudly announced that he was assuming the dictatorship of Sicily in the name of Italy* and Victor Emmanuel II. He took the first step towards making this boast a reality when he encountered the Bourbon troops at Calatafimi on 15 May.

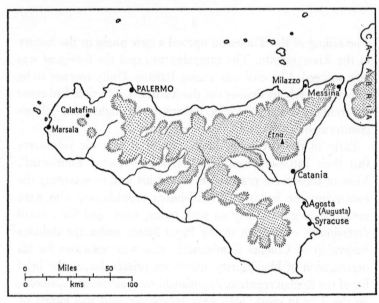

Sicily 1860

A detachment of young Sicilians had now joined the Thousand, and the combined force won a notable victory, largely with the bayonet. The Neapolitan troops were well trained and disciplined, but it is not surprising that they quailed before a ferocious attack led by a commander and senior officers wearing the red shirts made famous in Rome and South America and followed by a motley throng of volunteers of all ages, wearing everyday clothes. It was this Bourbon defeat which sent rumours about the 'red

---

* This was quite unintelligible to many Sicilians, who did not know what Italy meant. 'L'Italia, or rather la Talia, was for years thought by some to be the name of the king's wife.' (Mack Smith, *A History of Sicily*, III, p. 441.)

devils', who fought with bayonets, not with guns, flying all over Sicily. When Brancaccio di Carpino, a young Sicilian nobleman who was held as a political prisoner in Palermo, asked his gaoler why the Neapolitans did not shoot down the charging Garibaldini, he was answered: 'Signore, the Garibaldini, as you call them, are not men but devils, and bullets cannot penetrate their bodies.'[9]

The victory of Calatafimi was one of the decisive events of the Risorgimento. It gave proof that Garibaldi was in no danger of suffering the fate of Pisacane and the Bandiera brothers. In theory everything was against him. His small band of volunteers was opposed by 25,000 Neapolitan troops, supported by cavalry, artillery and gendarmerie; and these troops were well armed and well trained. But the Bourbon generals had no experience of irregular warfare, in which an invading force was given great assistance by local guerrilla bands; they 'were not prepared for a situation where the local people cut water supplies, destroyed the mills needed for grinding wheat, interrupted telegraph wires and killed any stragglers with the greatest ferocity'.[10] For the first time a southern landing was being enthusiastically backed up by the local inhabitants. The popular initiative of which Mazzini had dreamed for so long was at last in being.

It was all a triumph for Garibaldi. Evading the Bourbon forces which came out from Palermo to look for him, he marched on with an ever-increasing army, as thousands of Sicilian rebels hurried to join the volunteers. On 26 May he was at the gates of Palermo, where hundreds of citizens had risen against the government in expectation of his arrival. This time the battle was brief but sanguinary; again the Garibaldians could not be checked and they were able to take possession of most of the city, leaving the Bourbon troops isolated in the royal palace and its neighbourhood. After a few days the Neapolitan general decided to withdraw all his troops from Palermo. Garibaldi was master of the whole city.

With Palermo in his hands, Garibaldi had at once to take up the reins of government and to divide his time between the council chamber and the battlefield. On 9 June he set up a council of state, which passed a number of laws, some going back to the Sicilian revolution of 1848-9, others based on the current law of

Piedmont. At the same time he was incorporating fresh batches of volunteers into his army, for new expeditions began to leave Genoa within five weeks of his own sailing, culminating in large reinforcements in August which brought his numbers up to 20,000.

The first stages of this impressive build-up of Garibaldi's forces, which gave him the strength needed for the eventual conquest of all Sicily and most of the mainland territory of Naples, were mainly sponsored by the National Society. The society's existence in this crucial period is, indeed, an illustration of the precarious way in which Italy achieved unity; if the Thousand had sailed a few years earlier there would have been no strong organization ready to supervise an immediate supply of further volunteers and the expedition might have been forced to a halt. In 1860 the National Society was not only on the spot but was favoured by the government; it was thus able to arrange new expeditions until Bertani and the party of action were ready to take over the work by using the resources of the Million Rifles Fund. The August expeditions were almost entirely organized by Bertani.

It was at this time too that Garibaldi joined issue with Cavour on the question of annexing Sicily. The initiative was taken by Cavour, who sent La Farina to Sicily as his personal representative soon after the capture of Palermo. In some ways the choice of La Farina seemed obvious. He was a Sicilian by birth and had done much to help the Garibaldians. Yet he was the wrong man to send, for he and Garibaldi were not on good terms and the party of action still distrusted the National Society because of its alliance with Cavour.

Even after Garibaldi's unexpected success Cavour was not yet thinking of the unification of all Italy, but only of adding Sicily to Victor Emmanuel's kingdom. His plan was for a speedy annexation of the island, so that the great powers would be faced with a *fait accompli*; but his friend Nigra, who was then in Paris, warned him against being over-hasty. 'We must not show ourselves too hurried or too greedy,' he wrote on 6 June. 'Put your hands in your coat pockets and go and walk, smiling, under the arcades, and you will have Sicily, in spite of everything, even in spite of yourself.'[11] But Cavour was not sure that time was as much on his side as Nigra imagined. He felt it was important to get Sicily settled without delay. La Farina agreed with him, and showed his sympathies openly by starting a paper in Palermo called *L'Annessione* and putting up posters calling for annexation to Victor Emmanuel's kingdom.

Sooner or later annexation was inevitable, though Sicilian autonomists still hoped that their island might be given self-government. But when should annexation take place? Garibaldi and Crispi, who was the dictator's right-hand man in the island's administration, were firmly against the immediate action proposed by Cavour.

They had several reasons for preferring delay. They claimed that annexation could wait because the island already regarded itself as part of the kingdom of Italy, and they did not want to be bothered with a plebiscite while military operations were still in progress. And that was not all. They also wanted to use Sicily as a base for further action, which would include the conquest of Naples, Rome and Venice and the proclamation of a united Italy from the Capitol. They were afraid that Cavour would make the annexation of Sicily an excuse for closing the southern campaign, leaving Naples undisturbed and barring the road to Rome and Venice. Their views were shared by the Lombard nationalist, Cattaneo, who feared also that Cavour might sacrifice more Italian territory to France in exchange for the annexation of Sicily. 'To avoid all such claims by France,' Cattaneo wrote on 9 June to Alberto and Jessie White Mario (the former Jessie White, now married to a handsome Italian revolutionary), 'it is imperative that Sicily should remain free as long as possible ... We must make it the barracks and the arsenal for all that still remains to be done.'[12]

As the argument continued, Crispi became increasingly suspicious of La Farina's activities and accused him of encouraging hostility to Garibaldi. The finishing touch came when La Farina stated in the official Sicilian newspaper that the National Society had provided *all* the funds for Garibaldi's expedition. On 9 July Garibaldi had La Farina arrested and sent him back to Piedmont. He also asked Cavour to send a more acceptable politician,

Agostino Depretis, to take over the civil administration of Sicily. Cavour agreed, and Depretis, who was himself a future prime minister of Italy, was installed at Palermo as pro-dictator.

But Garibaldi had not yet completed his conquest of Sicily. His army was now enlarged by the new expeditions sent south by the National Society, and more volunteers were being collected by his own northern representative, Bertani. In this same month of July Garibaldi set out to seize Messina, which was still in the hands of the Bourbon army.

As they marched across the island the Garibaldians were accompanied by Alexandre Dumas, who was reporting the campaign for the Paris newspaper *La Presse* with the help of his nineteen-year-old mistress, Emilie Cordier ('the Admiral'), who sat on his knee and occasionally pinched him while he was writing.* Other new arrivals at Garibaldi's headquarters were Alberto and Jessie White Mario. Jessie had surprisingly transformed herself from revolutionary firebrand into hospital nurse and organizer, and is said to have looked after Garibaldi's wounded with the devotion of a second Florence Nightingale.

The decisive battle in this phase of the campaign was at Milazzo on 20 July, when the Garibaldians again routed the Bourbon army. But the victory was an expensive one, as the Garibaldians lost 755 dead or wounded, about one-fifth of their total force, while the beaten Neapolitans' casualties were no more

* Dumas, who was then fifty-seven, had left Marseilles for an eastern cruise in his schooner *Emma* on 9 May, but on reaching Genoa he had decided to follow Garibaldi to Palermo, where he was welcomed and lodged in a royal palace. Dumas's schooner party included one woman, the slim and attractive Emilie Cordier, who was soon to be the mother of his third recognized illegitimate child. Emilie was known on board as 'the Admiral' because she always wore her own version of naval uniform – a short jacket and trousers for day-time and a trouser suit in violet velvet with blue and gold lanyards for evenings. The presence of this exotic young female on the march from Palermo must have been something of a surprise to the Thousand. She was a lively girl. Brancaccio di Carpino, who was billeted with Dumas, Emilie and a number of Sicilian volunteers, mentions her 'unusual talent of being able to chop off a fly's head with a knife without injuring its body', an operation 'at which she was so expert that she never missed'. She would then drop the headless bodies in Dumas's wine when he was not looking. (Alexandre Dumas, *On Board the Emma*, p. 63; A. Craig Bell, *Alexandre Dumas*, p. 320; F. Brancaccio di Carpino, *The Fight for Freedom: Palermo, 1860*, pp. 188–9.)

than 162. One of the Sicilian volunteers felt that Garibaldi's heavy losses were inevitable, since the Neapolitans were fighting from prepared positions and were supported by artillery, while the Garibaldians had no artillery and had to attack the enemy's positions one after another. In the circumstances their success was remarkable, and it had the invaluable effect of cutting off Messina from all contact with the rest of the island.

Realizing that their position was hopeless, the Neapolitans surrendered the whole of Messina to the conquering invaders, with the single exception of the citadel, where a Bourbon garrison still held out. Since the Bourbons had now withdrawn from Syracuse and Agosta, all Sicily was Garibaldi's, except for this citadel. He was dictator in fact as well as in name.

3

Garibaldi's exploits had dazzled the world, and he had won particular admiration in liberal England. A Garibaldi committee was set up in London to raise funds for the volunteers and later to enlist Englishmen for 'an excursion to Sicily and Naples'; but though a British legion of more than 600 men was enrolled, it did not reach Italy until the fighting was nearly over. Another British effort was the Ladies' Garibaldi Fund, of which Jessie White Mario became the local representative in Naples a few weeks later. But while other countries watched Garibaldi's movements with pleasurable excitement the question of where he would go next was a matter of deep concern in Naples and Turin.

Francis II, the young king of the Two Sicilies, was definitely alarmed. When Garibaldi entered Palermo, Francis 'was seized with such a panic', as Odo Russell reported to his uncle Lord John, 'that he telegraphed five times in twenty-four hours for the pope's blessing', and 'Cardinal Antonelli, through whom the application had to be made, sent the last three blessings without reference to His Holiness, saying that he was duly authorized to do so.'[13] Subsequently, in a desperate effort to save his mainland territory and win back the Sicilians, he gave a statute to both Naples and Sicily, with an additional promise of considerable Sicilian autonomy; but this death-bed repentance had little effect on his rebellious citizens. Francis's kingdom was doomed.

Garibaldi was coming to Naples. Even a letter from Victor Emmanuel asking him not to cross the straits of Messina could not deter him from his appointed task.*

Cavour was thoroughly alarmed at the thought of Naples falling into Garibaldi's hands. Writing to Nigra on 1 August, he observed: 'If Garibaldi can pass to the mainland and take possession of Naples, he becomes the absolute master of the situation . . . King Victor Emmanuel loses almost all his prestige; in the eyes of the great majority of Italians he is no more than Garibaldi's friend . . . The king cannot take the crown of Italy from Garibaldi's hands; it would be too unsteady on his head.' With Garibaldi in Naples, the letter continued, the king's only course would be to attack the Quadrilateral, since the capture of Verona and Venice would cause Palermo and Milazzo to be forgotten. 'For a prince of the House of Savoy it is better to perish in war than in a revolution.'[14]

But the event which Cavour dreaded, the event which would make Garibaldi 'the absolute master of the situation', now seemed certain to happen. As a last hope Cavour tried to forestall him. By making contact with a venal Bourbon minister, Liborio Romano, and sending southern exiles to Naples as *agents provocateurs*, he made desperate efforts to promote a liberal revolution in the city before Garibaldi could reach it. But there was no revolution. Naples remained apathetic. Cavour could do no more.

---

* It has been suggested that Garibaldi did not take the king's orders seriously because he had also received a private letter from Victor Emmanuel telling him that he could disregard the official instructions. But was the second letter ever delivered? Certainly the king *wrote* two letters to Garibaldi – the official one telling him not to cross the straits and the private one giving him permission to disobey; both letters were taken to Sicily by the king's orderly, Count Litta, and the private note in the king's own handwriting was discovered among the count's papers in 1909. But Denis Mack Smith points out in *Cavour and Garibaldi* (p. 126) that the seal was unbroken when the letter was found. 'Possibly', he writes, 'the king had instructed his private orderly to sound Garibaldi first, giving him the official letter as the cabinet had asked, but if he found the dictator bent on further conquest the success would be condoned.' In any case, if the letter had been delivered it would surely have turned up in Garibaldi's papers rather than Count Litta's. We are left to conclude that the king did not actually encourage Garibaldi to cross the straits, though he would have been ready to do in certain circumstances.

Garibaldi crossed the straits of Messina on 18–19 August. Popular risings in Calabria and Apulia greeted his arrival, the Bourbon troops were reluctant to face the invincible Garibaldians, and his advance on Naples was virtually a military promenade. He entered the city by train on 7 September.

Francis II was not there. He had realized that Garibaldi could not be stopped, and he had no wish to make his capital city a battlefield. It would be better to let Naples go and to re-enter it, if fortune favoured him, at a later date. Francis had two choices for action. Either he could go south and try to put some life into the Bourbon army which was making so little resistance; or he could go north, retreating to Capua or Gaeta, behind the Volturno, there to assemble all the loyal Bourbon troops and await his opportunity for a counter-attack on the invaders. He chose the second course, and on 6 September, the day before Garibaldi's entry, he left Naples for Gaeta in a small warship. In Naples harbour his vessel signalled to the rest of the fleet to follow her, but no ship moved, as the Piedmontese Admiral Persano had already made secret arrangements to take over the Neapolitan navy. Many regular soldiers deserted and went to their homes, but when Francis II arrived at his new headquarters he was able to assemble an army of about 50,000 men to pit against Garibaldi's volunteers.

The problem of the future administration of Naples was now added to the Sicilian problem. The clashes which had occurred at Palermo between Crispi and La Farina were repeated at Naples between Garibaldi and Cavour's nominees to high administrative posts. And throughout this period of dispute Cavour was afraid that at any moment Garibaldi might upset Italy's international relations by invading the Papal States and marching on Rome, where a clash with the French garrison of 6000 men could have provoked a disastrous war with France and the consequent loss of everything that Italy had gained since 1859.

For the time being Garibaldi remained dictator of Sicily, and for six weeks or so he was also dictator of Naples, where he surprisingly gave Dumas the post of director of excavations and museums. ('The Admiral' had gone back to France to have her baby.) The problem of the annexation of Sicily was still unsolved.

It was generally agreed that the island *must* be annexed, but there was no agreement over time and method. Cavour wanted early action, Garibaldi favoured postponement. Cavour wanted the quick decision of a plebiscite, Crispi and the radicals preferred the election of an assembly which could pass the necessary vote. Both Cavour and Garibaldi were against the Sicilian autonomists, though many of the leading islanders were among them and they had great influence on public opinion.

Relations between Cavour and Garibaldi went from bad to worse. On 11 September Garibaldi wrote to Victor Emmanuel, asking him to send a civil administrator to Naples, and also demanding the dismissal of Cavour and his principal minister, Farini. The king refused to dismiss them, but the split between Cavour and Garibaldi was now irreparable.

Garibaldi was again considering an immediate march on Rome, and he told Sir Henry Elliot, the British minister at Naples, 'that he did not even look upon it as an enterprise of any considerable difficulty'. Most historians think that this was a foolish boast, though Denis Mack Smith observes: 'At Naples, and even at Turin, it was quite possible to believe that the French would prefer to abandon Rome than risk a war with the last ally they had in Europe.'[15] That was a tenable theory, but if, as seems more likely, the French had held firm the Garibaldians would have found a serious encounter with French troops very different from their battles with the Neapolitans. As it happened, Garibaldi had no chance of testing his belief that Rome would fall without difficulty. Cavour was already preparing the bold counterstroke which undermined Garibaldi's position at Naples.

4

At the end of June Cavour had received an important letter from Prince Napoleon, who was not only the husband of Princess Clotilde but was also a genuine well-wisher of the Italian cause. In this letter the prince hinted that if ever Cavour wished to attack southern Italy, he could do so without fear of the emperor's veto. 'Daring alone can save you today', wrote Prince Napoleon. 'Be strong . . . No more *finesse*; that served your turn for Tuscany; it will not serve your turn with Sicily, Naples and Rome. Explain to him [Napoleon III] your views of the future, not only your end but your means and your conduct.'[16]

It was in the Papal States that daring was needed. The conquest of Sicily had finally convinced Cavour that the unification of all Italy, with the exception of Rome and Venetia, was an immediate practical possibility. But this would clearly require the occupation of the papal provinces of Umbria and the Marches, so that northern and southern Italy might form a continuous territory, with the consequent restriction of the pope's temporal power to the city of Rome and the 'patrimony of St Peter' – a strip of territory on the Tyrrhenian coast with an average depth of about forty miles.

Pius IX could not be expected to agree to such a proposal. He was so jealous of his temporal power and his independence that he was enlarging the papal army with the help of a French general, de Lamoricière, while Cardinal Antonelli was negotiating with the French ambassador for the early and complete evacuation of the French garrison which had been in Rome since 1849. He was fully aware of the threat to the papal provinces. He called it a plot to confine him to 'Rome and a garden'.

He returned to the gardening metaphor in an audience given to Odo Russell on 12 July 1860. 'The emperor,' he said, 'wants to make a gardener of me, and leave me the Vatican and a garden only, instead of my present dominions, but in the end the pope will be in possession of his eternal power when perhaps neither his Majesty nor his ally King Victor Emmanuel will have a throne to rest upon. The popes are gardeners in one sense, but they have been soldiers too.'[17]

But Cavour went on with his plans. After the annexation of Romagna he had hoped that further transfers of papal territory might be effected by a treaty with the pope, but Pius repeated in a letter to Victor Emmanuel that he would not sacrifice 'the Church's patrimony'. The idea of a treaty was abandoned. Open seizure was the only way forward, but Napoleon's attitude had first to be established, since it would have been madness to take Umbria and the Marches at the cost of a war with France. Prince Napoleon's letter encouraged Cavour to sound out the emperor directly.

On 28 August two Italian envoys, Farini and General Cialdini, went to Chambéry to see the emperor and ask for his approval of an invasion of the Papal States. Garibaldi's progress in southern Italy had made the enterprise more urgent than ever; it also enabled the envoys to claim that Piedmontese troops must go south to preserve order and to prevent the triumph of revolution in Naples. Though Napoleon had never wanted to see a unitary Italy on his frontier, he felt that the project was now justified. '*Bonne chance, mais faites vite*,' were his parting words to the envoys.[18]

French intervention was not the only danger which had to be guarded against. Austria might also act if the pope were threatened. Cavour thought such action improbable because of the instability of the Austrian empire, and he was willing to take a chance on it. 'I believe an aggressive move on the part of Austria unlikely', he wrote to Nigra. 'In the actual internal conditions of the country the slightest reverse would be very dangerous for her. It might mean the total ruin of the empire. But it is all the same possible.'

With the French emperor's approval assured, all that Cavour needed was a *casus belli*. He found it on 7 September in the foreign troops whom the pope had enrolled to defend his territory and replace the French garrison in Rome. An ultimatum was sent to Antonelli, calling for the foreign troops' disbandment. When Antonelli refused, the Piedmontese army crossed the frontier into the Marches on 11 September. The civil war which Garibaldi had begun in Sicily and continued in the kingdom of Naples was thus extended by Piedmont to the Papal States.

In one sense this southward trek through the Papal States was an anti-revolutionary, anti-Garibaldian movement. From the Italian government's point of view it was intolerable that Garibaldi should remain the dictator of southern Italy. The best way to 'stop Garibaldi' was to make the war against Naples 'official', and this could be done only by sending Piedmontese troops to take part in it. But the invasion of the Papal States was also a revolutionary act on the part of Cavour and Victor Emmanuel, a political master-stroke which made Italian unity possible. Unity could never have been established if the Papal States had remained as a geographical barrier between northern and southern Italy. Cavour's bold decision to annul the barrier by invasion and annexation was truly, as Salvatorelli asserts, 'a revolutionary initiative', 'a Mazzinian thought given life by Cavourian politics'.[19]

The smoothness of the invasion tends to make it look drab and conventional in comparison with Garibaldi's dramatic victories. Yet it was as crucial for the making of Italy as was Garibaldi's sailing from Quarto, and it was certainly no less audacious. If Austria had intervened, no help would have come from France, and Italy would have had to 'go it alone' at last. But Austria did not move. The Piedmontese army moved slowly south in the congenial if somewhat disingenuous guise of an army of liberation.

It consisted of two army corps led respectively by Generals Della Rocca and Cialdini, under General Fanti as commander-in-chief, with three army corps left at the Mincio and the Po to guard against Austrian attack. This was a new army, which Fanti had built up in the year since Villafranca. It was no longer a solely Piedmontese army, but it was not yet the army of Italy. It was the Italian army of Victor Emmanuel's kingdom.

Its task on its first appearance was not exacting: most of the towns and cities of the Marches welcomed the invaders as their liberators from papal misrule, though in Perugia the redoubtable Schmidt, who had sacked the town in the previous year, put up a stout resistance with his papal troops in the fortress. After losing 136 men killed or wounded, Schmidt surrendered, and the Italians took 1700 prisoners and 6 field guns. Their own casualties were 90 killed or wounded.

Apart from Perugia, the only serious clash with Lamoricière's papal army was at Castelfidardo, a small village between Osimo and Loreto, on 18 September. Lamoricière had 5000 infantry, 500 cavalry and 12 guns, and was heavily outnumbered by Cialdini's 13,000 to 14,000 men, 1000 cavalry and 24 guns. It was a vigorous battle. The papal mercenaries fought well so long as they were facing the Italians on more or less equal terms; but as soon as Cialdini was able to deploy his whole army corps the issue was decided. The Italians lost 61 dead and about 200 were wounded; on the papal side 88 men were killed, 400 wounded and 600 taken prisoner. Three guns and a regimental flag were captured.

Castelfidardo was not a great victory. It was not comparable with Garibaldi's successes. But it gave the new army some useful prestige. It showed the world that Italy had a reasonably efficient regular army, and was not dependent on volunteers of dubious political allegiance.

The army had another chance of showing its mettle at Ancona, where Lamoricière had retreated with the greater part of the papal force. Though barely defensible against invasion by sea, Ancona had strong natural defences on its landward side. Under the command of General Fanti himself, Piedmontese troops invested the landward side of Ancona between 20 and 24 September; but Fanti decided that there was no time for a long siege and the issue must be forced by his men's *élan*. Covering fire was given by the guns of a Piedmontese frigate, *Vittorio Emanuele*, and after five days' struggle the attackers had gained positions which left the defenders helpless, and with no alternative to surrender. Lamoricière and two other generals were taken prisoner, together with 7000 men, and the victors also acquired 154 guns. Thereafter there was no papal army to dispute their advance.

After the fall of Ancona Victor Emmanuel came south to put himself at the head of his army. He brought with him his mistress Rosina, who evidently saw herself as 'the forces' sweetheart', for she wore her most sparkling jewels and her most revealing dresses. The king's intention in joining his army was to ensure that there would be no trouble when the regular forces met the Garibaldians. As self-appointed dictator, Garibaldi might have taken a high line with one of the king's generals. His strong sense of loyalty made it certain that he would not affront the king himself.

Garibaldi's military position had worsened in the weeks while the Piedmontese troops were advancing through the Marches and Umbria. If there had ever been the possibility of a lightning dash to Rome, it had now disappeared. Some 40,000 or 50,000 Bourbon troops barred the way. Garibaldi's army had grown to about 20,000, but many of his men were still poorly armed, and the deeds of the original Thousand seemed unlikely to be repeated.

The first clash between the main Neapolitan army and the Garibaldians was in early September, while the dictator was engaged with political affairs in Sicily. General Türr, a Hungarian member of the Thousand, had been left in command of the army.

Eager for action, Türr decided to attack Caiazzo, a fortified post on the northern bank of the Volturno, which would have made an excellent bridgehead for a a later crossing in force. At first the operation seemed to go well. A body of 300 Garibaldians crossed the river and entered Caiazzo without opposition on 19 September. But Garibaldi, on his return from Sicily later in the day, at once realized that 300 men were too few to hold such an important position on the enemy's side of the river. On the next day 600 men were sent as reinforcements.

They were not enough. The whole plan had been misconceived. On 21 September the Bourbon army attacked Caiazzo with 7000 men and 8 guns. After some hours' resistance the Garibaldians fled. Two-thirds of them were able to escape across the river, but 250 were left behind, dead, wounded or prisoners. Türr's blunder had led the Garibaldians to their first defeat.[20]

But there was still a victory to come – the last of Garibaldi's victories and the last of his battles as dictator of southern Italy. After Caiazzo the Neapolitan generals were heartened to know that the 'red devils' were no longer invincible. They decided to cross the Volturno and recapture Naples before they were faced with a flank attack by General Fanti's Italian army.

Fortunately for Garibaldi, the Neapolitans divided their forces and attacked simultaneously from two directions. Garibaldi's position south of the Volturno was on a line from Santa Maria to Maddaloni; one Bourbon army was to attack Santa Maria from the Capua direction, while another was to start from Ducenta and advance on Maddaloni. Their hope was to meet at Caserta, in the centre of the Garibaldian line.

The Neapolitans had every technical advantage when they crossed the Volturno and began their attack on 1 October. Some 30,000 well-trained and well-equipped troops were matched against Garibaldi's 20,000, who were not only inferior in arms but were becoming weary after their many months in the field. They were suffering from sicknesses of various kinds, owing to overwork and shortage of rations, and occasional deserters were beginning to steal back to Naples. But to offset his deficiencies Garibaldi had one great tactical advantage: the two-pronged Bourbon attack allowed him to operate on interior lines, and the railway between Santa Maria and Maddaloni was ideally placed for the quick movement of reserves.

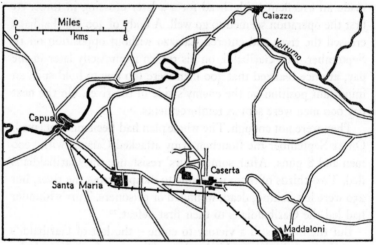

The battle of the Volturno

Garibaldi's ease of movement was, indeed, the deciding factor in the two-day battle of the Volturno, which began on 1 October. It was purely a defensive battle for the Garibaldians. In the west Garibaldi held out in the Santa Maria area against superior numbers of Neapolitans; in the east the Neapolitan general advancing on Maddaloni made the mistake of further dividing his forces, so that he actually faced 5600 Garibaldians, holding a strong position, with only 3000 Bourbon infantry. Neither of the Neapolitan attacks succeeded, and though a detached force of about 5000 infantry was able to occupy Caserta, this isolated success had no real effect on the progress of the battle.

The issue was decided by the evening of 1 October and confirmed by further fighting on 2 October. The Neapolitans again failed to break through and had to abandon their attack, leaving 2000 prisoners in Garibaldi's hands. There were about 300 dead on each side.

The battle of the Volturno has a double significance in the history of the Risorgimento. It was certainly, as Mack Smith asserts, 'a tremendously important victory' for Garibaldi, though at the time it was played down by the politicians and official historiographers at Turin.[21] Naples was saved for Italy. Francis II could not go back to his capital. The Italian army could enter Naples and Victor Emmanuel could annex the entire kingdom of the Two Sicilies. Cavour and the king were spared the international complications which would certainly have arisen if Piedmontese troops had had to attack the king of Naples in his own capital and subject the city to a long siege. The next stage of the unification of Italy was brought appreciably nearer by Garibaldi's success on the Volturno.

That is one side of the picture. But the very limitations of Garibaldi's victory were also immensely valuable in the making of Italy. The Bourbon army had been defeated but by no means routed, and Ruggero Moscati shrewdly points out that 'the heroic resistance of the Bourbon soldiers on the Volturno unintentionally facilitated the national task'.[22] If the Bourbons had fled and opened the road to Rome the whole course of history might have been changed; a new Garibaldian coup might have overshadowed the Piedmontese march through Umbria and given a new impetus to the forces of revolutionary republicanism. By standing firm in its old position the Neapolitan army gave precious help to the Italian monarchists in their urgent task of 'stopping Garibaldi'.

5

Cavour had more than one reason for wishing to end Garibaldi's irregular regime as quickly as possible. He knew that Victor Emmanuel's personal prestige was of great importance for the future of Italy, and it would not do for the king to be regarded only as 'Garibaldi's friend'. Cavour was also alarmed by Garibaldi's conduct as dictator, since it seemed that his aim was to rule without parliament and without genuine liberty. He was suspicious, too, of Mazzini's influence on Garibaldi, and of the consequent danger of republican revolution in spite of Garibaldi's protestations of loyalty to Victor Emmanuel.

Cavour was wrong about Mazzini's influence. Garibaldi was always a Mazzinian at heart, but he did not seek his former master's advice on forms of government. Mazzini had gone to Genoa soon after the Thousand had left and had stayed there till September, making unsuccessful efforts to raise and equip an expeditionary force for an invasion of the Papal States. He went on to Naples in mid-September. He was very busy there ('From morning to night my room is full of people', he wrote to an English friend)[23] and he met Garibaldi, but there was no close contact between the two men. Mazzini had little or no direct influence on events at this period.

After his victory on the Volturno Garibaldi was fighting a losing battle over the control of the Two Sicilies. His military power was diminishing, for his army was dispirited at having to stay in the field and its numbers were still being reduced by desertions. He could guess that his civil power was threatened too, for Victor Emmanuel and the Italian army would soon be leaving Ancona for Naples. Garibaldi felt obliged to say that he would meet the king on his way to Naples, though he was conscious that he would lose the initiative by doing so. He was also losing the long struggle over annexation.

The arguments over whether annexation should be immediate or put off till a later date, and whether the decision should be taken by plebiscite or by an elected assembly, were cut short on 11 October. On that day the Italian parliament in Turin approved the annexation, by means of a plebiscite, of any Italian territory which wished to become part of Victor Emmanuel's kingdom.

This forthright decision was inspired by Cavour, who had good reason for choosing a plebiscite rather than a decision by an elected assembly. Though plebiscites are inexact methods of settling complex issues he was afraid that an assembly might put too much power in the hands of those Garibaldians who still dreamed of establishing a republic. Cavour had accepted many of Mazzini's principles, but republicanism was not one of them.

The Italian parliament's decision was quickly followed by

action. The plebiscites for Naples and Sicily were held on 21 October, and those for Umbria and the Marches a few days later. Voters were asked to say 'Yes' or 'No' to the question whether they wished to form an integral part of an Italy one and indivisible under Victor Emmanuel as their constitutional king. The votes were: Sicily, 432,053 to 667; Naples, 1,302,064 to 10,312; the Marches, 133,072 to 1212; Umbria, 99,628 to 380. On paper Cavour's triumph was complete. Italy was made. But the meaning of the overwhelming votes for annexation was by no means so obvious as it seemed from the comfortable distance of Turin.

There was no doubt that Umbria and the Marches genuinely wished to escape from the papal government and were happy to be fused with the rest of Italy. Their huge majorities in favour of annexation were as truly representative of public opinion as were the similar votes in Emilia and Tuscany. But in Sicily and Naples the case was different. The Sicilians gave their vote for annexation in the firm belief, encouraged by Cavour, that they could expect a considerable measure of local autonomy; they were to feel a sharp sense of grievance when they realized that they were being placed under an Italian government without any autonomy at all. In Naples too the vote was far from being a sign of approval of Piedmont and all that Piedmont stood for. It was given at an extraordinary time, when three separate armies – Francis II's, Garibaldi's and Victor Emmanuel's – were on Neapolitan soil. In these circumstances the plebiscite vote was really a vote for peace and order; since the people disliked the Bourbons and were afraid of the revolutionaries, their only course was to vote for Victor Emmanuel; but an impartial observer who went to Naples in December reported to Cavour that the friends of annexation were in a very small minority.[24] Northern Italian politicians were at fault in failing to recognize that Naples and Sicily had voted for fusion only because nothing better was offered them.

The votes were the death-knell of Garibaldi's dictatorship. Victor Emmanuel and the Italian army were now heading for Naples, having easily routed some 5000 Bourbon soldiers who tried to dispute their advance. On hearing that the king was near, Garibaldi crossed the Volturno with a few regiments on 25

October, bivouacked for the night in the valley between the hills of Cajanello and Vajrano, and rode next day to a cross-roads to wait for the Piedmontese army.

The encounter is familiar – the bearded Garibaldi in his red shirt, the heavy-moustached Victor Emmanuel II in field uniform, both mounted. The deliciously banal conversation has a deathless charm:

> 'I salute the first king of Italy!'
> 'How are you, dear Garibaldi?'
> 'Well, your Majesty. And you?'
> 'First rate.'

They rode and talked together for a short time before separating, the royal army keeping on the main road to Teano, while Garibaldi and his men went back by country lanes to Calvi. As they rode, the king told the dictator that his volunteers would no longer be needed. The professionals would finish the job.

Dismissal can hardly have been a surprise to Garibaldi, but it was still a heavy blow. To his friend Admiral Persano he said: 'This is what happens, Persano, they just treat men like oranges, pressing out the juice to the last drop, and throwing the peel away';[25] and to Jessie White Mario: 'Jessie, they have sent us to the rear.'[26]

The great adventure which began at Quarto in May was ended. One last gesture remained. On 7 November King Victor Emmanuel II entered Naples in a carriage, with Garibaldi sitting at his side. Garibaldi asked to be made civil and military governor of the Two Sicilies for a year with full powers; but the king turned down his request, and Garibaldi refused the king's offer of various financial and material rewards for his services. Two days later the ex-dictator left by boat for Caprera. All that he took with him was a bag of seed-corn for his farm and some borrowed money for immediate expenses. He had made nothing for himself out of his months of power.

But he had served Italy well. Without the exploits of the Thousand the fusion of Naples and Sicily with the rest of Italy might have been put off for several years. Garibaldi's sword, Cavour's diplomacy and Mazzini's inspiring genius had given a

Cardinal Antonelli

Urbano Rattazzi

Jessie White Mario

Baron Ricasoli

*" How are you, my dear Garibaldi ? " : the meeting of Garibaldi and Victor
Emmanuel II, 1860*

Italian troops entering Rome at Porta Pia, 20 September, 1870

united Italy to a king who had used his own position to advance
the Risorgimento. Happily for Italy, the task had been done
without interference by the great powers. Though Venice and
Rome had still to be incorporated in the new kingdom, Italy was
free, largely independent and largely united.

It had been a near thing. After a conference at Warsaw
Austria, Prussia and Russia had joined in condemning the invasion
of the Two Sicilies. Even Napoleon III, in spite of his connivance
with Cavour's envoys at Chambéry, formally withdrew his
minister from Turin in September. But there was no intervention
by any power.

One factor which tended to ease the international tension was
the sympathy for Italy openly shown by England's liberal statesmen, Palmerston and Lord John Russell. Writing to Sir James
Hudson, the Italophile British minister at Turin, on 27 October,
Russell observed: 'Her Majesty's government can see no sufficient
ground for the severe censure with which Austria, France,
Prussia and Russia have visited the acts of the king of Sardinia.
H.M. government will turn their eyes rather to the gratifying
prospect of a people building up the edifice of their liberties and
consolidating the work of their independence.'[27]

Russell's dispatch, which took account of the fusion of the Papal
States (excluding Rome) and the Two Sicilies with the rest of
Italy, was warmly welcomed by Italians when it was published a
few days later. Omodeo considers that this note 'was the basis of
continued Anglo-Italian friendship up to 1935', the year in which
Mussolini invaded Abyssinia.[28]

XIV

CAVOUR'S ITALY

Creating the kingdom   *Cavour's last battle*   *The Roman*
       question   *The southern question*

THE fusion of Naples and Sicily with the new kingdom of Italy in
1860 and the recognition of Victor Emmanuel II as the first king
of Italy in March 1861 are sometimes taken as the terminal points
of the Risorgimento, and the various centenaries of the period
were widely celebrated in Italy in 1960–1. Both Cavour and
Azeglio spoke as if the task of making Italy had been completed
by 1861. Cavour's last words before he died, less than three
months after Victor Emmanuel's assumption of his new title,
were: 'Italy is made. All is safe.'[1] Azeglio expressed the same
view, though reaching a different conclusion, when he said:
'*L'Italia è fatta. Restano a fare gli italiani.*' ('Italy is made. We
have still to make the Italians.')[2]

But Italy was not made. When one looks at the problems
confronting the Italian government in 1860–1 it is clear that the
Risorgimento had still a long way to go. A new kingdom had been
created, but two of Italy's brightest jewels – Rome and Venice –
were no part of it. War with Naples dragged on through the
winter: Francis II and the remains of the Bourbon army kept
up their resistance in the fortress of Gaeta, where the French
fleet at first prevented an Italian attack by sea, and it was only in
February 1861, when Napoleon III gave up his attempt to
protect Francis and withdrew his ships, that the fortress surrendered and the king and queen of Naples escaped to Rome.
The disposal of the Bourbon army raised difficult problems for
the Italian government, which was already harassed by the even
greater complexities of disbanding Garibaldi's southern army
without arousing lasting resentment.

The government was also faced with the problem of fusing

together a number of states with different traditions and social structures, of governing 22,000,000 people who had been divided for twelve centuries and of forming a ruling class which would be neither Piedmontese nor Tuscan nor Neapolitan, but Italian. Such fusion was particularly difficult in the south, where the standard of living was conspicuously lower than it was in the north, and the new Italy soon understood that it had a 'southern question' on its hands as well as the 'Roman question' of persuading the pope to give up his remaining temporal power. These were daunting problems, and the new state could not be firmly based until some of them had been resolved. An Italian historian has suggested that all the Italian governments between 1860 and 1866, the year of the restoration of Venetia, should be regarded only as provisional governments.[3] One might go even further and say that they were all provisional governments until the entry into Rome in 1870 removed the greatest weakness that had hampered the new Italy.

An urgent task in 1860–1 was to give some kind of homogeneity to the fused kingdom. Cavour's general principle was that Italy should be based, as Piedmont had been, on monarchy, army and parliament. Much had now to be built on this foundation. The army had to be truly Italian, and the new state must have a fleet which would not be disgraced among the navies of the world. Legislation and public debt should be unified, and an effort made to restore the national finances after the upheavals of the preceding years. Yet this was no time for retrenchment. A complete educational system had to be created. If Italy were to be economically and politically viable, it needed more roads and railways, not only for trade purposes but to bring together the people of a country where the Apennine mountains and the great internal distances, both from north to south and from the Alps to the Austrian frontier, were serious barriers to unification. And all these things had to be done by a government which, because of a restricted franchise, was more oligarchic than democratic, and had little contact with the people.

The first step towards all these objectives was the creation of a common legislative system and a new civil administration. For many years Cavour and the moderate party had thought that a federal Italy would be preferable to a unitary state, and it was not, perhaps, until the invasion of Umbria and the Marches that Cavour had publicly shown that he accepted the unitary principle. It might have been thought that some trace of these old federal leanings would be found in the organization of the new state, but in fact the government chose to impose a centralized bureaucracy on the whole country. Since Turin was the capital, and Piedmont's laws and treaty relations with foreign countries were imposed on all Italy, there was much resentment in other areas at the forced adoption of Piedmontese institutions.

It has been said that Piedmontization 'was too suddenly and too universally introduced, it ignored the human element, over-stressing symmetry and rounded edges, and assuming that society could easily be taken apart and put together again'. Moreover, 'many susceptibilities were offended by the insensitive and high-handed treatment which was sometimes allotted to the rest of Italy by the Piedmontese.'[4] But in fairness to Italy's rulers it must be recognized that the policy of centralization was forced on the Turin government because there was no practicable alternative.

Cavour certainly considered the possibility of decentralization. Early in 1860 he asked Farini to prepare a scheme for regional autonomy which would not endanger the safety of the state. Farini produced a plan for sub-dividing Italy into regions, each to be administered by a governor appointed by the central government and by twenty commissioners elected by provincial councils. In the end Cavour rejected Farini's scheme because he saw the dangers of decentralized government. One of these was the lack in certain areas of suitable men to run it. Such men could probably have been found in north and central Italy, but there were fewer of them in the south, where the opposition of republican democrats and the clergy (who were still faithful to the Bourbon regime) might have reduced local government to chaos. Piedmontization might arouse bad feeling, but the only way of running the country and preserving unity was by means of a strong bureaucracy, independent of the local population.[5]

While centralization appears to have been unavoidable, it is still open to question whether some method of paying more respect to local susceptibilities might not have been found. It would certainly have been useful in Sicily, where Cavour's policy strengthened, rather than weakened, the Sicilian desire for autonomy. But no attempt was made to adapt national institutions to special local situations. The whole body of Piedmontese legislation was imposed on the peninsula; Charles Albert's statute became the Italian corner-stone. The predominance of Piedmont was suggested even in the king's designation: he remained Victor Emmanuel II, the title he had borne as king of Piedmont, though he should really have become Victor Emmanuel I of the new kingdom of Italy. This act of royal pedantry gave some colour to the fanciful theory advanced in later years that the Risorgimento was not really the rebirth of the Italian nation but only the conquest of Italy by the House of Savoy.

The maintenance of Charles Albert's statute was to have a great influence on Italy's future development. The statute was strongly monarchical; the king was head of the state, and had his own share in its legislative, juridical and executive functions. Ministers were the king's ministers, the senate was nominated by him. This was Cavour's wish, but it was certainly not Mazzini's, nor was it in keeping with general democratic advance in western Europe. Many Italian historians consider that the king's predominance was a permanent hindrance to the proper development of Italian democracy.

2

The disposal of two unwanted armies – the Bourbon army of Naples and Garibaldi's southern army – was a pressing matter for Cavour in the early part of 1861. The Bourbon soldiers were more easily dealt with, though their case was unusual. They were a defeated army, which had recently been fighting against King Victor Emmanuel; but since Naples was now fused with the kingdom of Italy they had automatically become an Italian army. The awkward question was whether they should, or should not, be accepted as part of the national force.

In the end it was found necessary to dissolve the Bourbon army, since the soldiers refused to accept order and discipline. But by sending the Neapolitan soldiers home General Fanti, as

Italian minister of war, was unfortunately turning them into potential brigands, to be used for political purposes by the ex-king of Naples and his supporters in Rome. The position of the Bourbon officers was rather different. They had had an orthodox military training and were reasonably competent in their work. Since the Italian army was short of regular officers it absorbed many of those who had held Bourbon commissions. It also allowed them to keep their Neapolitan ranks, even including recent promotions won in fighting the Garibaldians.

This generosity towards former enemies disgusted the Garibaldians, who were not at all satisfied with their own treatment by the Italian government. Army and cabinet had been at loggerheads over this matter. As early as October 1860 Cavour wrote to Farini about the danger of the government's showing itself ungrateful to men who had fought and shed their blood for Italy. 'I do not thereby mean that we must retain all the ranks given by Garibaldi or by others on his behalf,' he observed. 'Heaven forbid that such an absurd idea should enter my head. But on the other hand we cannot do as Fanti wishes and send all the Garibaldians home with a simple gratuity.'[6]

In the end the professionals had their way, and the Garibaldians were treated with a great lack of generosity. Respect was shown for those who had served with the original Thousand: many were given regular commissions and sixteen of them ended their careers as generals. The others – those who had joined Garibaldi as the campaign proceeded – were regarded with something like contempt by the war office, and commissions were granted to only a quarter of the volunteer officers who wished to transfer or return to the regular army.[7] Though Cavour was not responsible for Fanti's ungenerous conduct, the treatment of the volunteers increased Garibaldi's resentment against the government. He did not want the southern army to be disbanded at all. He wanted it to be kept in being for early assaults on Venice and Rome. It was the last straw that it should be not only disbanded, but disbanded in such a shabby way.

Soon after his return to Caprera from Naples in November Garibaldi began to call loudly for war in the spring of 1861. His slogan was 'an armed nation'; his appeal for the mobilization of a million armed men was published in all the democratic press in December. His militant propaganda was so insistent that the British government became disturbed, and in February Lord John Russell somewhat eccentrically wrote him a letter asking him 'seriously to reconsider' his announcement that he would make war in the spring, since no individual, 'however distinguished, has a right to determine for his country the momentous question of peace or war'. It was a measure of Garibaldi's unique position in Europe that a British foreign secretary should have written to him in such a vein. Queen Victoria had protested against the letter being sent at all, since she felt, with some justice, that it 'implied a recognition of the general's position as a European power'.[8]*

In fact, the only war that Garibaldi waged that spring was one of words. A new chamber of deputies – the first truly Italian parliament with deputies from north, centre and south – was elected in January, and Garibaldi was one of the eighty deputies who were recognized as Mazzinians or Garibaldians. Apart from these and a few clericals, the great majority of the 443 deputies were pledged to follow Cavour.

One of the first tasks of the new chamber was to elect its president (the equivalent of the Speaker of the House of Commons) and Cavour astutely nominated his old democratic ally, Urbano Rattazzi, with whom he was no longer on good terms. The reason for Cavour's action was that Rattazzi would be less dangerous to the government if he were in the neutral position of president of the chamber than if he were at large among the deputies. Rattazzi was elected by a large majority, but he showed no gratitude to Cavour. The deputies were treated to the unusual spectacle of a prime minister and a president of the chamber who did not even exchange a greeting when they passed in the corridor.

When the chamber had formally approved the king's new title of Victor Emmanuel II, king of Italy, Cavour made the bold

---

* Russell's view of Garibaldi's importance was certainly shared by Geoffrey Marsh, the United States minister at Turin, who told his government in 1861 that 'though but a solitary and private individual, he [Garibaldi] is at this moment, in and of himself, one of the great powers of the world'. (Mack Smith, *Garibaldi*, p. 115.)

gesture of submitting his resignation, so that parliament could have a new premier, possibly from some other region than Piedmont. It was only a gesture. All the politicians whom the king invited to form a ministry replied that Cavour was indispensable. He therefore resumed office with a cabinet which included, for the first time, ministers from Naples and Sicily.

Cavour was now ready for his last great political battle. In a series of debates which began on 25 March he had to defend his policies against vigorous attacks by Garibaldians and other deputies who disagreed with him on particular issues. In spite of the government's big majority in the chamber he was in serious danger, for any failure to carry conviction would have put his whole unitary policy at risk. The debates formed a running battle for several weeks, from which Cavour emerged with enhanced credit. His victory meant that the new kingdom of Italy would follow the course he had charted for it.

The first attack concerned Cavour's resolve that Rome should eventually become the Italian capital. In the previous October, when the chamber had given its approval to annexation by plebiscite, he had definitely stated that Rome must become the capital and had thus envisaged the ending of the pope's temporal power. This proposal had become the subject of keen controversy. In December a similar call for the separation of the pope's temporal and spiritual powers was made in a French pamphlet called *France, Rome and Italy*, another of those curious literary productions in which Napoleon III aired his views without putting his name to them; and to Cavour's delight the same note was struck by his friend Prince Napoleon in the French senate a few days later. In Italy, however, the pamphlet aroused the indignation of the still formidable Azeglio, who was convinced that it was morally undesirable and practically impossible for Rome to be made the Italian capital. In a pamphlet of his own, published in March 1861, he denounced 'this mania for Rome', 'this folly of climbing the Capitol', and declared that Rome, as the seat of the papacy, could not be absorbed in Italy like Florence, Naples, Milan or Venice. The head of the Church, Azeglio argued, must live in Rome, and he 'must have the name, independence, great and exceptional position of a sovereign'.

Florence, he argued, would be a far more suitable capital than Rome, which in any case was still in the hands of the pope and the French garrison.[9]

Azeglio was not at this time a deputy, and Audinot, one of his close friends, offered to raise the matter in the chamber. He did so on 25 March, and Cavour had to uphold his Roman policy against two different kinds of opponent – Azeglio's right-wing friends, who urged that Rome should be left alone, and the Garibaldians, who wanted the kingdom of Italy to be proclaimed from the Capitol at the earliest possible moment.

Cavour had a reasoned answer for each set of opponents. To those who said that Rome would not be a suitable capital he replied that it was, in fact, the only possible capital because it was the only city in Italy which did not possess an exclusively municipal past. To the hotheads who wanted Rome to be annexed at once he retorted that two conditions must be satisfied before Italy could make Rome its capital: Italy must 'go to Rome' in full agreement with France, and it must go there in such a way that Catholics both inside and outside Italy could not interpret the occupation of Rome as a sign of the enslavement of the Church. The pope's independence must be guaranteed; with the acquisition of Rome the new Italy would separate the Church from the state and would give the Church the widest possible liberty.

But Rome was not the only issue on which Cavour had to defend himself; he had also to explain the government's attitude towards Austrian-held Venetia. He surprised the chamber by announcing that he was 'giving up conspiracy' after conspiring with all his might for twelve years – conspiring to attain and secure independence for his country, but conspiring 'in a singular way' by proclaiming in press and parliament the scope of his conspiracy. In future, however, his diplomacy would be correct and irreproachable, and for that reason he was taking no immediate action about Venice. He warned the chamber that Italy could not make war against Austria single-handed, and he asked: 'Will the deliverance of Venice come by arms or diplomacy? I do not know. It is the secret of providence.' Thus in typically Cavourian fashion he simultaneously rebuked the fanatics who wanted an immediate march on Venice and gave formal notice to Europe that Italy regarded Venetia as an integral part of the new kingdom.[10]

The debate was resumed two days later. This time Cavour summed up his arguments about Rome in an appeal to the pope, assuring him that the sacrifice of the temporal power would give him a greater independence than the popes had ever enjoyed. 'We are ready,' he said, 'to proclaim in Italy this great principle – the free Church in the free state.'

Cavour had won. His two speeches convinced the chamber. A motion approving the government's policies was passed by a huge majority, with only the left and right extremists voting against it. The vote of 27 March was not only a personal triumph for Cavour, it was also a political event of the first magnitude. Crispi, Garibaldi's former lieutenant who was now a Sicilian deputy, might grumble about the indignity of 'going to Rome only when Louis Napoleon allows it', but the decisive vote and Cavour's speeches were an eloquent message to Europe. The vote, says a recent student of the period, 'took the Roman question out of the sphere of intrigues and revolutionary dreams and placed it before the chancelleries of the great powers as a European problem which could not be postponed.'[11] World opinion was thus conditioned to accept, in 1870, the Italian entry into Rome as a necessary factor in the making of Italy.

The two speeches of 25 and 27 March were Cavour's last major addresses to the Italian parliament. But another clash with the Garibaldians – indeed, with the general himself – had still to come in this critical session.

Garibaldi, who was not present for the March debates in the chamber of deputies, left Caprera for Turin at the beginning of April. On his way to the capital he showed his hostility to the government in a speech he made to a deputation of Milanese workmen who met him at Genoa. On this occasion he spoke contemptuously of the government's 'unworthy' policy and the 'crowd of lackeys' who supported it; he said that the king was surrounded by 'a poisoned atmosphere', but he hoped to put him on the right road. His words caused great indignation at Turin, where Ricasoli declared in the chamber that Garibaldi's remarks had 'wounded the feelings of every deputy, offended the majesty of parliament and the inviolability of the king'. With some charity Ricasoli ended by suggesting that Garibaldi had probably been misquoted.

Cavour recognized the ominous note in the general's outburst. He knew that Fanti's tactics had exposed the government to censure for its mean treatment of Garibaldi's volunteers, and that Garibaldi was now calling for the formation of a national guard, which would be a military organization in rivalry with the army. He looked round for a compromise, and thought he had found one by drafting a decree establishing a volunteer corps of three divisions, to be commanded by former Garibaldian officers. But this proposal satisfied no one. It was clear that Cavour would have to fight hard for its acceptance.

The debate on the new decree was on 18 April. It had been in progress for some time before Garibaldi made a sensational entry in red shirt and grey poncho, which looked very bizarre among the sober suits of the other deputies. He was loudly cheered by the spectators and a number of deputies, and after taking his seat he listened to General Fanti's explanation of his plans for army reorganization and for using the services of Garibaldian officers. But soon he was on his feet to introduce his own proposal for setting up a national guard.

Garibaldi began by reading a prepared speech, but before long he put it aside and launched into a passionate denunciation of Cavour. After general charges that Cavour had hindered the sailing of the Thousand and had only accepted the idea of Italian unity at the last minute, Garibaldi was carried away by his anger about the cession of Nice and Savoy and the government's treatment of the volunteers. He declared that it would always be impossible for him to shake the hand of the man who had sold his country to the foreigner, and he accused the government of having checked the Garibaldians' successes with its 'cold and hostile hand' and of having been ready to provoke 'a fratricidal war'.

The chamber was in an uproar after these startling accusations, which Cavour indignantly refuted. 'It is not permissible that he should insult us in this fashion,' said Cavour. 'We protest! We never had such intentions.' But Garibaldi repeated his charges, in which he had at last released his long repressed antipathy to the prime minister, and Rattazzi suspended the session to allow tempers to cool down.

Cavour was justified in denying the general's charges. His correspondence shows that in a private letter of September 1860 he had spoken of 'throwing the Garibaldians into the sea', but he had never made any attempt to do so; and the invasion of Umbria and the Marches was designed to restrict civil war, not to provoke it. When the debate was resumed he tried to appease Garibaldi by making a reasoned defence of the government's treatment of the volunteers. The difficulty, he pointed out, was that the volunteers were not trained soldiers; even their high officers had pursued no military studies. Fanti also tried to convince the Garibaldians that there was no wish to humiliate them, but the bitter argument ended with the gulf between government and Garibaldians, between Cavour and Garibaldi, entirely unbridged.

The vote was taken on a motion agreeing to leave the treatment of the volunteers to the ministry's discretion. It was carried by 194 votes to 77. A few days later Garibaldi went back to Caprera, and Cavour wrote to a colleague: 'I do not think that we have finished with Garibaldi, but I believe that he will stay quiet for some time. *C'est déjà beaucoup de gagné.*'[12]

3

Cavour had little more than two months to live after these crucial debates. Much of the last period of his life was devoted to the Roman question.

His statements about the temporal power on 25 and 27 March were based on the policy he had been following secretly for some months. In the autumn he had opened private negotiations with the Roman court through the intermediacy of Diomede Pantaleoni, a Roman doctor, who had made contact on the papal side with Father Passaglia, a personal friend of Pius IX. The two men sent Cavour a draft agreement on future relations between Italy and the papacy, and then, on their own initiative, took the matter to a higher level by bringing in two of the more liberal cardinals, Santucci and D'Andrea. In January 1861 Cavour was sufficiently optimistic to refer in a letter to the hope of 'at last bringing about, by direct agreement with the Holy Father, a durable reconciliation between the Church and civilization'.[13]

Matters continued to go well in February. Cavour wrote to Passaglia that if peace could be achieved before Easter, 'the joy of the Catholic world will be even keener than that which, nearly nineteen hundred years ago, greeted the entry of Our Lord into Jerusalem'. It was a different story in March. Reactionaries made their moves in Rome. Passaglia and Pantaleoni were expelled. The pope flatly refused to exchange his temporal power for any guarantee of independence. His attitude was the same as it had always been: 'This corner of the earth is mine. Christ has given it to me. I will give it up to Him alone.'

The policy of direct approach to Rome had failed. Cavour turned once more to his old ally, the French emperor. But here the position was changed. Napoleon was not pleased by the establishment of a united Italy instead of the separate states he had proposed at Plombières. He showed his displeasure by declining to recognize the new kingdom.

This refusal was a serious embarrassment to Cavour and Victor Emmanuel. Recognition had been given by Britain, Switzerland and the Scandinavian countries, and could be expected from Prussia in the near future. But French recognition was essential if Italy were to take her rightful status as a European power.

In spite of this break in the friendly relations between France and Italy, Napoleon was willing to consider a compromise over the Roman question, with which both countries were closely concerned. This compromise, which was described as Napoleon's extreme concession, reached Cavour in mid-April in a letter from Prince Napoleon. It provided for recognition of Italy by France and the withdrawal of French troops from Rome, on condition that Italy would promise not to attack the pope's present territory and would prevent, by force if necessary, any attack by others, and that it would acquiesce in the formation of a papal army of 10,000 men, who might come from foreign Catholic countries.

It was an ingenious compromise. It would please the French Catholics, since Napoleon, in spite of his earlier anti-papalism, would now appear to be supporting the temporal power; in Italy it could be presented as a big step forward, since Rome would at last be free of French troops. Cavour recognized the importance of the French withdrawal, but he also realized that Napoleon's terms would postpone indefinitely the Italian occupation of Rome, and that it would be hard to get them accepted by the chamber. He was ready to try, but Napoleon would not confirm his offer and for the time being no action was possible.

In essence the scheme was very much like the September convention which Minghetti, then prime minister of Italy, signed in 1864. But 1861 was too soon. Cavour's death gave Napoleon the opportunity to withdraw his offer altogether, and the French garrison stayed in Rome.

4

Venice and Rome could wait; another problem had already raised its head and was to loom over Italian life for decades to come. This was 'the southern question' – the tremendous problem of restoring order in the former kingdom of the Two Sicilies and of bringing southern living standards up to the northern level.

Garibaldi had not stabilized the south. Comparatively few southerners had joined his army of liberation, and the changes introduced under his dictatorship had only disorganized the existing administration. Popular support for Italian unity had never been strong in the south; it was now in danger of dis-appearing because of dislike of Piedmontization and resentment of the superior attitude too often adopted by northern officials, who behaved as though they were dealing with a rather backward colony. The more enlightened northerners were themselves aware of this danger. Cavour's friend Nigra, who had gone to Naples in December 1860 as lieutenant to the new governor, Prince Eugenio of Carignano, complained in February: 'Three more Piedmontese organizers have just arrived, and they tell me others are coming . . . Tell our dear Minghetti [minister of the interior] to stop this immigration of organizers.'[14]

Rural disorders were the first sign of southern dissatisfaction.

On the mainland these were mainly in the form of brigandage. While the urban middle classes could expect to profit from the new regime, the rural populace had no such hope, and anti-bourgeois hostility became a prominent feature of country life. It was expressed in the formation of large bands of brigands, in which soldiers and non-commissioned officers of the disbanded Bourbon army took a big part. To make things worse, these bandits were encouraged from Rome by ex-King Francis II, who fantastically dreamed that brigands and cut-throats could be transformed into a legitimist army which would win him back his throne. For years to come the activities of the Neapolitan brigands were virtually a guerrilla war without quarter.

Sicily's problem was different. It too had its share of banditry, but its great scourge was the Mafia, which grew rapidly after 1860 and spread its criminal network throughout the island. Murder was a common occurrence, and there were ten times as many assassinations in Sicily as in Lombardy or Piedmont. More generally, the Sicilians felt that they were being enslaved by Italy as they had formerly been enslaved by Naples. Conscription was imposed on them for the first time, and they deeply resented it; young men sank into the criminal underworld to avoid the call-up, and were joined there by deserters.[15] In Sicily, as in Naples, it was already clear that annexation had solved no problems. Both economically and in the sphere of public order 'the southern question' had come to stay. It was part of Cavour's legacy to his successors.

Yet the legacy, take it for all in all, was a noble one. Even in 1861, when all the states which had been fused with Piedmont were having difficulties in assimilating the Piedmontese legislative and administrative systems, a new Italy was in being. The impetus given by Mazzini's propaganda and Garibaldi's military leadership had created the opening for unity which Cavour had skilfully exploited with the encouragement of Victor Emmanuel. Now, with the last stage of the Risorgimento still to be covered, its great statesman was to pass from the scene.

Cavour's friends had noticed signs of strain during his clash with Garibaldi in the recent debate. For years he had not spared himself in the service of Piedmont and the making of Italy. On

5 June, after a few days' illness, he died from a cerebral haemorrhage. He was fifty years old.

Though excommunicate, Cavour was given the last rites of the Catholic Church by a sympathetic friar. He was thinking of Italy to the last. 'Friar, friar, a free Church in a free state,' he whispered shortly before he died. And then the last words of all: 'Italy is made. All is safe.'

His last diplomatic victory was won by his death. In homage to his old friend, Napoleon III agreed to recognize Italy without further argument, though he did so in a rather niggling way: instead of actually recognizing the kingdom of Italy, he announced that he was recognizing Victor Emmanuel's title of king of Italy.[16] An old colleague who had often crossed swords with Cavour wondered how Italy would fare without him. 'Who now is going to be the counterweight to Mazzini and Garibaldi?' asked Azeglio. 'Who now can keep the revolution safe indoors like some domesticated hyena?'[17]

VENICE RECOVERED

The 'Iron Baron' Aspromonte The September Convention
The Austro-Prussian war

CAVOUR'S death is sometimes pictured as an irreparable loss to the new Italy. That is an exaggeration. Certainly his hand on the helm would have been useful in a critical decade, but Italy had other competent politicians, and it is doubtful whether Cavour could have done any better than they did. For the two major events in the last stage of the Risorgimento were largely due to external forces. The Austro-Prussian war of 1866 gave Venice back to Italy; the Franco-Prussian war of 1870 created the opportunity for Italy's entry into Rome. Even Cavourian diplomacy might not have achieved these results at any earlier date.

The same can be said about home affairs. Rosario Romeo is surely right when he says that it did not matter whether Cavour lived or died in 1861: 'The profound and complex weaknesses of the new political organism were too great for a single statesman to eradicate in the course of a few years.'[1] It is generally agreed that the standards of political life fell after 1861, but this was due to the faults of the governmental system rather than to the death of Cavour.

A basic weakness of the new kingdom was that it was oligarchic rather than democratic. Owing to the limited franchise the people's share in public life seemed to be diminishing rather than increasing. The only voters were men who could read and write and paid not less than 40 lire a year in direct taxation, together with members of academies or orders of knighthood, teachers and public functionaries of the higher and middle grades; and even by 1871 there were only 530,000 electors out of a population of 25,000,000 – a mere 1.98 per cent. The position was particularly bad in Sicily, where landlords, their friends and their employees were often the only voters in an electorate of little more than 1 per cent of the population.[2] True democracy could not exist on such a narrow basis. A wider franchise was needed to save the Risorgimento from Giuseppe Ferrari's charge that it was 'the revolution of the rich'.[3]

The first statesman to inherit the dual task of administering a new state and completing the Risorgimento was the Tuscan Baron Ricasoli, who had worked so hard and so long in 1859–60 for the annexation of Tuscany to Piedmont. He was a man of high sentiments and rigid austerity, but he lacked, as his nickname of 'the iron baron' suggests, both the flexibility and the charm of Cavour. Though he was well accustomed to dealing with state affairs it was a drawback, which eventually proved fatal, that he had no experience of handling parliamentary business. Even so, his achievements at home during his short tenure of office included the unification of public debt, the beginning of new railway construction, administrative reorganization and a resolute attempt to restore order in Neapolitan territory, where General Cialdini was appointed royal lieutenant with the special mission of putting down brigandage.

While agreeing that both Rome and Venice were needed to complete the new kingdom, Ricasoli gave priority to the Roman question. It was, he thought, 'an inexorable necessity' that Italy should 'go to Rome', but Venetia could be left for later consideration. In this attitude he was directly opposed by Victor Emmanuel II. The king put Venice first, partly because, as a good Catholic, he was afraid of offending the Church by hasty action at Rome,* and partly because he saw more military glory in driving the Austrians out of Venice than in dislodging 'the good old man in the Vatican'. Without telling Ricasoli he was already thinking of using Garibaldi in a complicated plan for recovering Venice.

In these years after Cavour's death Italian politics were often confused through the personal interventions of Victor Emmanuel. It has been said of him that he stepped into the vacuum left by Cavour and gave free rein to his penchant for personal rule, but

---

* A French envoy at Turin once commented that Victor Emmanuel 'would rather gamble with his throne than with his place in paradise'. (Mori, *La Questione Romana*, p. 45 n.)

it was personal diplomacy, even more than rule, which especially appealed to him. In a moment of crisis some years later a British diplomat in Florence commented ruefully in a dispatch to London: 'You are aware, of course, that H.M. Victor Emmanuel is no joke under these circumstances, and is rather prone, as Lord Russell was wont occasionally to observe, to be making scores off his own bat.'[4] He was using 'his own bat' when he began his negotiations with Garibaldi in the early 1860s.

The dice were loaded against the 'iron baron'. The king disliked his emphasis on the Roman question and found him personally unsympathetic; his coldness and his austerity made him unpopular with the deputies. Strangely enough, it was his leniency towards Garibaldi which brought him down.

At this time the general was the key figure in a movement to set up 'action committees for Rome and Venice' all over Italy. The committees were attacked in the chamber. Ricasoli, knowing the king's attachment to Garibaldi, defended them. Though the chamber ultimately supported him, he was sharply reproved by the king, who complained that Ricasoli was pandering to the extreme left to secure a parliamentary majority. This was only a pretext for getting rid of a prime minister whom he disliked. Realizing that he had lost his sovereign's confidence, Ricasoli resigned, and the king was happy to ask his more congenial friend Rattazzi to form a new ministry. This was a coalition which excluded the really eminent moderates, such as Farini and Minghetti. Rattazzi himself took the ministries of the interior and foreign affairs, and an important newcomer in the cabinet was Quintino Sella, a Piedmontese scientist, who made his first appearance as minister of finance.

Ricasoli had held office from June 1861 to February 1862. He won no laurels for his premiership, but he had at least helped to consolidate unity on the lines laid down by Cavour. Grave trouble awaited his successor.

2

King Victor Emmanuel's plan for the recovery of Venice was a somewhat elaborate one of sending a new Garibaldian expedition into the Balkans to encourage insurrections among Austria's subject-peoples. It could be expected that Hungary would rise in revolt, and while Austria was engaged in suppressing the risings Italy, possibly with French support, would be able to occupy Venetia and the Tyrol without difficulty. The king thought so highly of his scheme that he sent General Türr, the prominent Garibaldian, to explain it to Napoleon III in Paris in January 1862, but the emperor coldly replied that he had no advice to give, as he wanted to have nothing to do with 'such an odyssey'. He was sure, he said, that Austria would at once be at war with Italy if Garibaldi made any move in Dalmatia.[5]

In spite of this rebuff Victor Emmanuel stuck to his plan and brought Rattazzi, the new prime minister, into his confidence. Early in March Garibaldi came to Turin and discussed the Balkan project with the king and Rattazzi. It was agreed that the plan should go forward, and that the government should give Garibaldi financial aid.

But conditions in 1862 were very different from those of 1860. In 1860 the party of action had moved on its own initiative, and Cavour had skilfully harnessed its force to the service of the monarchy. Victor Emmanuel and Rattazzi were mistaken in thinking that they could take the initiative in promoting a similar coup in 1862. On 20 March a hint about possible action for the recovery of Venice was conveyed to Italian diplomats abroad in a circular note from Rattazzi. Its reception by foreign governments was so adverse that Rattazzi abandoned the plan, withheld the promised aid for Garibaldi and gave up the foreign ministry to General Durando, a respected moderate whose appointment was a guarantee that there would be no revolutionary initiative.

Garibaldi did not give up so easily. After his interview with the king and Rattazzi he had made a triumphal tour of Lombardy, where his warm reception by ministers, senators, deputies, mayors and prefects made him think that Venice and even Rome were really within his grasp. Though the government had failed him he decided to move on his own and began to gather volunteers for an expedition. He had decided, however, to invade the Tyrol, not the Balkans.

The king and Rattazzi were now aware of the international dangers of a new Garibaldian *coup*. In the middle of May the government acted. More than a hundred Garibaldians were arrested at Sarnico, Palazzolo and Alzano Superiore on the frontiers of Trentino, and a Garibaldian demonstration was suppressed by force at Brescia. The expedition was stopped, but in view of his own complicity Rattazzi refused to hold a parliamentary inquiry into the incident and quietly released the prisoners without prosecution.

But Garibaldi was still in fighting mood. He went back to Caprera, to prepare for the first of his two unhappy attempts to take Rome. In June he left for Sicily, where he proclaimed at crowded meetings that Rome would soon be Italian. It was at one of these meetings that he accepted the cry of 'Rome or death!' as his future watchword. After revisiting the battlefields of his 1860 campaign he raised 3000 volunteers at Palermo and took possession of Catania, where the regular troops retreated to the castle without opposing him.

In surprising contrast with the government's recent action at Sarnico, the military authorities in Sicily made no attempt to interfere with Garibaldi's movements. The reasons for their inertia are not clear, though they probably suspected that Garibaldi was in league with Victor Emmanuel. The king's private admission that Garibaldi had been carrying out orders 'to a certain extent' shows that he had some complicity in the enterprise;[6] he may well have thought that a new Garibaldian rising, even if it were unsuccessful, would be a good way of persuading Napoleon to withdraw the French troops from Rome.

If this was the king's idea, he had completely misjudged the situation. French Catholic opinion was aroused by the new threat to the pope. Napoleon, always fearful of losing Catholic support, telegraphed from Paris that Garibaldi's actions were making it impossible for him to withdraw his Roman garrison. And on 3 August Victor Emmanuel washed his hands of the whole affair by issuing a royal proclamation against 'blameworthy impatience and rash action'. The proclamation, which was countersigned by all the ministers, said bluntly:

> When the hour for the completion of the great enterprise comes, the voice of your king will make itself heard. Every call which does not come from him is a call to rebellion, to civil war.[7]

A fortnight later Garibaldi was denounced as a rebel and martial law was declared in Sicily, to be quickly followed by a similar declaration in Naples. Yet even then the Italian navy was not clearly instructed to prevent Garibaldi from crossing the straits of Messina. At the end of August he seized two steamers and crossed to Calabria with several thousand men. His march to 'Rome or death' had begun.

He found neither. For the government acted at last. General Cialdini came out from Naples with a body of regular troops and met Garibaldi while he was still in the southernmost part of Calabria. A 'battle' was fought on the massif of Aspromonte on 29 August, but it was not really a battle, since Garibaldi did not want to begin a civil war and had ordered his men not to reply to the regulars' fire. In spite of this order a few shots were exchanged, seven soldiers and five volunteers were killed, and Garibaldi himself was wounded in the ankle and taken prisoner. He was carried down the mountain to an Italian gunboat.

The new expedition had ended ignominiously, but with no diminution of Garibaldi's heroic stature. The government, on the other hand, was much criticized for its conduct both before and after Aspromonte. Volunteers who were army deserters were shot without trial, but the ministers were fearful of taking action against Garibaldi himself. The open rebel went free with a compound fracture in his right ankle.

Mazzini, who had resumed his life in London after the annexation of southern Italy, was deeply stirred by the news of Garibaldi's movements. 'They will not go to Rome without me', he proudly wrote to a young English girl who had offered her services to the Italian cause,[8] and late in August he went to Lugano to be ready to join Garibaldi on the road to Rome. Even when the enterprise was in ruins Mazzini could not believe that all was lost. Jessie White Mario, who went to Switzerland to meet him, wrote to the Stansfelds that Mazzini 'did not doubt for a moment that the Italians would rise as one man to avenge their outraged chief'.[9] But there was no rising. Mazzini's faith in popular insurrections was again misplaced.

3

The Aspromonte affair was a setback to Italian hopes of the early acquisition of Rome and Venice. The Austrians were still in Venetia, the French garrison stayed in Rome, Pius IX still refused to consider any agreement that would leave him with less than his former territory. The familiar claim was set out at length in a letter from Cardinal Antonelli to Earl (formerly Lord John) Russell on 11 November 1862: 'The pope did not hold the States of the Church as an inheritance from his ancestors and could not dispose of them at his will before or after death. As Vicar of Christ he held them in trust for the Catholic world, and as he received them, so he had to leave them to his successor according to the oath taken by the pontiffs on ascending the throne of St Peter.'[10]

On this showing the Italian government might have had to wait indefinitely for a settlement of the Roman question, but a new prime minister approached the matter in a different way. Rattazzi had resigned after Aspromonte, and after a month or two in which the king tried the experiment of a purely administrative government, headed by Pasolini, the premiership was briefly held by Farini, who was persuaded to retire after giving unfortunate signs of mental instability.* He was followed by Marco Minghetti, a Piedmontese moderate, who was anxious to renew the former close relations between France and Italy. In these negotiations he was greatly helped by his foreign minister, Emilio Visconti Venosta, a Lombard who had fought in Milan's Glorious Five Days and in 1859 had been Cavour's representative with Garibaldi at Varese. His appointment to high office at the age of thirty-four caused much surprise, but time was to show that he was Italy's best foreign minister since Cavour.

Minghetti's government was better than Rattazzi's, but it badly needed some action that would enhance its prestige. Garibaldi had not lost his magic: half-a-million people lined the London streets to welcome him when he visited England in the spring of 1864, and Minghetti felt that his ministry was

---

* The finishing touch was when he 'threatened the king with a knife to force a declaration of war on Russia'. (Mack Smith, *Italy*, p. 64.)

being weakened by such demonstrations of Garibaldian hero-worship.

He had other troubles also, with national finance and the unrest in Sicily as the chief causes for concern. Financially the country was stumbling from one budget deficit to another – 446 million lire in 1862, 382 in 1863, 367 in 1864 – and the continuing need for roads and railways gave little hope of breaking even in the foreseeable future.[11] The situation in Sicily was virtually civil war; the Italian government was no more popular there than the Bourbons had been. The island's real need was for economic and social reforms, but instead of approaching the problem from that angle the government chose to restore order by means of harsh repression. General Govone was sent to Sicily with full power to hold military tribunals and shoot convicted persons. Arrest and imprisonment without trial, the taking of hostages, torture and threats to cut off water supplies were among the weapons that Govone used against rebellious villages and their inhabitants.

Conscious of the bad 'image' that the government was acquiring Minghetti looked round for some kind of Cavourian master-stroke that would restore its reputation. He thought he had found one in a partial solution of the Roman question.

Though Pius IX was still impervious to argument, Minghetti felt that it would be a step forward if agreement could be reached with Napoleon III over the withdrawal of French troops from Rome. His negotiations with the emperor were successful; a pact, which became known as the September convention, was signed on 15 September 1864. By this pact the emperor agreed to withdraw his troops from Rome within two years and pledged himself to observe the principle of non-intervention. In return, Italy would guarantee the pope's territory against any attack, and would transfer its own capital from Turin to Florence within six months. It was also agreed that the pope should have the right to enlist from foreign countries an armed force of not more than 10,000 men.

Omodeo says of the September convention that it 'satisfied no one and resolved nothing; it gave only some years of uncertain truce in the thorny diplomatic struggle'.[12] It saddened the pope, who realized that he could never hope to regain his lost provinces and must count himself happy if he could succeed in keeping the small territory which had been left to him. It shocked Mazzini, who issued a manifesto claiming that plebiscites, government, parliament and people had decreed that Italy should be one and Rome its metropolis, and that the convention cancelled this solemn collective decree. Yet it was not entirely without merit. Napoleon felt that he was at last freeing himself from the embarrassment of maintaining a French garrison in a foreign country; Minghetti thought that the departure of the French troops would bring Italy appreciably nearer to a final solution of the Roman question. The transfer of the capital from Turin to Florence would have practical advantages, as Azeglio had pointed out in 1861, and there was no need to interpret it as a renunciation of the Italian claim to Rome. That claim could still be enforced when the right moment came.

The September convention was to remain in force for six years, but Minghetti's hope that it would raise the government's prestige was not fulfilled. It was unpopular in Turin, especially among the aristocracy and upper classes, who promoted rioting which lasted for two days and caused an experienced observer to comment that the Turinese 'have shown, and still show, a municipalism and an indifference to the general good of Italy that is painful to all the *buoni*'.¹³ The king felt bound to dismiss a government which had lost public confidence, and the able Visconti Venosta left the foreign ministry for five years. The eminently safe General La Marmora – one of the king's own men – succeeded Minghetti as prime minister.

Besides being upset by the convention's provisions, the pope was angry that neither he nor Antonelli had been consulted about an agreement concerning Roman affairs. A few weeks later he published his *Syllabus of Errors*, which made it clear that the papacy had no intention of coming to terms with contemporary liberal thought.

The syllabus was not, as some thought at the time, an answer to the September convention; it had been in preparation for several years, and the convention had no influence on its appearance. Its full title was 'A Syllabus, containing the principal

Errors of our times, which are noted in the Consistorial Allocutions, in the Encyclicals and in other Apostolic Letters of our most Holy Lord, Pope Pius IX.' It was a list of eighty propositions which Pius IX considered to be erroneous, and its tone was set by the sweeping clause which condemned those who taught that 'the Roman pontiff can and should reconcile himself to progress, liberalism and modern civilization'.[14] Some of the errors denounced were specifically Italian, and the document could be generally interpreted as a condemnation of the Italian government, Mazzini and Garibaldi and an attempt to stifle the growth of liberal catholicism.

The pope's forthright attack on liberal thought caused great excitement in most Catholic countries, and especially in France, where it disappointed those who had hoped for a reconciliation between Church and state and delighted the Church's enemies, who thought that the pope had put a valuable weapon into their hands. But it was taken calmly in Italy, where the pope's views were well known and democrats had long been convinced that liberty and the Church were irreconcilable.

If Pius had hoped that the syllabus would strengthen his own position he must soon have been disappointed. In the end it was helpful neither to the Church of Rome nor for the preservation of the temporal power. By its confirmation of the pope's inflexible attitude it gave violent impetus to the anti-clericalism it was designed to combat.

4

During Minghetti's premiership Victor Emmanuel had kept up his personal contacts with revolutionaries both inside and outside Italy, and he had not entirely abandoned his plan for recovering Venice by means of a Balkan rising. Minghetti himself was involved in this secret royal work, and unsuccessful efforts were made to associate Britain with it. It was only after Minghetti's resignation that a new and more practical way of regaining Venice was presented to Italy.

By 1865 the September convention was beginning to take effect. The Italian capital was transferred to Florence. The first detachments of French troops prepared to leave Rome. Recruits for a new papal army were enlisted in France, Belgium, Germany and Switzerland. The pope's clerical minister of war was replaced by a general. For the time being it seemed as though Italy could take no further step along the roads to Venice and Rome. But once again a foreign country was to play an important part in the Risorgimento.

That country was Prussia, whose chancellor, Count Otto von Bismarck, needed to eliminate Austrian influence in Germany before he could unite the German states in an empire led by Prussia. In 1862 he had freely admitted to Disraeli that he was going to make war on Austria at the earliest opportunity,[15] and now in the mid-60s he was ready to put his threat into action. His plans called for an Italian alliance, so that Austria would be attacked from both north and west and would have to fight on two fronts. Venetia would be the price for Italy's help.

La Marmora, the Italian prime minister, was delighted to listen to Bismarck's approaches. He had little faith in the king's dream of winning back Venice by means of a Garibaldian coup. The Prussian alliance seemed far more hopeful, and was even favoured by Napoleon III, who was inclined to support Italy's claim to Venice. An Italo-Prussian treaty was signed in April 1866, though La Marmora insisted that Italy would not take action until Prussia began the war.

Austria was alarmed at the prospect of having to fight on two fronts and tried to buy off Italy. An Austrian offer to give up Venetia in exchange for Italian neutrality was conveyed to La Marmora through Napoleon, who advised acceptance. But La Marmora was not prepared to break his pledge to Prussia. He held to the treaty, which was for three months only and so left open the possibility of accepting Austria's offer if Prussia did not begin the war within that period.

But Prussia acted before the three months had expired. The war began on 15 June; Bismarck pretended that Austria had provoked it, but even Moltke, commander of the Prussian armies, admitted afterwards that Prussia had deliberately planned the attack. Italy declared war on 20 June.

It was a short war – six weeks for Prussia, five for Italy – but it was long enough to give proof both of Prussia's military might and of Italy's lack of good generalship. Within three weeks Moltke and the Prussian crown prince crushed the main Austrian army after a stiff battle at Sadowa (Königgratz), and the way to Vienna lay open. But Bismarck feared French intervention if the war went on. He thought it wisest to yield to Austria's demand for an armistice, which was signed on 25 July.

While Prussia fought so brilliantly, Italy suffered the humiliation of defeat on both land and sea. The battle plan was for La Marmora and the king to attack with twelve divisions from the Mincio, while Cialdini, with six divisions, advanced from the lower Po, and Garibaldi, who had been summoned from Caprera to lead a force of 35,000 volunteers, invaded the Tyrol. The main advance collapsed after the Italian army's defeat in a series of engagements in and around Custoza; at sea Admiral Persano bombarded the island of Lissa but was then attacked and soundly beaten by a smaller Austrian fleet; only Garibaldi, operating with half his volunteers from headquarters at Salo, on Lake Garda, was able to give Italy a small victory by pushing the Austrians back and advancing into the Tyrol.

In the end, as in the war of 1859, Italy had to cease fighting in accordance with an armistice made without reference to Italian wishes. Yet there was one bright spot in this sorry tale of blunders and disaster. Italy had undoubtedly helped to win the war, for its armies had engaged 130,000 Austrians, who might otherwise have turned the scale against Prussia.[16]

The price for Italy's help was duly paid, though in a rather humiliating way. Venetia was ceded by Austria to Napoleon III, who then gave it to Italy. The transfer was confirmed by a plebiscite and Venice was once again an Italian city, but the rejoicing was tinged with disappointment. Italy had wanted more than the province which Austria called Venetia. It had hoped to conquer both Trentino (south Tyrol) and Venezia Giulia (the territory including Trieste, Gorizia, Pola and Fiume) before the war ended, and to retain them afterwards. Now both these territories remained in Austrian hands.

The war of 1866 was not one of the happier stages in the fulfilment of the Risorgimento. It would have been better for Italy's future if Venetia had been regained by the force of its own arms.

Its restoration as a gift from France after defeat in the field gave the Italians a military inferiority complex which was to last for many years. Their later thirst for military glory may well be traced back to their defeat at Custoza.

THE ROAD TO ROME

*Mentana   The Franco-Prussian war   Porta Pia   The
reckoning*

By 1866 it seemed that brigandage was virtually suppressed in
southern Italy. Highway robberies continued, and would do so
for many years, but stern repression with the aid of some 120,000
troops had ended the state of civil war. It had been a costly
business. In the work of putting down brigandage 'there were
more regular soldiers who died from malaria alone than were
killed in all the campaigns of 1860, and more people perished in
it than were killed in all the other wars of the Risorgimento put
together.'[1]

Unhappily for the new kingdom, the withdrawal of troops
from southern Italy to take part in the Austro-Prussian war gave
an opening for another revolt in Sicily, where armed bands,
formed of autonomists, Bourbon supporters, army deserters and
peasants and other workers, rose at Palermo and overwhelmed the
small Italian garrison of 3000 men. It was a strange rising, in
which Mazzinians and Bourbonists, Mafia and clergy found themselves on the same side. Their opening success was followed by a
week of anarchy; an organizing committee, including Baron Riso
and three princes, then took control, but by that time the end of
the Austro-Prussian war had released troops who could be sent
south to restore order. The insurgents had no chance against
40,000 soldiers and the guns of the Italian fleet, and the rising
was quickly suppressed. It had shown again that Sicily could not
be easily assimilated into the general pattern of the Risorgimento.
The island had still to be garrisoned by a substantial military
force, which made Sicilians feel that they were living under
foreign occupation.

In Florence, which was now the Italian capital, Ricasoli had succeeded La Marmora as prime minister at the end of the war, and was at once faced by the parlous condition of the national finances. In 1866 the budget deficit rose to 721 million lire; the public debt, which had been 2450 million lire in 1861, was now more than doubled.[2] It was a grim position for a new state. W. E. Gladstone, writing to Sir James Lacaita at the end of 1867, commented severely: 'The truth is that no good can be done by Italy, and she cannot act with dignity and effect, until, instead of consuming her own vitals, she has balanced her income and expenditure. Until this is done she will not really have made herself a nation.'[3]

This was also the opinion of the remarkable Quintino Sella, who was finance minister in several coalition and right-wing ministries from 1862 onwards. He was a man of the greatest integrity, with a wide range of cultural and intellectual interests, who deliberately chose the thankless post of finance minister because of his deep conviction that Italy must be able to pay its way. His political sense told him that a country which was always in financial trouble would exert little influence abroad and would be in danger of losing its authority at home, and he was not held back by the knowledge that rigorous fiscal measures would certainly make him unpopular. His policies pressed hardly on the Italian people, but his efforts to restore the national finance were at last rewarded by Italy's first balanced budget in 1876.

Riscasoli's return to office in 1866 was of short duration. In 1867 Rattazzi was prime minister again with a largely left-wing ministry. His previous ministries had been ended by the defeat of Novara in 1849 and the Aspromonte affair in 1862. He was again destined for trouble, and again, as in 1862, it was Garibaldi who caused it.

At the end of 1866 the last of the French troops left Rome, in accordance with the September convention, and a papal army of 11,000 foreign mercenaries took over the defence of the city and of the temporal power. In the following year the new situation encouraged both Mazzini and Garibaldi to make plots for the seizure of Rome. They were working, however, along different lines.

At that time Mazzini was looking for help from a new and

unexpected quarter. In November the champion of liberty and republicanism had actually opened negotiations with a conservative monarchist, none other than Bismarck, the Prussian chancellor. Mazzini warned Bismarck (both prematurely and incorrectly) that a Franco-Italian alliance was being prepared, and he asked for 1 million lire and 10,000 rifles which he would use to overthrow the Italian government. Bismarck, who was already planning to make war on France and knew that a Franco-Italian alliance would make victory more difficult, did not reject Mazzini's suggestion out of hand, but asked for proof of the coming pact. Since Mazzini had no proof, his request was left in abeyance, and nothing came of it.[4]

But Mazzini still had his eye on Rome, and it is clear from his correspondence that he wanted something more than a mere insurrection, which would probably have been followed by Italian intervention, a plebiscite and annexation. 'I want Rome to be the metropolis of the nation,' he wrote to a young English friend, 'and I want her rising to give a new watchword to Italy, to instil a new life in our people.'[5] The new watchword was not given. There were no more Mazzinian risings in Italy.

Garibaldi's approach was on the old 'Rome or death' lines. He decided to collect a band of volunteers, enter papal territory from the north and march on Rome. At the same time he hoped to promote an insurrection in the city, so that its capture would be made easier. Mazzini disapproved of Garibaldi's venture, as he felt that it would make it impossible for him to go ahead with his own plot.

The attitude of the king and Rattazzi towards Garibaldi's venture is not entirely clear. Garibaldi claimed that he was encouraged to march on Rome by emissaries of the Italian government, which hoped to use the disturbance as an excuse for entering Rome to restore order; Rattazzi denied this, but the king's private statements to the French and British ambassadors tend to confirm Garibaldi's claim.* It is certain, at all events,

---

* According to a despatch from Baron de Malaret, the French ambassador in Florence, after an interview with Victor Emmanuel, the king had hoped to use Garibaldi's expedition as an excuse for occupying Rome, and had devised a remarkable plan for the occasion. 'This plan,' de Malaret wrote on 29 November 1867, 'consisted in letting the Garibaldians enter Rome and

that the government did nothing to stop the assembly of volunteers on the papal frontier, and that secret service funds were used to supply them with arms.[6] Rattazzi may, perhaps, have been hoping that the mere prospect of a Garibaldian invasion would lead to a spontaneous insurrection in Rome, after which (as Mazzini surmised) the city and its surrounding territory could be annexed by plebiscite.

Insurrection by the Romans was, in fact, an integral part of Garibaldi's plan, and on 16 September, after assuming his old title of general of the Roman republic, he issued a proclamation calling on the Romans to rise against their oppressors and assuring them that 'there will be many Italians on hand to share your glory'. This was too much for Rattazzi, who was fearful of arousing Napoleon III's displeasure by breaking the September convention. Garibaldi was arrested and sent back to Caprera.

This was only a half-measure. The volunteers were still at liberty. Armed bands under Menotti Garibaldi, the general's son, crossed into papal territory, and attempts were made to send arms to Rome and to persuade the Romans to rise on behalf of their own liberty. But the Romans, like the Neapolitans in 1860, were apathetic. They were content to be rescued, if that might be. They were not willing to share the responsibility by starting an insurrection on any considerable scale. A small rising was actually begun on the evening of 22 October, but it was suppressed by the following morning, and a body of seventy-eight Garibaldians, who arrived by boat expecting to find the city in full revolt, were surprised and defeated by papal troops on the next day. One of their leaders, Enrico Cairoli, was killed, and his brother Giovanni was taken prisoner, together with all the other survivors.

concentrate there to the strength of twenty or thirty thousand. When that was done, and while the Pope was safe in Castel Sant'Angelo, the king would have entered the eternal city in his turn at the head of his troops, and the massacre of the revolutionary bands would have been such that no trace would have been left of them. With the ground thus cleared, his Majesty said he was convinced that it would have been very easy to make an arrangement with the Pope.' (Alessandro Luzio, *Aspromonte e Mentana*, pp. 432–3). Perhaps it was a good thing for 'the honest king's' contemporary reputation that Napoleon III, to whom he confided his bloodthirsty project, would not allow him to carry it out.

Garibaldi's last 'Rome or death!' expedition moved to its destined failure. He escaped from Caprera, returned to the volunteers and began the march on Rome. With 3000 men he defeated the papal troops at Monterotondo on 24–26 October, but after advancing further on the road to Rome he heard that a French army had landed at Civita Vecchia and he went back to Monterotondo. On 3 November he decided to retreat towards Tivoli and was attacked on the way by papal troops at Mentana. For a time the Garibaldians held their own, but the issue was soon decided when the French army came to the aid of the papalists.

Napoleon had decided that it was France's duty to protect the papal territory, as it had done from 1849 to 1866. He forbade the Italian government to send troops against Garibaldi, and a French expeditionary force, armed with the brand-new *chassepot* rifle, was sent from Toulon to Civita Vecchia. At Mentana the volunteers had no chance against the well-armed French troops, who substantially outnumbered them. The French had only two men killed, the papal troops lost thirty, but 1600 Garibaldians were taken prisoner. The rest of the volunteers dispersed; Garibaldi escaped across the frontier and was ignominiously arrested by the Italian police. After three weeks in custody he went home to Caprera, where his movements were watched so closely that he was virtually a prisoner.

Since Garibaldi was still a national hero, the Mentana episode aroused bitter anti-French feelings in Italy. These feelings were exacerbated when the commander of the French expedition reported to Paris: 'The *chassepots* have done marvels!' – a phrase which unhappily suggested that the aim of the expedition was to try out the new weapon on the Italians.* Another consequence of Mentana was that it re-established the French in Italy. Since the Italian government had failed to prevent Garibaldi from crossing the papal frontier Napoleon felt it his duty to protect the pope by sending a French garrison back to Rome. This garrison,

---

* Napoleon III himself thought that the *chassepots* phrase was unfortunate, and asked for it to be changed to 'The *chassepots* produced a terrible effect.' His request was ignored. The ex-Empress Eugénie told Maurice Paléologue in 1903 that Marshal Niel 'was bristling with pride in his new gun and retained the original text'. (Paléologue, *The Tragic Empress*, p. 81.)

which was later stationed at Civita Vecchia, was to be a serious embarrassment to him in the near future.

2

The two years which followed Mentana have been described as 'the years of the new kingdom's deepest moral depression'.[7] It was a period of bitter anti-clericalism and of weakened faith in the monarchy. Rattazzi had resigned in the middle of the Mentana crisis, and the king turned, as he had done before, to a general who could be trusted to do his bidding. This was General Menabrea, a former officer of the royal household. Under his uninspiring guidance political and social problems remained unsolved and the budget was still unbalanced, though Sella, who was again finance minister, ruthlessly attacked the mounting deficit by the imposition of new taxes.

His efforts were not always successful. Increased taxes on salt and tobacco brought no extra revenue because consumption was reduced. At last, in spite of opposition from his own colleague Giovanni Lanza and the parliamentary left, he reintroduced the tax on grinding wheat and corn which had been abolished on the formation of the unitary state. This was expected to produce 100 million lire a year, but only at the cost of imposing great hardship on the poorer classes, who lived largely on foodstuffs made from flour.

The new measure came into force in January 1869. Rioting followed, and there were 250 deaths, 1000 people wounded and 4000 imprisoned. The rioters' cries of 'Long live the pope and Austria' were a grim sign that the new kingdom had no firm hold on the people. Though Sella's policies were successful in the end, he can hardly escape criticism for laying so much of the fiscal burden on those who were least able to bear it.

In December 1869 Menabrea was succeeded as prime minister by the much abler Giovanni Lanza, a right-wing politician who shared Cavour's views on the Roman question. Visconti Venosta was again foreign minister, a post he was to hold for the next nine years. Lanza's early months in office were marked by a few small revolutionary outbreaks in Romagna and Calabria, which were quickly suppressed by the army, and by the prefect of Genoa's failure to arrest Mazzini when that incorrigible conspirator turned up in Italy in disguise in the hope of guiding a new insurrection. But Mazzini was less fortunate when he left Genoa and went south to stir up trouble in Sicily; in spite of his disguise and the false name on his passport he was recognized, arrested and imprisoned in the fortress of Gaeta, where he was treated with every courtesy.

In Rome Pius IX's attention was diverted from temporal to spiritual power, as the first Vatican council, which opened in December 1869, proceeded to define the fundamentals of the Catholic faith and to declare that papal infallibility was one of the articles of that faith. The council was a sign of Pius IX's confident belief in the universality of the Church; Odo Russell told Lord Stanley, the British foreign secretary: 'The pope believes his oecumenical council to be the result of divine inspiration and that he is chosen to become the shepherd of one single united Christian flock of the future.'[8] To Roman Catholics the Council presented a reassuring picture of the fathers of a world-wide Church grouped devotedly round their spiritual leader; to others the proclamation of papal infallibility seemed to raise an impenetrable barrier between the Roman Catholic and other Churches. The pope's last efforts to preserve his temporal power were not helped by the apparent centralization of his Church's spiritual forces in the person of one man.

While the Vatican council was sitting in Rome France was blundering into war with Prussia – the war that Bismarck had skilfully planned and allowed France to provoke by its indignation at a German prince's candidature for the Spanish throne. It was an expected war, and in the preceding months Napoleon had tried to strengthen his position by forming an alliance with Italy. The French garrison in Civita Vecchia was the stumbling-block in the way of a pact.

Victor Emmanuel would have liked an alliance with France. He enjoyed making war, his favourite daughter had married a Bonaparte and he felt sure that France would win. In one of his frequent endeavours to 'make scores off his own bat' he began private negotiations with Napoleon, to whom he offered 10,000 soldiers to immobilize Bavaria if Austria also came in with

France. But he wanted his price. Napoleon must give up Rome to Italy.[9]

In these secret negotiations Victor Emmanuel was backed by some prominent Italian military leaders and right-wing politicians, but Italian public opinion favoured neutrality or was even pro-Prussian; and a French alliance would have been most unpopular in Italy.[10] The project broke down over Italy's demand for Rome. Austria agreed that this was a just demand, but Napoleon would not accede to it in face of the opposition of his wife and many of his ministers. 'Better the Prussians in Paris than the Italians in Rome,' said the Empress Eugénie, and a leading minister assured the chamber of deputies that the French flag would never cease to fly at Civita Vecchia as guardian of the Vatican.[11]

The pope's supporters carried the day. Napoleon lost a valuable alliance because of the ill-chance which had taken French troops to Italy twenty-one years earlier and had sent them back again in 1867. Prince Napoleon, a keen supporter of a Franco-Italian alliance, was hardly exaggerating when he said later that the attempt to maintain the pope's temporal power cost France Alsace and Lorraine.

France declared war on Prussia on 15 July 1870. The early Prussian victories showed that the French armies would need every man they could raise. In August the French troops at Civita Vecchia sailed for France, in accordance, the French government politely informed the Italian, with the terms of the September convention, which was still in force. The road to Rome was open at last. The pope had no foreign protector. Only his own mercenary army was left to defend him.

The recall of the French garrison was greeted in Italy with left-wing demands for the immediate seizure of Rome. Lanza, the prime minister, declined to move; he agreed with France that the September convention was still in force. His attitude infuriated the left, who threatened to leave the chamber of deputies and appeal to the people, but a swift intervention by Sella averted a political crisis. Sella had a passionate faith that Rome must be Italy's capital; he now told the left-wing leaders that the September convention would not prevent the government from 'going to Rome', that it *would* go, and that he would resign and join the opposition if it did not do so. His sincerity carried conviction. The left agreed to wait for the government to act.

As the war continued to go badly for France Napoleon made a final effort to enlist Italian and Austrian aid. In the middle of August Prince Napoleon was sent to Florence on an urgent mission. The emperor hoped that Victor Emmanuel's own son-in-law, who was a known friend of Italy, might succeed where he and his ministers had failed.

Prince Napoleon was told that it was too late. There was no time to raise an expeditionary force. The size of the army had been cut as one of Sella's economy measures. Even a partial mobilization was impossible; the only help that could be offered was so trivial that it would be useless to France and would endanger Italy.

Inquiries from Vienna drew an equally discouraging answer. Intervention would be fruitless at the point which the war had now reached. Prince Napoleon went back to Paris with the painful knowledge that the French empire was lost.*

Italy and Austria were right. It was far too late to save France. Napoleon had made the fatal blunder of trying to maintain the pope's temporal power (which he had criticized so much in the past) even at the cost of a vital military alliance. He paid for his blunder at Sedan on 1 September.

3

On Sella's insistence, the Italian government had begun to discuss

---

* In view of the general gloom in Italy in 1859 when the fifteen-year-old Princess Clotilde married the raffish, middle-aged Prince Napoleon it is pleasant to know that she was still a loyal wife to him eleven years later, in spite of his own infidelity. When the fall of France was imminent Clotilde flatly refused her father's suggestion that she should go back to Italy. In a superb letter, which Massari quotes in *La Vita ed il Regno di Vittorio Emanuele II* (II, p. 374) she declared that, out of regard for her husband, her sons, her adopted country, her native country, she could not leave Paris at such a time. 'One is not a princess of the House of Savoy for nothing,' she proudly informed her father. Massari also tells us that, when the war was lost and she could no longer stay in France, 'she did not flee from Paris; she went quietly away, serene and imperturbable, admired by all, a daughter truly worthy of her father'.

plans for the early occupation of Rome within a few days of the French troops' departure from Civita Vecchia on 19 August. At first, instead of considering the ways and means of ending the pope's temporal power, the ministry became involved in a strange debate on whether Rome, after annexation, should become the capital of Italy or should just be regarded as an Italian provincial city.[12] It is true that it was only five years since the capital had been transferred to Florence, yet even so it seems astonishing that an Italian cabinet should ever have thought it possible to deny Rome the primacy among Italian cities. The idea appears to have lingered on, as a matter of debate, till a week before the occupation. It may only have been finally dispelled when Count Ponza di San Martino, who had been on a government mission to Rome, came back to tell the cabinet: 'The Romans will demand a republic rather than agree to become an Italian provincial town.'[13]

Early in September the government was ready for action. An army commanded by General Raffaele Cadorna was waiting on the frontier of the papal territory. The cabinet was agreed that the pope should be left with complete independence within the boundaries of the Leonine city (which is now more generally known as Vatican city), and that there should be no interference with his spiritual powers. But one question still divided the ministers. Some, like Sella, felt that there was no obstacle to the immediate military occupation of Rome, provided that the major powers were informed in advance and raised no objection; it was Sella's contention that, in the changed circumstances, the September convention did not prohibit such an occupation. Other ministers, including Visconti Venosta, were not so sure about the legality of immediate occupation and wished to safeguard Italy against any accusation of aggression; they thought it advisable to wait for a suitable incident, such as a popular rising or a mutiny in the papal army, which would justify Italian intervention to maintain public order.[14]

King Victor Emmanuel was at first opposed to an immediate march on Rome, but after demonstrations in Florence and threats of mass resignations by the parliamentary left, he agreed to follow whatever advice his ministers gave him. He was ready, says Salvemini, 'to destroy the pope's dominion, so as to avoid seeing both the pope's dominion and that of his own dynasty destroyed simultaneously.'[15]

While the exact date of the occupation was still undecided, the situation was dramatically changed by Napoleon's surrender and the proclamation of the French third republic. Even the legalists could no longer argue that the September convention, which had been made with Napoleon III and the ministers of the Second Empire, was still binding. Formal notes, which varied slightly according to the probable reaction of the receiving countries, were sent by Visconti Venosta to the European powers, to inform them of the reasons which made the Italian occupation of Rome imperative.

At the same time Victor Emmanuel made a last appeal to Pius IX for a friendly settlement. Count Ponza di San Martino was sent to Rome with a personal letter to the pope. Writing 'with the affection of a son, the faith of a Catholic, the loyalty of a king and the soul of an Italian', Victor Emmanuel announced that his troops were obliged to go beyond the papal frontier to maintain the security of Italy and of the Holy See. He appealed for the pope's benevolent co-operation.[16]

The pope's reply was a blunt refusal of Victor Emmanuel's request for a friendly settlement and a complete rejection of the principles on which it was based. In the audience he gave to San Martino the pope further declared that he would yield only to violence and that he reserved the right to make at least a formal resistance to the Italian army.[17]

The issue was now decided. The answers from the powers raised no insuperable objections. On 12 September Cadorna's troops crossed the papal frontier and began a leisurely advance on Rome. As they approached the city Pius IX made his last appearance outside the walls of the Vatican, his last appearance as a European sovereign, the temporal ruler of Rome. On 19 September he drove to the church of St John Lateran to review the papal army, which was drawn up before it. Supported by a friend, he climbed the Scala Santa on his knees. On reaching the top he first prayed, and then turned to bless the troops. Afterwards he drove back to the Vatican, where he was resolved to stay.

On 20 September, at half past five in the morning, the Italians were at the gates of Rome. Almost up to the last moment the Italian government hoped for a popular rising, so that the troops could enter as guardians of order; but the Roman people did nothing. A detachment of papal troops attempted to bar the army's entry into Rome. It was only a token resistance, and was soon abandoned, but nineteen papal soldiers and forty-nine Italian soldiers were killed. Then the Italians made a breach in the city wall at Porta Pia, which at that time adjoined the rural area of the Campagna. The troops entered the city and took possession of all Rome except the Vatican palaces and Castel Sant'Angelo. The pope's temporal power – the oldest sovereignty in Europe – was ended.

Twelve days later the military occupation of Rome and the surrounding territory was confirmed by a plebiscite, in which 133,681 votes were cast in favour of annexation to the kingdom of Italy and 1507 against. Lanza and Sella announced the result to Victor Emmanuel in Florence. In a public statement he declared grandiloquently: 'The arduous enterprise is finally accomplished. The fatherland is made.'[18] Guns boomed in salute, and Sir James Hudson, the British minister, poetically fancied that the portrait of Dante in the Bargello let fall a sympathetic tear.[19]

Victor Emmanuel's private reaction to the news had been rather different from his public declaration. When the two ministers said politely that they were sure his Majesty must be very happy, the king replied in broad Piedmontese: 'Oh, shut up. There's nothing left for me now but to shoot myself. For what remains of my life there will be nothing else to take.'* It was this remark which made Sella call him 'the last of the conquistadors'.

4

The Risorgimento was completed. The Tyrol and Venezia Giulia were still in Austrian hands, and would remain so until after the first world war, but Rome was now the capital of united Italy.

---

* 'Ca staga ciutô; am resta nen aut che tireme un culp d'revolver; per l'on c'am resta da vive ai sarà nen da pié.' (F. Martini, *Confessioni e Ricordi*, pp. 152–3, quoted by Gramsci, *Il Risorgimento*, pp. 171–2.)

Mazzini, who was released from Gaeta under the amnesty which followed the occupation of Rome, might say ruefully, 'I thought to call up the soul of Italy, and I see only its corpse.' Yet his dream of liberty, unity and independence had been realized in his lifetime, and his own driving force, together with the constructive acts of Cavour and Garibaldi and the support of Victor Emmanuel II, had helped to build resurgent Italy.

Roman Catholics all over the world protested at the rape of the pope's temporal power, but no government took action against Italy. The Cavourian principle of 'a free Church in a free state' was put into practice by the law of guarantees which was passed in November and regulated the relations of Church and state in Italy until Mussolini made the Lateran treaty with Pope Pius XI in 1929. The law of 1870 allowed the pope the full attributes of a sovereign within the Vatican city, authorized him to have his personal guard, postal and telegraph services, and offered him an annual payment of more than 3 million lire a year in return for his lost territories. But this was not a treaty between Italy and the papacy and it was ignored by Pius IX and his successors, who refused to recognize the Italian government and regarded themselves as 'prisoners of the Vatican'. The effect of the loss of temporal power on the propagation of the faith is outside the scope of this book, but it may be mentioned that one of Pius IX's orders to the faithful had a baleful influence on Italian public life for years to come. This was his stern injunction that no Italian catholic should take part in his country's government, either as voter or as deputy.

One of the great architects of the Risorgimento was already dead. Of the others Mazzini died in Pisa in 1872, and Victor Emmanuel II in Rome in 1878. An English resident said of the king's passing: 'No death in the world ever called forth a more passionate expression of grief. It was as if the nation had lost a father.'[20] Garibaldi died in Caprera in 1882, married at last to his mistress Francesca Armosino. 'His wish to be cremated in an aromatic pyre was disregarded,' says one of his biographers. 'He was buried near the house in the presence of dignitaries of the Crown and government under a solid block of granite bearing the single word, *Garibaldi*.'[21] Another great Italian died in the same year as Victor Emmanuel. Pius IX's long reign was over at last, and the Roman people, whose fathers held torchlight processions in the pope's honour, had come to dislike him so much that it was unsafe to carry out a prearranged plan of taking his coffin from the Vatican to the church of San Lorenzo fuori le Mura. It was taken there at night three years later and rests in a pseudo-mediaeval funerary chapel.

Faced by the unrelenting opposition of the Catholic Church, the Italy of the Risorgimento moved rather uneasily into its life of unity and independence. Years were to pass before it became a genuine democracy; it began as an 'oligarchy of notables' and it was not until 1912 that suffrage became almost universal. A dozen years later the Risorgimento's achievements were temporarily overthrown by Mussolini's fascist state, and it took a second world war to create the Italian republic that Young Italy had called for in Marseilles more than a century earlier.

What is the final reckoning? There are those who say that the Risorgimento was not the resurgence of Italy at all, but only the conquest of Italy by the Savoy monarchy. But that is not really what happened. In spite of all the Piedmontization of the 1860s, Italy is not, and never has been, simply an enlarged Piedmont. As Ruggero Moscati observes, Italy drew the House of Savoy to itself, and the history of Savoy merged into Italian history. The royal 'conquest' was actually the royal acceptance of the new Italy.[22]

Others again, like Gobetti in *Risorgimento senza eroi*, look upon the Risorgimento as a *rivoluzione mancata*, a revolution which never came off. They condemn it for its lack of social and agrarian reconstruction, of conscious economic advance and of religious reform, and for the fact that it was made by the leadership of the few rather than the initiative of the whole people. But surely it is academic to say that the Risorgimento *should* have been different from what it was. It must be taken as it stands. Its architects did what they could, and they were well aware that they could not do everything at once.

In his diary of the years 1858–60 Giuseppe Massari has recorded Cavour's prophetic answer to those who attack the Risorgimento for its lack of social significance. Relations between capital and labour, said Cavour, were undoubtedly the great problem of the future. 'This will be seen in Italy,' he added, 'but it is a matter for our successors to deal with. We can think of nothing but the national question.'[23]

That was the point. It was, above all, the national question which mattered in the years of the Risorgimento. Between 1815 and 1870 the separate states of Italy were united into a single free and independent nation, and that was enough for the time being. It was not, of course, a great popular uprising, but the minority who made the union were working, as Omodeo remarks, *for* the people and believed *in* the people.[24] At certain stages in the Risorgimento governmental and popular initiative marched together, but at all times the movement succeeded only when it was able to win the acceptance of the people of Italy. In the long run it is that acceptance which has made resurgent Italy a living nation.

SELECT BIBLIOGRAPHY

HISTORIES

Arrivabene, Count Charles. *Italy under Victor Emmanuel.* 2 vols. London, 1862.

Berkeley, G. F.-H. and J. *Italy in the Making.* 3 vols. Cambridge, 1932–40.

Bersezio, Vittorio. *Il Regno di Vittorio Emanuele II.* 8 vols. Turin, 1878–95.

Cambridge Modern History. Vol. X. Cambridge, 1907.

Catalano, F., Moscati, R. and Valsecchi, F. *L'Italia nel Risorgimento dal 1789 al 1870.* Verona, 1964.

Clough, Shepherd B. and Saladino, Salvatore. *A History of Modern Italy.* New York and London, 1968.

Croce, Benedetto. *Storia del Regno di Napoli.* 2nd edition. Bari, 1931.

Farini, Luigi Carlo. *The Roman State from 1815 to 1850.* 4 vols. London, 1851–4.

Fisher, H. A. L. *A History of Europe.* London, 1936.

Grant, A. J. and Temperley, Harold. *Europe in the Nineteenth and Twentieth Centuries.* 6th edition. London, 1952.

Guedalla, Philip. *The Second Empire.* London, 1922.

Heriot, Angus. *The French in Italy, 1796–1799.* London, 1957.

Lucas-Dubreton, J. *La Restauration et la Monarchie de Juillet.* Paris, 1926.

King, Bolton. *A History of Italian Unity.* 2 vols. London, 1899.

Mack Smith, Denis. *A History of Sicily.* Vol. III. London, 1968.

——. *Il Risorgimento italiano.* Bari, 1968.

——. *Italy : a Modern History.* Ann Arbor and London, 1959.

——. *The Making of Italy.* London, 1968.

Mario, Jessie White. *The Birth of Modern Italy.* London, 1890.

Marriott, Sir John A. R. *The Makers of Modern Italy.* Oxford, 1931.

New Cambridge Modern History. Vol. X. Cambridge, 1960.

Omodeo, Adolfo. *L'Età del Risorgimento italiano.* Naples, 1946.

Romeo, Rosario. *Dal Piemonte sabaudo all'Italia liberale.* Turin, 1963.

——. *Il Risorgimento in Sicilia.* Bari, 1950.

Rosi, Michele. *Storia Contemporanea d'Italia.* Turin, 1914.

Salvatorelli, Luigi. *Sommario della Storia d'Italia.* Turin, 1938.

Spellanzon, Cesare. *Storia del Risorgimento e dell'Unità d'Italia.* 7 vols. Milan, 1934–51.

Sprigge, C. J. S. *The Development of Modern Italy.* London, 1943.

Thayer, W. M. *The Dawn of Italian Independence*. Boston, 1893.

Tivaroni, Carlo. *L'Italia durante il dominio austriaco*. 3 vols. Turin and Rome, 1892–4.

Trease, Geoffrey. *The Italian Story*. London, 1963.

Trevelyan, Janet P. *A Short History of the Italian People*. Revised edition. London, 1956.

Whelpton, Eric. *A Concise History of Italy*. London, 1964.

Whyte, A. J. *The Evolution of Modern Italy*. Oxford, 1944.

Woolf, S. J. *The Italian Risorgimento*. London, 1969.

CRITICAL STUDIES

About, E. *La Question Romaine*. Brussels, 1859.

Azeglio, Massimo d'. *Degli Ultimi Casi di Romagna*. Italy, 1846.

Blakiston, Noel. *The Roman Question*. London, 1962.

Bonanno, Carlo. *I Problemi del Risorgimento*. Padua, 1961.

Cattaneo, Carlo. *L'insurrection de Milan e le Considerazioni sul 1848*. New edition. Turin, 1949.

Gentile, Giovanni. *I Profeti del Risorgimento italiano*. 2nd edition. Florence, 1928.

Ghisalberti, Alberto M. *Gli Albori del Risorgimento italiano, 1700–1815*. Rome, 1931.

Gioberti, Vincenzo. *Del Primato Morale e Civile degli Italiani*. New edition. Turin, 1932.

Gobetti, Piero. *Risorgimento senza eroi*. Turin, 1926.

——. *Scritti Politici*. Turin, 1960.

Gramsci, Antonio. *Il Risorgimento*. 9th edition. Turin, 1966.

Greenfield, Kent Roberts. *Economics and Liberalism in the Risorgimento*. Revised edition. Baltimore, 1965.

Grew, Raymond. *A Sterner Plan for Italian Unity*: the Italian National Society in the Risorgimento. Princeton, 1963.

Jemolo, Arturo Carlo. *Chiesa e Stato in Italia negli ultimi cento anni*. Turin, 1955.

Luzio, Alessandro. *Aspromonte e Mentana*. Florence, 1935.

Mack Smith, Denis. *Cavour and Garibaldi, 1860*. Cambridge, 1954.

Matter, Paul. *Cavour et l'Unité Italienne*. 3 vols. Paris, 1922–7.

Maturi, Walter. *Interpretazioni del Risorgimento*. Turin, 1965.

Mori, Renato. *Il Tramonto del Potere Temporale*. Rome, 1967.

——. *La Questione Romana*. Florence, 1963.

Moscati, Ruggero. *Risorgimento liberale*. Catania, 1967.

Omodeo, Adolfo. *Difesa del Risorgimento*. Turin, 1951.

——. *L'opera politica del Conte di Cavour*. 2 vols. Florence, 1945.

Pieri, Piero. *Storia militare del Risorgimento*. Turin, 1962.

Salvatorelli, Luigi. *Pensiero e azione del Risorgimento*. Turin, 1960.

——. *Spiriti e Figure del Risorgimento*. Florence, 1961.

Salvemini, Gaetano. *Mazzini*. London, 1956.
——. *Scritti sul Risorgimento*. Milan, 1961.
Sanctis, Francesco de. *Mazzini*. Bari, 1920.
Taylor, A. J. P. *The Italian Problem in European Diplomacy*. Manchester, 1934.
——. *The Struggle for Mastery in Europe, 1848–1918*. Oxford, 1954.
Valsecchi, Franco. *Italia ed Europa nel* 1859. Florence, 1965.
——. *L'alleanza di Crimea*. 2nd edition. Florence, 1968.
Woodward, E. L. *Three Studies in European Conservatism*. London, 1929.

BIOGRAPHIES

Acton, Harold. *The Last Bourbons of Naples*. London, 1961.
Bell, A. Craig. *Alexandre Dumas*. London, 1950.
Belloc, Hilaire. *Napoleon*. London, 1932.
Bibl, Victor. *Metternich, 1773–1859*. Paris, 1935.
Cerro, Emilio del. *Giuseppe Mazzini e Giuditta Sidoli*. Turin, 1909.
Colomb, Vice-Admiral P. H. *Memoirs of Sir Astley Cooper Key*. London, 1898.
Croce, Benedetto. *Maria Cristina di Savoia*. Naples, 1924.
Curatulo, Giacomo Emilio. *Garibaldi e le Donne*. Rome, 1913.
Dansette, Adrien. *Louis-Napoléon à la Conquête du Pouvoir*. Paris, 1961.
Decaux, Alain. *La Castiglione; Dame de Coeur de l'Europe*. Paris, 1953.
Dicey, Edward. *Cavour: a Memoir*. London, 1861.
Driault, J.-E. *Napoléon en Italie*. Paris, 1906.
Entreves, E. Passerin d'. *L'Ultima Battaglia Politica di Cavour*. Turin, 1956.
Espitalier, Albert. *Napoleon and King Murat*. London, 1912.
Garnier, Jean-Paul. *Murat, Roi de Naples*. Paris, 1959.
Griffith, Gwilym O. *Mazzini: Prophet of Modern Europe*. London, 1932.
Grunwald, Constantin de. *La Vie de Metternich*. Paris, 1938.
Hales, E. E. Y. *Mazzini and the Secret Societies*. London, 1956.
——. *Pio Nono*. London, 1954.
Halperin, S. William. *Diplomat under Stress* (Visconti Venosta). Chicago, 1963.
Hammond, J. L. and Barbara. *James Stansfeld*. London, 1964.
Hancock, W. K. *Ricasoli and the Risorgimento in Tuscany*. London, 1926.
Hermant, Abel. *La Castiglione*. Paris, 1938.
Hibbert, Christopher. *Garibaldi and his Enemies*. London, 1956.
Hinkley, Edith. *Mazzini: the story of a great Italian*. London, 1924.
James, Henry. *William Wetmore Story and his Friends*. Vol. I. Boston, 1903.

King, Bolton. *The Life of Mazzini*. Revised edition. London, 1912.

Lacaita, Charles. *An Italian Englishman* (Sir James Lacaita). London, 1933.

Luzio, Alessandro. *Carlo Alberto e Giuseppe Mazzini*. Turin, 1923.

——. *Giuseppe Mazzini, Carbonaro*. Turin, 1920.

Mack Smith, Denis. *Garibaldi*. London, 1957.

Malmesbury, Earl of. *Memoirs of an ex-Minister*. New edition. London, 1885.

Marshall, Ronald. *Massimo d'Azeglio*. London, 1966.

Martin, Sir Theodore. *Life of the Prince Consort*. Vol. III. London, 1877.

Massari, Giuseppe. *Diario dalle cento Voci*. New edition. Bologna, 1959.

——. *La Vita ed il Regno di Vittorio Emanuele II*. 2 vols. Milan, 1878.

Mastellone, Salvo. *Mazzini e la 'Giovane Italia'*. 2 vols. Pisa, 1960.

Maurois, André. *Alexandre Dumas*. London, 1955.

Mazzini, Giuseppe. *Life and Writings*. 6 vols. London, 1864–70.

Morelli, Emilia. *Mazzini in Inghilterra*. Florence, 1938.

O'Meara, Kathleen. *Frederic Ozanam*. Edinburgh, 1876.

Packe, Michael St John. *The Bombs of Orsini*. London, 1957.

Paléologue, Maurice. *Cavour*. Paris, 1929.

——. *The Tragic Empress* (Empress Eugénie). London, 1928.

Parris, John. *The Lion of Caprera* (Garibaldi). London, 1962.

Pasolini, Pietro Desiderio. *Memoir of Count Giuseppe Pasolini*. London, 1885.

Phillimore, Vice-Admiral Augustus. *Life of Admiral of the Fleet Sir William Parker*. London, 1880.

Polnay, Peter de. *Garibaldi*. London, 1960.

Rodolico, Niccolo. *Carlo Alberto*. 3 vols. Florence, 1930–43.

Romeo, Rosario. *Cavour ed il Suo Tempo, 1810–1842*. Bari, 1969.

Simpson, F. A. *Louis Napoleon and the Recovery of France*. London, 1923.

——. *The Rise of Louis Napoleon*. London, 1909.

Trevelyan, G. M. *Garibaldi and the Defence of Rome*. London, 1907.

——. *Garibaldi and the Thousand*. London, 1909.

——. *Garibaldi and the Making of Italy*. London, 1911.

——. *Manin and the Venetian Revolution of 1848*. London, 1923.

Venturi, Emilie A. *Joseph Mazzini*. London, 1875.

Vidal, C. *Charles-Albert et le Risorgimento Italien*. Paris, 1927.

Whyte, A. J. *The Political Life and Letters of Cavour, 1848–1861*. London, 1930.

LETTERS

Cavour, Camillo di. *Cavour e l'Inghilterra*. 2 vols. Bologna, 1933.

——. *Il carteggio Cavour-Nigra dal 1858 al 1861*. Bologna, 1926–9.

Chiala, Luigi (edited by). *Lettere Edite ed Inedite di Camillo Cavour.*
6 vols. Turin, 1883–7.
Huxley, Leonard (edited by). *Jane Welsh Carlyle : Letters to her Family,*
1839–1863. London, 1924.
Kenyon, F. G. *Letters of Elizabeth Barrett Browning.* London, 1897.
King, Mrs Hamilton. *Letters and Recollections of Mazzini.* London,
1922.
Richards, Mrs E. F. (edited by). *Mazzini's Letters to an English Family*
3 vols. London, 1920–2.

OTHER BOOKS

Bandini, Gino. *Giornali e scritti politici clandestini della Carboneria*
Romagnola. Rome and Milan, 1908.
Brancaccio di Carpino, F. *The Fight for Freedom : Palermo, 1860.*
London, 1968.
Cobbett, James P. *Journal of a Tour in Italy.* London, 1830.
Connell, Brian. *Regina v. Palmerston.* London, 1962.
Dumas, Alexandre. *On Board the Emma.* London, 1929.
Dunant, J. Henry. *Un Souvenir de Solferino.* Geneva, 1863.
Ellesmere, Earl of (translated by). *Military Events in Italy, 1848–1849.*
London, 1851.
Elliot, Frances. *Roman Gossip.* London, 1894.
Enciclopedia Italiana.
Nicolson, Harold. *The Congress of Vienna.* London, 1946.
Ottolini, Angelo. *La Carboneria.* Modena, 1936.
Trollope, Theodosia. *Social Aspects of the Italian Revolution.* London,
1861.

A NOTE ON REFERENCES

References to authors' names are to their works which appear in the bibliography. To simplify references to authors of more than one of the books referred to, the following abbreviations are used:

Hales, *Mazzini*	E. E. Y. Hales, *Mazzini and the Secret Societies*
Hales, *Pio*	E. E. Y. Hales, *Pio Nono*
King, *Unity*	Bolton King, *History of Italian Unity*
King, *Mazzini*	Bolton King, *Life of Mazzini*
Mack Smith, *Garibaldi*	Denis Mack Smith, *Garibaldi*
Mack Smith, *Sicily*	Denis Mack Smith, *History of Sicily*, vol. III
Mack Smith, *Risorg.*	Denis Mack Smith, *Il Risorgimento Italiano*
Mack Smith, *Italy*	Denis Mack Smith, *Italy : a Modern History*
Mack Smith, *Cav.-Gar.*	Denis Mack Smith, *Cavour and Garibaldi, 1860*
Mack Smith, *Making*	Denis Mack Smith, *Making of Italy*
Mori, *Questione*	Renato Mori, *La Questione Romana*
Mori, *Tramonto*	Renato Mori, *Il Tramonto del Potere Temporale*
Omodeo, *Difesa*	Adolfo Omodeo, *Difesa del Risorgimento*
Omodeo, *Età*	Adolfo Omodeo, *L'Età del Risorgimento italiano*
Omodeo, *O.P.C.*	Adolfo Omodeo, *L'opera politica del Conte di Cavour*
Paléologue, *Cavour*	Maurice Paléologue, *Cavour*
Paléologue, *Empress*	Maurice Paléologue, *Tragic Empress*
Romeo, *Piemonte*	Rosario Romeo, *Dal Piemonte sabaudo all'Italia liberale*
Romeo, *Sicilia*	Rosario Romeo, *Il Risorgimento in Sicilia*
Romeo, *Cavour*	Rosario Romeo, *Cavour ed il Suo Tempo*
Salvatorelli, *Sommario*	Luigi Salvatorelli, *Sommario della Storia d'Italia*
Salvatorelli, *Pensiero*	Luigi Salvatorelli, *Pensiero e azione del Risorgimento*
Salvatorelli, *Spiriti*	Luigi Salvatorelli, *Spiriti e Figure del Risorgimento*
Salvemini, *Mazzini*	Gaetano Salvemini, *Mazzini*
Salvemini, *Scritti*	Gaetano Salvemini, *Scritti sul Risorgimento*
Trevelyan, *Defence*	G. M. Trevelyan, *Garibaldi and the Defence of Rome*
Trevelyan, *Thousand*	G. M. Trevelyan, *Garibaldi and the Thousand*
Trevelyan, *Making*	G. M. Trevelyan, *Garibaldi and the Making of Italy*
Trevelyan, *Manin*	G. M. Trevelyan, *Manin and the Venetian Revolution of 1848*

REFERENCES

CHAPTER I

1. Oriani, *La lotta politica*, pp. 689–690, quoted by Maturi, p. 398.
2. Salvatorelli, *Pensiero*, pp. 34–5.
3. Omodeo, *Età*, p. 165.
4. Salvemini, *Scritti*, p. 613.
5. Mack Smith, *Risorg.*, pp. 1–14.
6. Salvatorelli, *Spiriti*, p. 92.
7. Thayer, p. 4.
8. Salvemini, *Scritti*, pp. 496–8.
9. Salvemini, *Scritti*, pp. 526, 531.
10. Maturi, 'Risorgimento' in *Enciclopedia Italiana*, XXIX, p. 434.
11. Ghisalberti, pp. 64–5; Clough and Saladino, p. 16.
12. Salvemini, *Scritti*, p. 533.
13. Salvemini, *Scritti*, p. 560.
14. Ghisalberti, p. 90.
15. Driault, p. 2.
16. Fisher, p. 823.
17. Salvatorelli, *Spiriti*, p. 131.
18. Salvemini, *Scritti*, pp. 614–15.
19. Mack Smith, *Sicily*, p. 338.
20. Romeo, *Sicilia*, p. 125; Mack Smith, *Sicily*, p. 342.
21. Espitalier, p. 7.
22. Garnier, pp. 191–4.
23. Garnier, p. 224.
24. Garnier, pp. 274–5; Mack Smith *Risorg.*, pp. 20–2.
25. Mack Smith, *Risorg.*, pp. 18–19.

CHAPTER II

1. Bibl, p. 128.
2. Nicolson, p. 253.
3. Simpson, *Rise of Louis Napoleon*, p. 11.
4. Salvemini, *Scritti*, p. 397.
5. King, *Unity*, I, p. 45.
6. Nicolson, pp. 186–8.
7. Rodolico, I, p. 27.
8. Spellanzon, I, pp. 693–4; Tivaroni, I, p. 607.
9. Spellanzon, I, p. 699.
10. Tivaroni, I, p. 3.
11. Spellanzon, I, pp. 700–1; Omodeo, *Età*, p. 243.
12. Omodeo, *Età*, p. 249.
13. Tivaroni, I, p. 609.
14. Tivaroni, II, p. 1.
15. Spellanzon, I, p. 729.
16. Tivaroni, I, pp. 592–5.
17. Omodeo, *Età*, p. 240.
18. Salvemini, *Scritti*, pp. 35–6.
19. Tivaroni, I, p. 326.
20. Mazzini, I, p. 4.
21. Spellanzon, I, pp. 715–16.
22. Tivaroni, II, p. 103.
23. Tivaroni, III, p. 5.
24. Salvatorelli, *Sommario*, p. 533.
25. Romeo, *Sicilia*, p. 163.
26. Salvemini, *Scritti*, p. 615.
27. Omodeo, *Età*, p. 239.
28. Ottolini, p. 26.
29. Ottolini, p. 94.
30. Thayer, pp. 196–201.
31. Farini, I, pp. 11–12.

CHAPTER III

1. Farini, I, p. 17.
2. Spellanzon, I, pp. 783–4.
3. Spellanzon, I, p. 793.
4. Spellanzon, I, p. 807.

5. Romeo, *Sicilia*, pp. 150, 154.
6. Romeo, *Sicilia*, p. 152.
7. Salvatorelli, *Sommario*, p. 542.
8. Spellanzon, I, p. 824.
9. Spellanzon, I, p. 831.
10. Croce, *Storia del Regno di Napoli* pp. 243-4.
11. Tivaroni, I, p. 38.
12. Rodolico, I, p. 61.
13. Rodolico, I, p. 97.
14. Spellanzon, I, p. 847.
15. Tivaroni, I, p. 46.
16. Rodolico, I, p. 135.
17. Tivaroni, I, p. 51.
18. Rodolico, I, p. 210.
19. Spellanzon, I, p. 857.
20. Tivaroni, I, p. 381.
21. Rodolico, I, p. 274.
22. Rodolico, I, p. 283.
23. Vidal, p. 17.
24. Vidal, p. 18.
25. Lucas-Dubreton, p. 90.
26. Vidal, p. 18.
27. Rodolico, I, pp. 384-7.

CHAPTER IV

1. Hancock, p. 19.
2. Salvemini, *Scritti*, pp. 43-4.
3. Mack Smith, *Sicily*, pp. 362-5.
4. Tivaroni, II, p. 177.
5. Ma nesbury, p. 26.
6. Spellanzon, II, p. 292.
7. Bonanno, p. 67.
8. Spellanzon, p. 296.
9. Spellanzon, pp. 372-6.
10. Cerro, p. 50.
11. Berkeley, I, pp. 91-2.
12. Pieri, p. 122.
13. Pieri, pp. 123-4.
14. Spellanzon, II, p. 427.
15. De Sanctis, pp. 40-2.
16. Farini, I, p. 60.
17. Farini, I, p. 61.
18. Hancock, p. 28.
19. Mack Smith, *Sicily*, p. 366.
20. Croce, *Maria Cristina di Savoia*, pp. 31-6, 60.

CHAPTER V

1. Griffith, p. 24.
2. Mazzini, I, p. 2.
3. King, *Mazzini*, p. 6.
4. Mazzini, I, p. 16.
5. Hales, *Mazzini*, p. 50.
6. Hancock, pp. 47-8.
7. Omodeo, *Età*, pp. 298-9.
8. Mazzini, I, p. 34-5.
9. Mastellone, I, p. 82.
10. Mastellone, I, p. 49 n.
11. Mazzini, I, 57-60; King, *Mazzini*, pp. 44-5.
12. Mazzini, I, p. 54.
13. Gentile, p. 83.
14. Salvemini, *Mazzini*, p. 125.
15. Omodeo, *Età*, p. 300.
16. Mastellone, I, p. 89.
17. Mastellone, I, p. 91.
18. Berkeley, I, p. 17.
19. Mazzini, I, pp. 96-112.
20. Omodeo, *Età*, p. 300.
21. Pieri, pp. 107-32.
22. Woodward, p. 277.
23. Salvemini, *Mazzini*, p. 103.
24. Salvemini, *Mazzini*, pp. 18-20; De Sanctis, p. 59; Gentile, pp. 16, 51.
25. Salvemini, *Mazzini*, p. 61; Gentile, p. 64.
26. Romeo, *Piemonte*, pp. 48-9.
27. De Sanctis, p. 67.
28. Hales, *Mazzini*, p. 69.
29. Mazzini, I, p. 221.
30. Mastellone, II, p. 12.
31. King, *Mazzini*, pp. 46-7.
32. Tivaroni, I, p. 134.
33. Vidal, p. 58.
34. Luzio, *Carlo Alberto e Mazzini*, p. 182.
35. Rodolico, II, p. 135.

36. Mastellone, II, pp. 132–5; Hales *Mazzini*, pp. 107–9.
37. Mastellone, II, pp. 184–5.

38. Pieri, pp. 140–1; Hales, *Mazzini* pp. 125–6.
39. Mack Smith, *Garibaldi*, p. 15.

CHAPTER VI

1. Romeo, *Piemonte*, pp. 52–4.
2. Vidal, p. 77.
3. Hancock, pp. 48–53.
4. Omodeo, *Difesa*, p. 477.
5. Gobetti, *Scritti Politici*, p. 932.
6. Greenfield, pp. 259–60.
7. Mazzini, III, p. 164.
8. Mazzini, III, p. 165.
9. Berkeley, I, p. 241.
10. Berkeley, I, p. 242.
11. Spellanzon, II, pp. 821–5.

13. Packe, pp. 52–5.
14. Vidal, pp. 122–3.
15. Vidal, p. 124.
16. Tivaroni, II, p. 151.
17. Griffith, pp. 165–7; King, *Mazzini*, pp. 103–5.
18. Berkeley, I, p. 225.
19. Tivaroni, II, p. 252.
20. Vidal, pp. 149–50, 171.
21. King, *Unity*, I, pp. 167–8.

CHAPTER VII

1. Bonanno, p. 82.
2. Omodeo, *Età*, p. 315.
3. Omodeo, *Età*, p. 317.
4. Vidal, p. 117.
5. Matter, I, p. 242.
6. Vidal, pp. 135–6.

7. Mack Smith, *Making*, p. 115.
8. Marshall, p. 82.
9. Matter, I, p. 266.
10. Romeo, *Cavour*, pp. 733–9.
11. Mack Smith, *Making*, pp. 101–8.

CHAPTER VIII

1. Hales, *Pio*, p. 36.
2. Maturi, p. 593.
3. Berkeley, II, pp. 41–2.
4. Spellanzon, III, iii–iv.
5. Hibbert, p. 27.
6. Berkeley, II, p. 47.
7. Farini, I, p. 218.
8. O'Meara, p. 263.
9. Farini, I, p. 232.
10. Tivaroni, III, p. 173.
11. Mack Smith, *Making*, p. 117; Omodeo, *Difesa*, p. 246.
12. Tivaroni, II, p. 291–2.
13. Spellanzon, III, p. 250.

14. Richards, I, p. 38.
15. Spellanzon, III, pp. 87–8.
16. Salvatorelli, *Spiriti*, pp. 259–60.
17. Salvemini, *Scritti*, pp. 266–7.
18. E.g. Griffith, pp. 174–5.
19. Connell, p. 84.
20. Connell, p. 85.
21. Vidal, p. 359.
22. Farini, I, p. 310.
23. Hales, *Pio*, p. 81 n.
24. Vidal, p. 312.
25. Vidal, p. 392.
26. Hancock, pp. 80–1.
27. Trevelyan, *Manin*, pp. 60–4.

CHAPTER IX

1. De Grunwald, p. 306.
2. Spellanzon, IV, iii.

3. Mack Smith, *Sicily*, p. 415.
4. Romeo, *Sicilia*, p. 312.

5. Mack Smith, *Sicily*, p. 418.
6. Romeo, *Piemonte*, p. 94.
7. Farini, I, p. 357.
8. Farini, I, pp. 367–83.
9. Blakiston, p. 41.
10. Bibl., p. 323.
11. Cattaneo, p. 204.
12. Hinkley, p. 95 n.
13. Cattaneo, p. 218.
14. Cattaneo, p. 222.
15. Mack Smith, *Making*, p. 145.
16. Vidal, pp. 532–3; Romeo, *Piemonte*, p. 109.
17. Mario, p. 153.

18. Farini, II, p. 25.
19. King, *Unity*, I, p. 223.
20. Pieri, p. 196.
21. Pieri, p. 218.
22. Pieri, p. 233.
23. Richards, I, p. 86.
24. Farini, II, p. 100.
25. Pasolini, p. 61.
26. Farini, II, p. 110.
27. Spellanzon, IV, p. 215.
28. Spellanzon, IV, p. 358.
29. Phillimore, III, pp. 390–1.
30. Mack Smith, *Sicily*, p. 425.
31. Salvatorelli, *Pensiero*, pp. 136–7.

CHAPTER X

1. Salvatorelli, *Spiriti*, p. 278.
2. Trevelyan, *Defence*, pp. 88–9.
3. Farini, III, p. 215.
4. Farini, III, p. 280.
5. Griffith, p. 207.
6. Farini, III, p. 303.
7. Rodolico, III, pp. 480–1.
8. Pieri, p. 281.
9. Ellesmere, p. 237.
10. Rodolico, III, p. 543.
11. Pieri, p. 293.
12. Dicey, pp. 110–11.
13. Mack Smith, *Making*, p. 166.
14. Omodeo, *Età*, p. 353.
15. Omodeo, *Difesa*, p. 234.

16. James, p. 164.
17. Farini, III, p. 219.
18. Griffith, p. 220.
19. Blakiston, p. 181.
20. James, p. 152.
21. James, p. 153.
22. Trevelyan, *Defence*, pp. 123–4.
23. Trevelyan, *Defence*, p. 153.
24. Colomb, pp. 199–203.
25. Trevelyan, *Defence*, p. 162.
26. Trevelyan, *Defence*, pp. 188–90.
27. Trevelyan, *Defence*, p. 227.
28. Trevelyan, *Defence*, p. 231.
29. Trevelyan, *Manin*, p. 231.

CHAPTER XI

1. Elliot, p. 116.
2. Griffith, pp. 238–9.
3. Valsecchi, *L'Alleanza di Crimea*, pp. 117–18.
4. Omodeo, *O.P.C.*, I, p. 78.
5. Romeo, *Cavour*, pp. 202–4, 220–2.
6. Salvatorelli, *Pensiero*, p. 144.
7. Paléologue, *Cavour*, p. 54.
8. Omodeo, *O.P.C.*, I, pp. 136–7.
9. Omodeo, *O.P.C.*, I, p. 135.
10. Salvatorelli, *Pensiero*, pp. 147–8.
11. De Sanctis, p. 52.

12. King, *Mazzini*, p. 140.
13. Kenyon, II, p. 78.
14. Morelli, p. 85.
15. Salvatorelli, *Pensiero*, p. 148.
16. Dicey, pp. 172–3.
17. Omodeo, *O.P.C.*, I, p. 145.
18. Cavour, *Cavour e l'Inghilterra*, II, 2, pp. 284–5; Mack Smith, *Making*, p. 338.
19. Omodeo, *O.P.C.*, I, p. 150.
20. Fisher, p. 942.
21. Valsecchi, *op. cit.*, p. 356.
22. Omodeo, *O.P.C.*, II, p. 23.

23. Matter, II, p. 284.
24. Simpson, *Louis Napoleon and the Recovery of France*, p. 299.
25. Omodeo, *O.P.C.*, II, p. 47.
26. Martin, III, p. 366.
27. Chiala, II, p. 158.
28. Omodeo, *O.P.C.*, II, p. 98.
29. Romeo, *Piemonte*, p. 150.
30. Omodeo, *O.P.C.*, II, p. 112.
31. Trevelyan, *Manin*, p. 245.
32. Salvatorelli, *Spiriti*, p. 305.
33. Omodeo, *Età*, p. 383.
34. Richards, II, p. 55.
35. Lacaita, pp. 96–8.
36. Marshall, p. 258.
37. Omodeo, *O.P.C.*, II, p. 218.
38. Hammond, p. 34.
39. Salvatorelli, *Spiriti*, p. 379.

CHAPTER XII

1. Packe, p. 227.
2. Packe, p. 248.
3. Packe, p. 273.
4. Packe, p. 278.
5. Paléologue, *Empress*, p. 159.
6. Matter, III, pp. 97–9.
7. Paléologue, *Cavour*, p. 209.
8. Malmesbury, p. 466.
9. Omodeo, *Difesa*, pp. 290–1.
10. Mack Smith, *Garibaldi*, p. 76.
11. Marriott, p. 108.
12. Trollope, p. 1.
13. Pieri, pp. 597–9.
14. Mack Smith, *Garibaldi*, p. 76.
15. Blakiston, p. 28.
16. Dunant, p. 37.
17. Arrivabene,I, pp. 256–7
18. Paléologue, *Empress*, p. 29.
19. Paléologue, *Empress*, p. 76.
20. Omodeo, *Età*, pp. 390–1.
21. Whyte, *Cavour*, p. 324.
22. Paléologue, *Cavour*, p. 246.
23. Trollope, pp. 52–6.
24. Blakiston, p. 39.
25. Salvemini, *Mazzini*, p. 141.
26. Salvatorelli, *Pensiero*, pp. 153–4; Griffith, pp. 299–300.
27. Hancock, p. 229.
28. Whyte, *Cavour*, p. 338.
29. Trollope, p. 197.
30. Whyte, *Cavour*, p. 340.
31. Blakiston, p. 77.
32. Moscati, p. 86.
33. Lacaita, p. 132.
34. Romeo, *Piemonte*, p. 152.

CHAPTER XIII

Passim : Trevelyan, *Thousand*.
1. Acton, p. 465.
2. Mack Smith, *Garibaldi*, p. 86.
3. Omodeo, *O.P.C.*, II, pp. 227–9.
4. Brancaccio, p. 31.
5. Mack Smith, *Sicily*, p. 433.
6. Acton, p. 426.
7. Chiala, III, p. 250; Clough and Saladino, p. 115.
8. Chiala, III, p. 251; Clough and Saladino, p. 116.
9. Brancaccio, p. 141.
10. Mack Smith, *Making*, pp. 309–310.
11. Omodeo, *Difesa*, p. 315.
12. Mack Smith, *Cav.-Gar.*, p. 521.
13. Blakiston, p. 110.
14. Cavour, *Cavour-Nigra*, IV, pp. 122–3; Mack Smith, *Cav.-Gar.*, p. 132.
15. Mack Smith, *Cav.-Gar.*, p. 214.
16. Trevelyan, *Making*, pp. 33–4.
17. Blakiston, p. 120.
18. Paléologue, *Cavour*, p. 424.
19. Salvatorelli, *Spiriti*, p. 354.
20. Pieri, p. 702.
21. Mack Smith, *Garibaldi*, p. 111.
22. Moscati, p. 316.
23. Richards, II, p. 246.
24. Lacaita, p. 159.
25. Mack Smith, *Cav.-Gar.*, p. 408.
26. Trevelyan, *Making*, p. 284.
27. Mack Smith, *Risorg.*, pp. 612–13.
28. Omodeo, *Età*, p. 404.

CHAPTER XIV

1. Whyte, *Cavour*, p. 463.
2. Salvatorelli, *Pensiero*, p. 174.
3. Jacini, quoted by Entreves, p. 14.
4. Mack Smith, *Cav.-Gar.*, pp. 419–20.
5. Salvemini, *Scritti*, pp. 431–3.
6. Chiala, IV, 34–5; Clough and Saladino, p. 123.
7. Mack Smith, *Cav.-Gar.*, pp. 419–20.
8. Hibbert, p. 319 and n.
9. Marshall, pp. 281–3.
10. Paléologue, *Cavour*, p. 298.
11. Mori, *Questione*, p. xiii.
12. Entreves, p. 318.
13. Salvatorelli, *Spiriti*, p. 421.
14. Entreves, p. 289.
15. Mack Smith, *Sicily*, pp. 448–9.
16. Mori, *Questione*, p. 9.
17. Marshall, p. 284.

CHAPTER XV

1. Romeo, *Piemonte*, p. 218.
2. Mack Smith, *Sicily*, p. 449.
3. Salvemini, *Scritti*, p. 462.
4. Halperin, p. 159.
5. Mori, *Questione*, pp. 72–4.
6. Mack Smith, *Garibaldi*, p. 133.
7. Clough and Saladino, pp. 134–5.
8. Hamilton King, p. 16.
9. Hammond, p. 47.
10. Blakiston, p. 240.
11. Bonanno, p. 209.
12. Omodeo, *Età*, pp. 411–12.
13. Lacaita, p. 197.
14. Hales, *Pio*, p. 248.
15. Fisher, p. 965.
16. Salvemini, *Scritti*, p. 427.

CHAPTER XVI

1. Mack Smith, *Italy*, p. 75.
2. Bonanno, p. 209.
3. Lacaita, p. 216.
4. Bersezio, VIII, p. 353.
5. Hamilton King, p. 58.
6. Mack Smith, *Garibaldi*, p. 161; *Italy*, pp. 92–3.
7. Omodeo, *Età*, p. 430.
8. Blakiston, p. 352.
9. Halperin, pp. 92–3.
10. Halperin, p. 148.
11. Bersezio, VIII, pp. 357–8.
12. Mori, *Tramonto*, p. 512.
13. Mori, *Tramonto*, p. 531.
14. Mori, *Tramonto*, pp. 517–18.
15. Salvemini, *Scritti*, p. 115.
16. Clough and Saladino, pp. 154–5.
17. Mori, *Tramonto*, p. 530.
18. Clough and Saladino, pp. 155–6.
19. Lacaita, p. 235.
20. Elliot, p. 137.
21. Parris, p. 324.
22. Moscati, pp. 9, 18.
23. Massari, *Diario dalle cento Voci*, p. 41.
24. Omodeo, *Difesa*, p. 444.

INDEX